DISASTER SURVIVAL HANDBOOK

DISASTER SURVIVAL HANDBOOK

AN ILLUSTRATED GUIDE TO SURVIVAL

**TORNADOES • EARTHQUAKES • TSUNAMIS
TERRORIST ATTACKS • FOREST FIRES • HEAT WAVES**

Alexander Stilwell

Thunder Bay
P·R·E·S·S
San Diego, California

Thunder Bay Press
An imprint of Printers Row Publishing Group
10350 Barnes Canyon Road, Suite 100, San Diego, CA 92121
www.thunderbaybooks.com

Copyright © 2019 Amber Books Ltd

All rights reserved. No part of this publication may be reproduced, distributed, or transmitted in any form or by any means, including photocopying, recording, or other electronic or mechanical methods, without the prior written permission of the publisher, except in the case of brief quotations embodied in critical reviews and certain other noncommercial uses permitted by copyright law.

Printers Row Publishing Group is a division of Readerlink Distribution Services, LLC.
Thunder Bay Press is a registered trademark of Readerlink Distribution Services, LLC.

All notations of errors or omissions should be addressed to Thunder Bay Press, Editorial Department, at the above address. All other correspondence (author inquiries, permissions) concerning the content of this book should be addressed to:
Amber Books Ltd
United House, North Road, London, N7 9DP, United Kingdom
www.amberbooks.co.uk

Project Editor: Michael Spilling
Design: Zoe Mellors
Picture Research: Terry Forshaw
Illustrations: Tony Randell and Patrick Mulrey

Thunder Bay Press
Publisher: Peter Norton
Associate Publisher: Ana Parker
Publishing/Editorial Team: April Farr, Kelly Larsen, Kathryn C. Dalby
Editorial Team: JoAnn Padgett, Melinda Allman, Traci Douglas

Library of Congress Cataloging-in-Publication Data

Names: Stilwell, Alexander, author.
Title: Disaster survival handbook / Alexander Stilwell.
Description: San Diego : Printers Row Publishing Group, 2019. | Includes index.
Identifiers: LCCN 2018050039 | ISBN 9781684126781
Subjects: LCSH: Emergency management--Handbooks, manuals, etc. | Survival--Handbooks, manuals, etc. | Natural disasters--Handbooks, manuals, etc. | Preparedness--Handbooks, manuals, etc.
Classification: LCC HV551.2 .S74 2019 | DDC 613.6/9--dc23 LC record available at https://lccn.loc.gov/2018050039

ISBN: 978-1-68412-678-1

Printed in China

23 22 21 20 19   1 2 3 4 5

Disclaimer
This book is for information purposes only. Readers should be aware of the legal position in their country of residence before practicing any of the techniques described in this book. This book does not provide medical advice and should not be used instead of professional emergency service help.

CONTENTS

Preparation	6
What to Carry and to Wear	44
Floods and Tsunamis	54
Earthquakes and Volcanoes	66
Fires	78
Storms	92
Heat Waves and Droughts	114
Landslides, Avalanches, and Caving	134
Terrorism	160
Transport Safety	186
Rescue	206
First Aid	220
Cyberattack	248
Appendices	249
Glossary	250
Index	252
Acknowledgments	256

PREPARATION

If you are going to survive any disaster situation, you need to be fit and healthy. This chapter explores physical preparation, including testing your fitness, getting fit, and following a healthy diet. We also look at effective mental preparation, including building concentration, thinking clearly in a crisis with an emphasis on stress management, meditation techniques, and enhanced decision-making. If you are fit, you will be better prepared to deal with a disaster.

Running provides the essential core fitness that will be a huge advantage in a disaster survival situation.

PHYSICAL PREPARATION

To test how fit you are, measure your resting heart rate (RHR), which will provide good insight into your cardiovascular health. It is best to test your RHR in the morning, when your body is unaffected by variables.

Your heart rate, measured by timing your pulse, indicates the number of times your heart beats per minute. This in turn indicates how hard your heart has to work in order to circulate blood around the body. A weaker heart has to work harder to push blood through the arteries, so the pulse rate is faster. A stronger heart gives you more bang for your buck—your heart can work at a slower rate, as it provides a boost for each beat.

As a yardstick to assess your fitness, the average RHR for an adult is between 60 and 100 beats per minute (bpm). An athlete may have an RHR of between 40 and 60 bpm.

In order to track your fitness, keep a log of your RHR over a few weeks, especially if you are engaged in a fitness-training regime. As you become more fit, you should see your bpm decline.

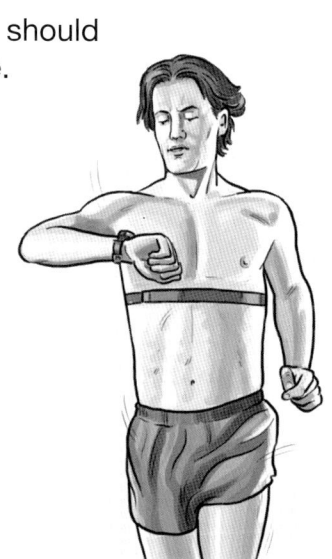

Heart rate monitor

A heart rate monitor that you wear on your wrist or chest can give you electronic indications of your resting heart rate and also track your heart rate during exercise. This should give you an idea of whether you reached the intensity that you were aiming for.

MEASURING RHR

Measure your RHR by finding your pulse in either your wrist or your neck.

WRIST
Hold out your hand, palm upward. Press the index and middle fingers on the inside of your wrist until you can feel the pulse.

NECK
Press the index and middle fingers on the side of your neck, under the jaw and next to the windpipe.
Move your fingers until you can feel the pulse.

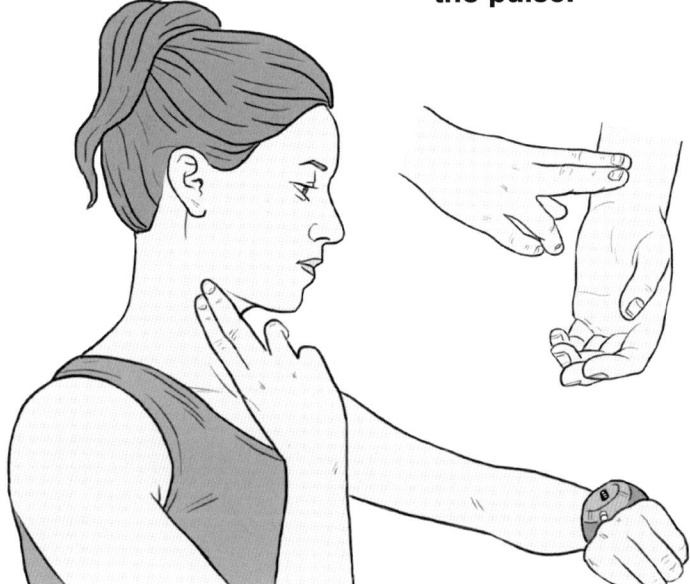

To measure your bpm, either count the number of beats for a full minute or count them for 30 seconds, and then multiply by two.

Maximum heart rate (MHR)

To measure your maximum heart rate (MHR), subtract your age from 220. This indicates the safe range you should work to when exercising. However, you also need to take into account your overall fitness, state of health, stress level, and other factors, such as climate. For example, your heart may have to work harder in a hot climate to lose heat. In general, aerobic exercise such as running should measure between 60 and 90 percent of your MHR.

If you are a woman, your heart is likely to beat about 5 bpm faster than a man's heart.

Training heart rate (THR)

Training heart rate (THR) is an indicator of how your heart beats when exercising. The THR is between 70 and 80 percent of your MHR.

PREPARATION

STRETCHING

There is often discussion among people in training about whether or not to stretch before exercise. This is because in static stretching a muscle may lose some of its efficiency.

However, stiff muscles are more likely to get injured than warmed and stretched muscles.
A good solution is dynamic stretching. This kind of stretching gradually begins the movements that you will be making anyway when you exercise.

Dynamic stretching

Start with slow, relatively limited movements, and gradually increase the range and pace as your muscles warm up and loosen.

- Do shoulder shrugs. First go forward, and then, backward.
- Make arm circles. To do so, first make big sweeps. Then make the sweeps smaller, and then gradually increase them again.
- Take lunges forward to stretch hip flexors.
- Walk or jog with high knees.

You can also target specific muscles. Here are a range of stretches that are useful for warming up the leg muscles.

Hamstring stretch

Gluteal stretch

PREPARATION 11

Calf stretch

Shoulder stretch

Iliotibial stretch

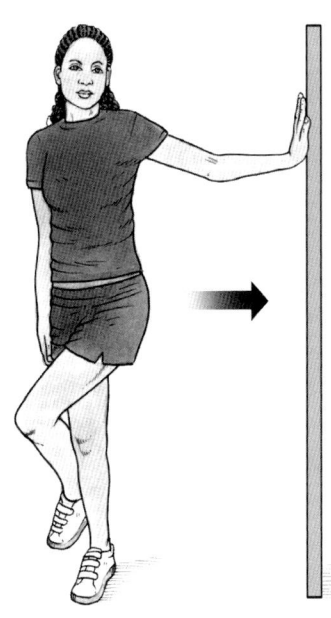

Inner thigh stretch

TEST YOUR FITNESS

These strength exercises will help you to assess your fitness before you start training. Do not be put off if you have a low score to begin with. Development begins with a single step.

Push-ups

The push-up tests upper-body strength, especially in the chest, shoulders, and triceps. It also improves proprioception (the body's ability to coordinate muscles).

Place your hands on the ground, shoulder width apart. Stretch out your legs, place them waist width apart, and balance on the balls of your feet. Bend your arms and lower yourself until your chest brushes the ground. Then push yourself back up to the previous position. Do as many push-ups as you can, and then try to do one or two extra the following day and so on.

Starter: 15–20 or less   Average: 20–30

Good: 30–40   Excellent: 40 plus

Abdominal plank

The abdominal plank tests and improves your core strength. Core strength is vital, as it provides essential stability, which can be used in all other forms of activity, including running and swimming. The plank helps to strengthen the lower back, hips, and buttocks.

Adopt the push-up position, and then set your feet waist width apart. Get down on your elbows and forearms, and then interlock your fingers. Hold the rigid position for as long as you can without any movement in your hips.

Starter: 1 minute or less

Average: 1 minute or more

Good: 2 minutes or more

Excellent: 3 minutes or more

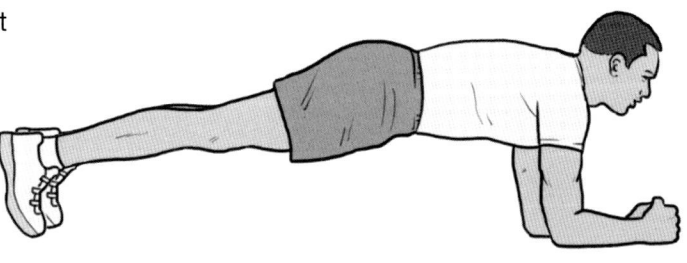

PREPARATION 13

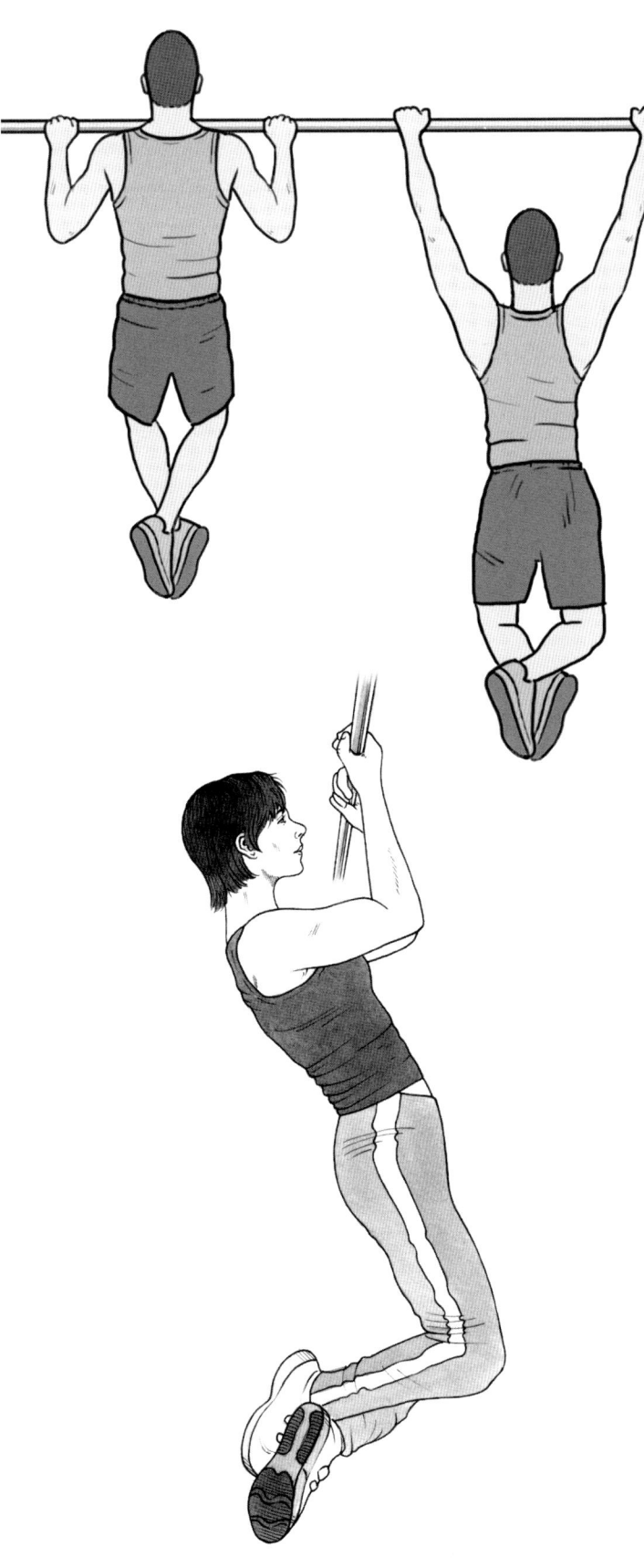

Pull-ups

The pull-up tests upper-body strength, including the strength of the lats, located on your sides, and the biceps in your arms. Stand beneath a secure horizontal bar, and grasp it with an overhand grip. Then pull yourself up in a smooth motion until your chin is over the bar. Let yourself gently down again, until your arms are straight, and then repeat.

You may start with one or two pull-ups, but try to increase the rate to about 10 as a baseline. You are doing very well if you can get to 20 and above.

Starter: 10 or less
Average: 10–15
Good: 15–20
Excellent: 20 plus

Sit-ups

Lie on your back on the floor. Put your hands near your ears. Bend your knees so that your feet are flat on the floor, and try to raise your body 30 degrees from the ground. Then lie back and repeat.

Rowing

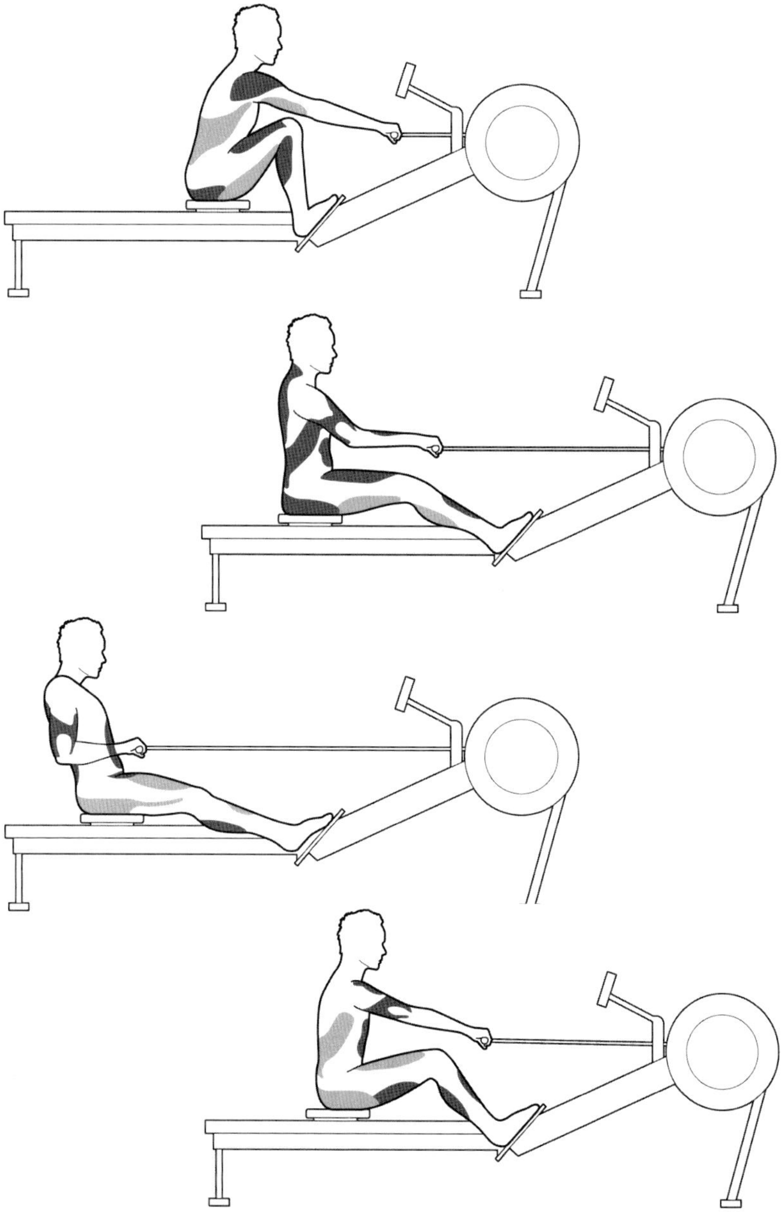

Using a rowing machine is a good way of developing overall body fitness. It is also a good way of losing weight.

Adopt the correct position, with your legs stretched and the handle of the rower pulled in toward your stomach. Then push your arms forward and slide forward, bending your knees. Then push back with your legs, while your arms are still stretched. Once you have pushed your body back with your legs, pull the handle back to your stomach. Try to perform the exercise as smoothly as possible.

Row for 500 yards (460 m). See how your time compares to the following:

Starter: 4.00 minutes plus
Average: 3.00–4.00
Good: 2.00–3.00
Excellent: Less than 2.00

RUNNING

Running will help improve your fitness, your health, and your sense of well-being. It is a total body workout that provides an excellent base for other fitness and strength-building activities.

DIFFERENT TYPES OF RUNNING

Mile run

The four-minute mile barrier was first broken in 1954. A reasonably fit runner may run a mile in 7 to 10 minutes. How fast you can run a mile (1.6 km) and how quickly you recover are good indicators of your overall fitness.

Long slow distance (LSD)

The long slow distance (LSD) run is designed to build endurance as a base for other activities. At a low-intensity pace, the run may last from 30 minutes to two hours, depending on your level of experience and fitness.

One benefit of LSD exercise is that it helps the body to burn fat instead of carbohydrates. This helps to explain why marathon runners are often very lightweight.

Fast continuous running (FCR), or tempo running

This is a high-intensity run for a relatively limited time or distance. The aim of tempo running, also known as fast continuous running (FCR), is to run at a pace that is challenging but still manageable for the whole distance. This way, you do not have to slow down. FCR means working near the top of your maximum heart rate (MHR) and just below your lactate threshold, the point where lactic acid accumulates in your muscles and makes you want to slow down. The run may be from 15 to 30 minutes long.

Tempo running not only helps to strengthen the heart, lungs, and body, it also improves your mental endurance and concentration.

RUNNING HINTS

POSTURE:
Stand straight, interlock your fingers above your head, and then push upward. This should help you to adopt the correct running posture, which is upright but leaning slightly forward. Strengthening your core with exercises such as planks will help you to improve your running posture.

CADENCE:
This is the number of times your feet hit the ground over a set time. The average runner takes between 160 and 170 steps per minute, whereas an elite runner takes over 200 steps per minute. Increasing your cadence by between 5 and 10 percent not only increases your speed, but it also helps prevent injury. Increased cadence reduces the strain on your knees, shins, and other areas.

STRIDE:
Try not to overstride. By maintaining a good cadence and reducing stride, you have a more upright stance. Try to move the impact of your foot on the ground from the heel toward the center of the shoe. Explore the use of running shoes with a reduced heel-to-toe drop.

FLEXIBILITY:
Running will create a certain amount of muscle tension. Your muscles may also become tight from other activities. Stretching helps to loosen the muscles and makes them more elastic, and therefore less susceptible to injury. Tight muscles are the ones that get injured from sudden movement.

PREPARATION 17

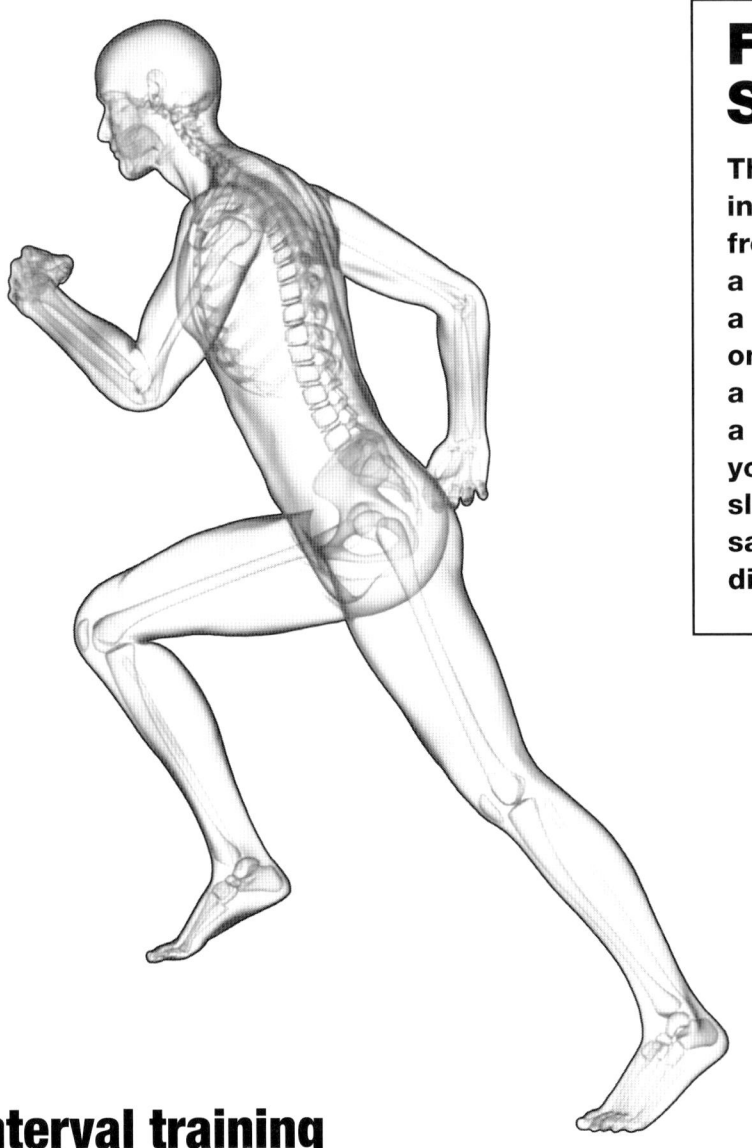

> # FARTLEK, OR SPEED PLAY
>
> This kind of running involves changes of pace, from a jog or steady run to a stride. You can either use a minute countdown timer on your watch or run toward a particular goal, such as a tree or a lamppost. Once you have reached your goal, slow down again for the same amount of time or distance.

Interval training

Interval training involves periods of intense workouts with short breaks for recovery. If you are a beginner, start with moderate intensity exercise at an aerobic level. As you become more fit, you may opt for anaerobic, high-intensity workouts.

Interval training can raise your lactate threshold (the point at which your muscles become swamped with lactic acid). Interval training is very effective at reducing fat and keeps your metabolism raised for an extended period beyond the exercise period. This means it is an effective way to lose weight.

18 PREPARATION

WEIGHT TRAINING

Weight training is an important component of your fitness program, as it will help to build the core stability and strength that provides a firm platform for other exercises.

The strong core muscles built up through weight training help to provide stability for walking and running, as well as for other strength-related activities.

Training with weights also builds the muscle needed to cope with some of the demanding aspects of military fitness testing. Weight training fits very well with the pursuit of military fitness because military life sometimes involves carrying weights, often over long distances. This requires short spurts of energy and strength. Soldiers, for example, may be required to walk a long distance with all their equipment and then dig a trench.

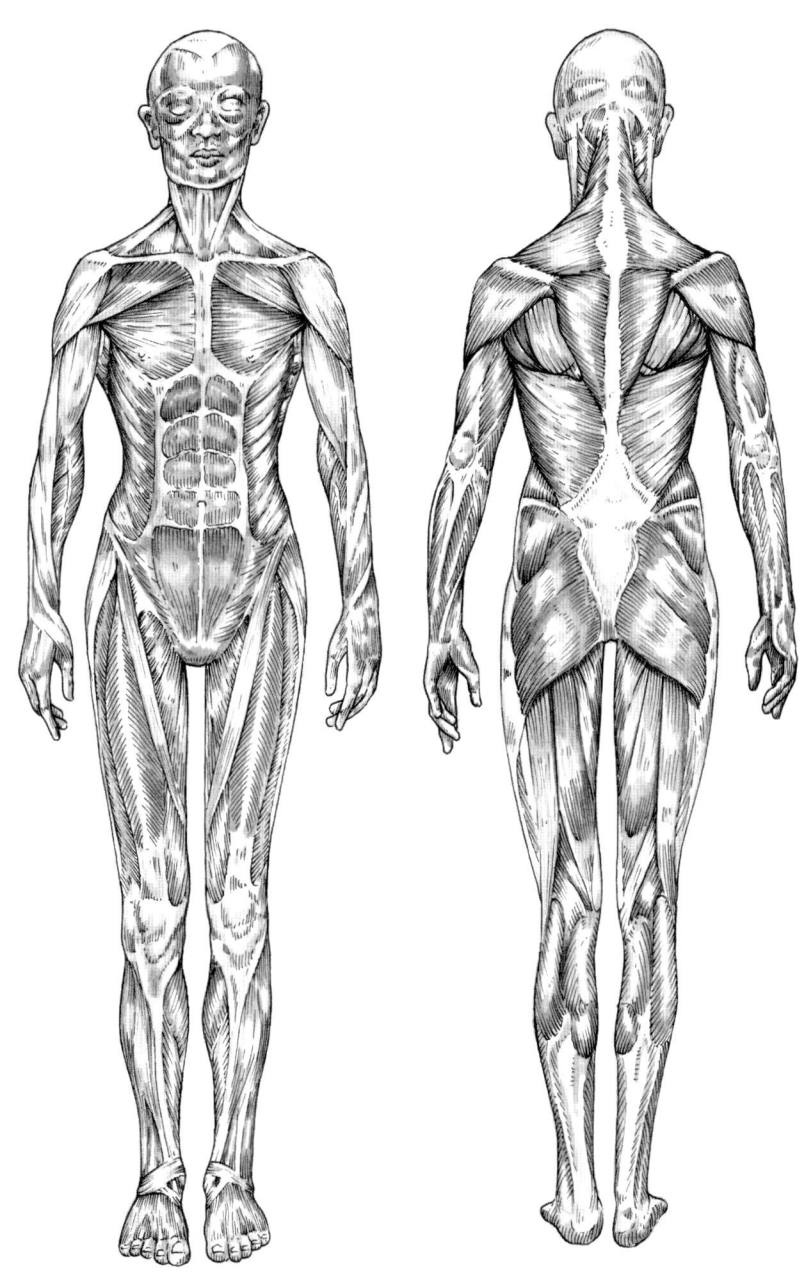

CHEST EXERCISES

Bench press

- Lie on a bench in a multigym, or use a manageable barbell.
- Place shoulders directly under the weights.
- Raise feet off the ground.
- Cross your legs.
- Grasp bar or handles.
- Push the weight until arms are almost straight (but do not lock the elbows).
- Lower slowly again.

Repeat about 20 times, depending on your level of strength and fitness.

Lateral raise

- Lie on a bench with your feet resting flat on the bench and your knees raised.
- Hold two dumbbells above the chest, one in each hand.
- Keep elbows bent.
- Lower the dumbbells to the sides.
- Then raise them again and bring the dumbbells together above your chest (but do not lock the elbows).

Do about 20 repetitions, depending on your level of strength and fitness.

SHOULDERS

Shoulder press

You can do this exercise one of three ways. You can be seated, or you can be on a multigym with support for your back. This can also be performed standing with a barbell.

- Place hands on the bar slightly under your shoulders.
- Hold the bar at the back of the neck.
- Slowly push the bar upward.
- Lower the bar slowly to the previous position.

Perform repetitions of 12, depending on your strength and fitness.

Dumbbell press

- Stand with feet shoulder width apart and with back straight.
- Hold a dumbbell slightly in front of each shoulder.
- Raise one above the head, and then return it to its position.
- Repeat on the other side.

Try doing sets of 18 repetitions, depending on your strength and fitness.

PREPARATION 21

Side lateral raise

- With your feet shoulder width apart and with back straight, hold a dumbbell in each hand by your waist.
- Raise both dumbbells simultaneously.
- Keep arms straight.
- Slowly lower the dumbbells to the previous position.

Try sets of 12 repetitions, depending on your strength and fitness.

Bent lateral raise

Bend forward, and hold the dumbbells in each hand near your knees. Then raise both arms until your straight arms are more or less parallel with the ground.

ARM EXERCISES

Curls

- Stand with your feet shoulder width apart and with your back straight.

- Holding either the curling bar from a multigym or a barbell at waist level; keep your elbows in at your sides.

- Curl the bar or barbell up to your shoulders and then back down again.

- Exhale when raising the weights, and inhale when lowering them.

Try to complete 20 repetitions in each set, depending on your strength and fitness.

Concentration curls

- Sit on a bench with one dumbbell in your hand.

- Rest your elbow on your leg.

- Slowly curl the dumbbell up toward your shoulder, and then lower it slowly.

Try doing sets of 12 repetitions, depending on your strength and fitness.

Tricep dip

This exercise helps to work your triceps. It is best performed using a pair of parallel bars in a gym, but you can also perform this using the seat of a chair.

- Hold yourself with your knuckles facing out.

- Hold your body at arm's length with your arms nearly locked above the bars.

- Push your legs out, lift your knees, maintaining a slight bend.

- Then slowly lower yourself down.

- Take the strain in your arms until your elbows are at 90 degrees, and then push back up through your arms until they are straight.

CORE FITNESS

Core muscles are central to supporting the whole body. A strong core will improve your performance in a range of activities, such as running or swimming. It will also improve your posture and reduce the risk of back injury.

ABDOMEN

Try doing abdomen exercises without locking your legs so that your abdomen muscles have to do the work, rather than your legs and lower-back muscles.

Crunches

- Lie on your back with legs bent and feet flat on the floor.

- Place your hands behind or next to your head, or on your thighs.

- Exhale as you raise your head and upper body off the floor, moving your elbows toward your knees.

- Hold the upward position for up to five seconds before lying back down on the floor.

Twist sit-ups

- Lie on your back with legs bent and feet flat on the floor.

- Place your hands behind or next to your head, or on your thighs.

- Exhale as you raise your head and upper body off the floor, moving one elbow toward the opposite knee (right elbow to left knee and vice versa).

- Then lie back and do the same for the opposite elbow and knee.

Leg raises

- Lie on your back with your hand next to your body or tucked under your buttocks.

- Keep legs straight, and raise your feet about 6 inches (15 cm) off the ground.

- Then raise them farther, to about 20 inches (51 cm) off the ground and then back down to 6 inches (15 cm).

- Repeat.

Try to do 30 repetitions in each set, depending on your strength and fitness.

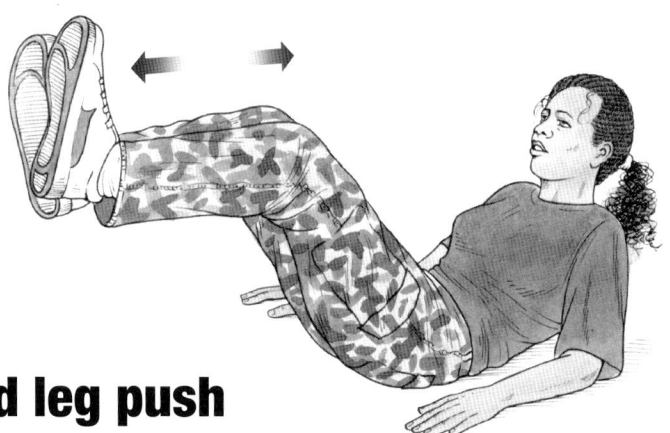

Seated leg push

Either sit on a bench or on the floor. Sit upright supported by your hands. Then bring your knees to your chest and straighten your legs. Keep your feet off the ground throughout the exercise. Do about 30 repetitions in each set, depending on your strength and fitness.

Dorsal raises

- Lie on your front with your legs stretched out and together.

- Clasp your hands behind your back.

- Push your toes into the ground, and then lift your head, shoulders, and chest 8 to 12 inches (20 to 30 cm) off the ground, using your back muscles.

- Hold the position for a few moments, and then relax back to your original position.

LEGS

Squat

- Stand up straight with your feet shoulder width apart and your hands by your sides.
- Slightly turn your feet out.
- Push your hips back, and then bend at the knees.
- Lower yourself until your thighs are parallel with the floor.
- Keep your back straight, and then push up through your heels back to the starting position.

Split squat

This exercise helps to work your hamstring and buttock muscles.

- Stand with feet shoulder width apart.
- Fold arms across your chest, and keep a straight back.
- Step forward with one foot while bending your standing leg, with your back foot resting on your toes.
- Lower yourself until the front leg is bent at 90 degrees and you can place your weight on the heel of the front foot.
- Push back up from the heel into the starting position.

Step-up

This exercise works your thighs, buttocks, and hamstrings.

- Fold your arms across your chest, and then place one foot on a step or platform that is about 16 inches (41 cm) high.

- Lean forward slightly, and then move your weight onto your front foot.

- Push through the heel of your front foot, and place your rear foot on the platform.

- Slowly step back down to the starting position.

Leg press

The leg press machine is a good way of building up strength in the knees and quad muscles.

- Place your feet shoulder width apart.
- Push to extend, but don't lock the knees.
- Slowly return to the start position.

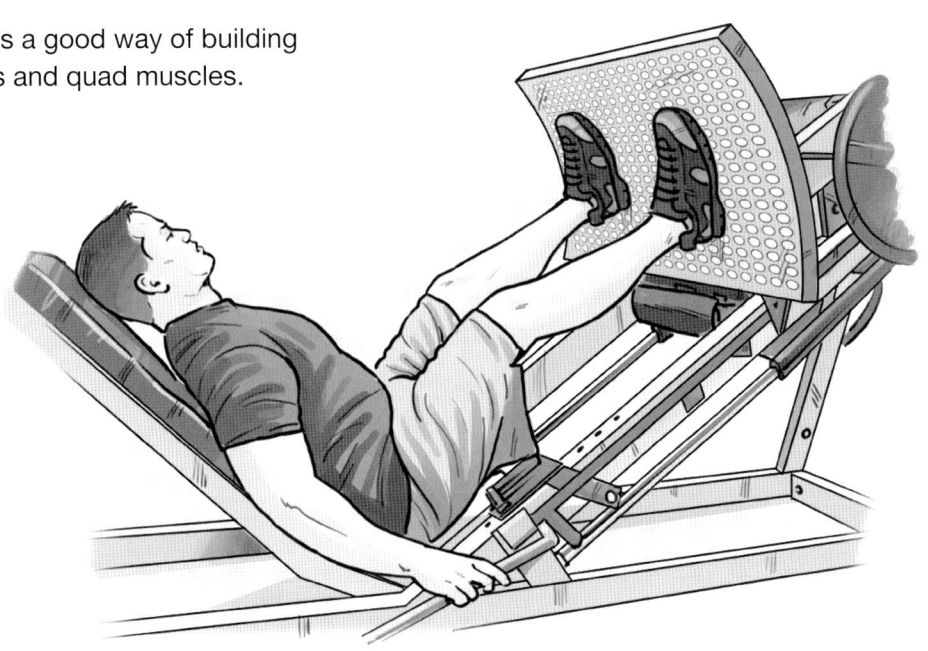

MILITARY FITNESS

Military fitness need not just apply to the military. There is increasing recognition that military-style all-round fitness with good core strength makes you fit for anything and will give you the versatility to survive disaster situations.

The aim of military-style fitness is to be both encompassing and functional because military personnel are faced with a myriad of practical tasks and challenges, such as hiking long distances with heavy loads, moving weapons and ammunition as quickly as possible, and digging trenches.

Bodybuilders may look strong, but their muscles are often not functional for everyday tasks, and bodybuilders may lack mobility. Long-distance runners may have speed and agility, but they may lack power for heavy lifting.

Leading military forces, such as the United States and British armed forces, have made their minimum fitness entrance tests reflect the realistic demands that military personnel will face in their work.

New British Army standard fitness test, in addition to beep test

Static lift:
Raising a 154-pound (70-kg) bag to simulate casualty extraction

Equipment carry test:
Carrying a 66-pound (30-kg) weight for 65 feet (20 meters) repeated 20 times

Push-ups:
44 in fewer than two minutes for males, 21 for females

Sit-ups:
50 in fewer than two minutes

1.5-mile (2.4-km) run:
14.30 to 9.40 minutes, dependent on soldier selection

MULTI-STAGE FITNESS TEST (MSFT), OR BEEP TEST

Several military forces around the world use the beep test, or multi-stage fitness test (MSFT). Special Forces use this kind of test as well. The MSFT sets minimum fitness standards before recruits can enter further training.

The beep test involves running between two lines that are 66 feet (20 m) apart in time with a beep. The beeps get faster, and your final score is taken from the last time that you keep up with the beep.

U.S. ARMY RANGER SOLDIER FITNESS

- 2-mile (3-km) run: 15.12 minutes maximum
- 49 push-ups in two minutes minimum
- 49 sit-ups in two minutes minimum
- 6 pull-ups minimum

DIET

A good diet is an essential part of your fitness regime. It will help you to reduce weight and to improve your BMI. The first thing to do is to cut down on excess carbohydrates and fats.

Carbohydrates can be found in excess in foods such as these:

- Desserts
- Candy
- Sugary soft drinks

Fats can be found in excess in sources such as these:

- Food cooked in saturated fat
- Margarine and butter
- Pastries
- Full-fat milk

Try to replace bad foods with good ones.

- Replace high-sugar breakfast cereals with low-sugar alternatives such as oatmeal.
- Replace sugary snacks with dried or fresh fruit, such as dates, raisins, or cranberries.
- Replace sugary drinks with plain water or with carbonated water with a slice of fruit, such as lemon or lime.
- Replace alcoholic drinks with low or zero alcohol alternatives, or with juice or water.
- Replace some high-caffeine drinks, such as coffee and tea, with low- or zero-caffeine substitutes, such as caffeine-free green tea or chamomile tea.

U.S. ARMY FITNESS GUIDE NUTRITION GUIDELINES

- **Strive for a diet in which two-thirds of nutrition comes from grains, vegetables, and fruits; one-third should come from low-fat or lean protein from the dairy or meat food groups.**
- **To lose weight, decrease calories while increasing exercise and activity. Limit high-fat and high-sugar foods.**
- **When engaged in a resistance-exercise program, increase calories to build muscle.**
- **Avoid or cut back on fast and processed foods.**
- **Drink 8 to 10 glasses of water per day.**
- **Adopt a food-first approach to good health and performance.**

BODY MASS INDEX (BMI)

Body mass index (BMI) is one of the key indicators used by military armed forces to assess the fitness of candidates. The score is based on your age, height, and weight. For example, to join the U.S. Army you normally need a BMI between 18.5 and 24.9.

Focus on essential foods such as these:

- Carbohydrates—bread, cereals, pasta, rice, and noodles
- Fats—milk, cheese, and butter
- Protein—meat, fish, eggs, and nuts. Eat oily fish twice per week.
- Vitamins and minerals—mainly found in vegetables, meat, and fruit. Eat five portions of fruit and vegetables per day.

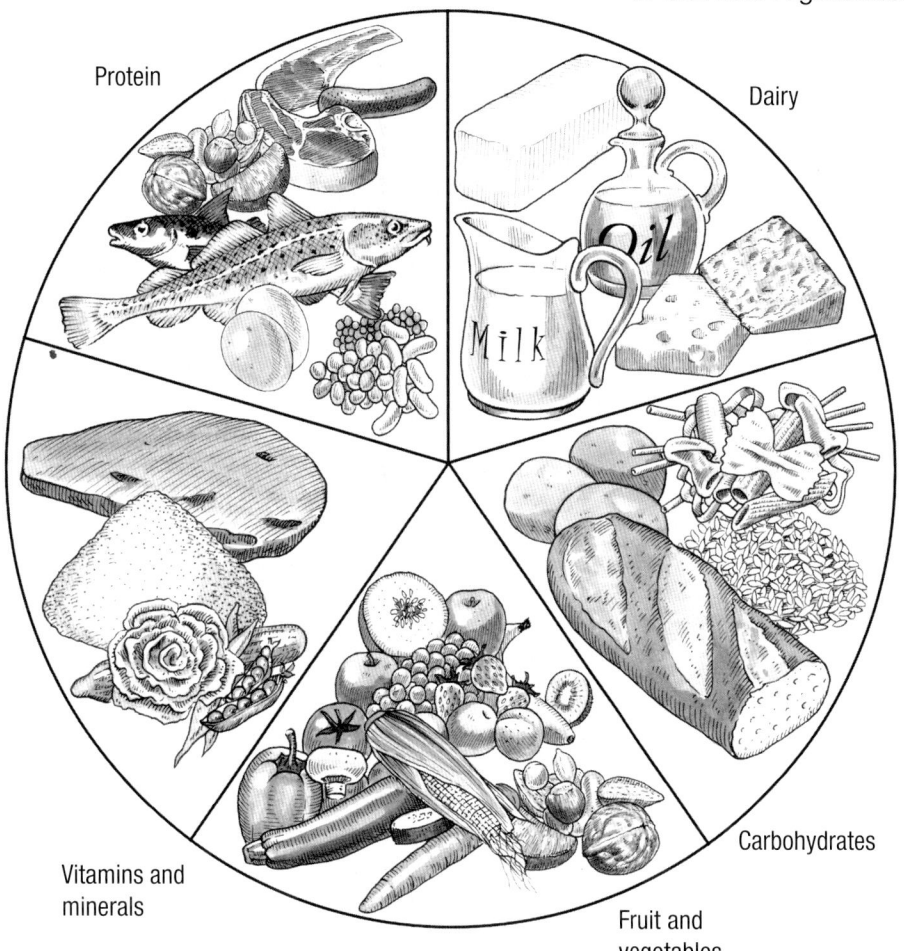

Note that fiber helps the digestive system to work efficiently and reduces hunger by adding bulk.

Prefer water to energy drinks when exercising. Energy drinks may have side effects; water does not.

Cut down on salt. Do not add salt to food, and check labels for salt content.

MENTAL PREPARATION

A disaster may be unexpected or appear at short notice and will be disorientating. It may include loss of equipment and threats to life and property.

The more prepared you are mentally to deal with the added stress you will suffer, the better your chances of coming through successfully.

After they have dealt successfully with a crisis, people in emergency services and the military sometimes say, "The training took over." This is a highly relevant phrase as it underlines the fact that it is difficult to plan and make decisions under the added pressure of a crisis, when there is little time to think. The more you can prepare yourself mentally, the better you will be able to cope.

Handling stress

The human mind and body are designed to handle stress for relatively short periods. The extreme version of the stress reaction is the "fight or flight" response, when hormones are released into the body and the brain closes down nonessential programs to focus on getting out of danger. One part of the brain that is closed down is the prefrontal cortex. This is a useful reaction in extreme danger, but it can be a problem in situations that require a more reasoned approach.

Training to step down the fight-or-flight approach can help you to maintain your ability to reason through a crisis while also being watchful and aware of present danger. Highly sensitive people are more prone to the fight-or-flight response and therefore need to focus more on desensitizing the triggers.

It is important to recognize the fundamental source of the reaction. This is always some form of fear. The next step is to judge the level of danger and to act accordingly. By controlling the fear reaction, you will be in a better position to make decisions that will get you out of trouble.

Practice by thinking about what might happen and how you may be able to minimize the danger. By creating a mental map, you will be better able to act in a calm and capable way when a crisis hits.

NEGATIVE EFFECTS OF STRESS

Stress can be overwhelming and lead to a range of negative side effects. Apart from the fight-or-flight response, another effect of stress can be the deer-caught-in-headlights effect, where you freeze or close down.

Mood swings, alcohol or drug use, loss of sleep, and short-term memory loss are all signs of a stress reaction. This may become extreme to the point where people become catatonic and unable to do anything for themselves or others.

Sleep

If you are in a constant state of stress, you will eventually wear yourself out, and your ability to act appropriately when necessary will be reduced. It is important to get good sleep when you can, so that your body and mind have a chance to reboot. This way, you can concentrate properly.

Concentration and planning

Some people are good at thinking on their feet and bouncing ideas off others, while some need time and space on their own to think clearly. Whichever works best for you, make sure that you give yourself enough time to make a plan when your mind is fully present. Then when things get stressful and there is a lot of pressure and need for action, you will have a clearer idea of how to respond.

BREATHING EXERCISE

Breathe in slowly through your nose, hold it for a few moments, and then breathe out slowly through your mouth. Focus on the breathing itself, rather than your thoughts or any external stimuli. If distracted, keep bringing your attention back to the breathing. This breathing exercise may last up to five minutes.

Breathing

Practice breathing deeply; inhale and exhale down into your stomach, releasing the breath slowly. This will help regulate the autonomic nervous system, which in turn will help to reduce the tendency to panic or overreact.

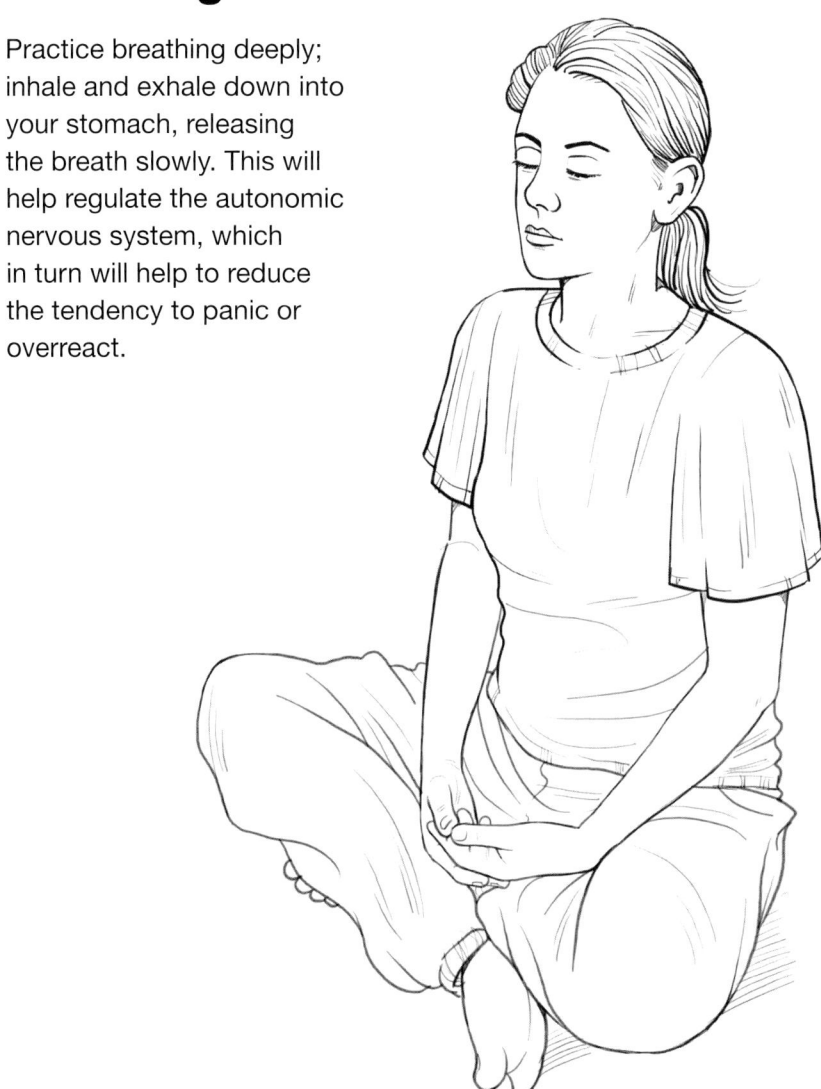

Meditation

Developing the habit of meditation will serve you well if you are faced with a crisis, as it will help you to take control of your mind when there may be a temptation to panic. Ideally, meditation should last between 20 and 30 minutes, but you can also practice taking two-minute meditation breaks to calm your mind.

When meditating, find a quiet place where you can be relaxed but also alert. Focus on a particular word or mental image that has a calming effect. Even during a crisis, you may find time to stop and collect your thoughts before making decisions.

Team building

If you are going on an expedition with other people, try to train with them beforehand. By exposing the team to tough challenges, you will build mutual confidence and also recognize each other's gifts and weaknesses. You will know whom you can rely on when the chips are down, and you will know whether others can rely on you.

MENTAL PREPARATION AND EMERGENCY CONDITIONING (EC)

However tough the physical conditions or your level of physical fitness and endurance, ultimately what decides whether you come through or give up is your brain. A shock or disaster will often leave the mind in confusion, partly because you have no previous experience of the event to draw on. Emergency conditioning (EC) is designed to create a special kind of file in your brain, which you can draw on in an emergency. EC can help to make your reactions more appropriate and effective.

Imagine coming across an unfamiliar situation and being able to consult a file, either in a filing cabinet or on your computer. Think about what you would like to find in that file. Probably it would include an easy-to-follow action list. The contents of the file may also include the information contained in the following chapters.

Visualization techniques

Use positive visualization techniques to imagine what you would do in various challenging scenarios. This will help you to think more clearly and act more efficiently during a crisis. It will also give you psychological strength, which will make you more resistant to panic and confusion.

Having positive images about how you might handle difficult situations will help to create a constructive mind-set. Imagine dealing with a challenging scenario in a competent, confident, and ultimately successful way. Imagine yourself being in control of the situation.

By thinking, planning, and guiding your imagination, you can create a positive virtual world on which your mind can draw during challenging situations, making it more likely that you will perform to the best of your ability and achieve success.

The human imagination is a powerful tool and is often more effective than trying to force yourself to learn a new skill. Make sure that you immerse yourself in the visualization so that it appears real to you.

Positive thinking

This requires creating a positive state of mind and focusing your resources so you can deal with whatever gets thrown at you.

Having an action plan gives you the confidence that you will know what to do in demanding circumstances. Planning enhances mental preparation. Work out the way of doing things that best works for you, and stick to it.

Practice makes perfect. Practice will also enhance the feeling of confidence that you can handle the challenges that arise.

Maintaining focus when under extreme stress will be key to surviving a disaster situation.

SITUATIONAL AWARENESS

One way of preparing for the unexpected is to be more aware of what is going on around you. Soldiers who have returned from a combat zone may be hyperaware for a period even though they are in a relatively safe civilian environment.

A car's backfiring, for example, may trigger an involuntary reaction, as if it were a gunshot. Within reason, this awareness is beneficial, especially when we live in a world where a car or truck may be used as a weapon.

If you are the sort of person who switches off during safety announcements or warnings, practice switching on. In addition, create your own safety analysis in crowded areas, cinemas, sports stadiums, and so on.

Look out for places to seek refuge if there is immediate danger. Keep an eye out for people acting suspiciously, wearing inappropriate clothing, or carrying suspicious baggage. Keep an eye out for possible allies in an emergency. In addition, keep a list of emergency contacts on your phone.

Disassociation

Disassociation can be a process with negative effects when someone is not able to engage with situations in his or her surroundings. However, it can be a positive tool if it helps to numb the pain of demanding situations that involve extreme cold, physical exertion, or other challenges. Disassociation can allow you to move your focus to something more pleasant. The process can engage your mind while allowing you to get on with what you have to do.

Sometimes being able to disassociate from your surroundings helps when concentrating on a challenging task.

Confidence

To build confidence, act as if you can do whatever is needed. Act despite feelings of fear. Remember that most people feel fear, but brave people push through it.

Preparation, whether physical or mental, will make you better prepared to cope. Look at the positive side of all your challenges and experiences. Instead of criticizing yourself for mistakes, look at the learning points and resolve to improve in the future.

Learn from both successes and failures. Strengthening your mental skills will help you to improve your confidence and commitment.

MOTIVATION

The will to survive requires a motive that remains with you throughout the experience and stops you from giving up. This may mean different things for different people. For some, it may mean the determination to see their family again or to not let down the members of their team.

Positive learning experiences and overcoming physical challenges help create a confident attitude.

GETTING RID OF WORRY

Worrying about negative scenarios achieves little more than making it more likely that those scenarios will come about. It also drains positive energy and creates more stress. Instead of worrying, shift your focus to plans and preparations.

Another way to shift worry is to focus on the present moment and what you are able to do here and now. Regret about the past is not helpful; fear of the future in not helpful, either. Both should be banished from your mind.

GOAL SETTING

Set a series of achievable short-term goals that will contribute to attaining the long-term goal, and focus entirely on the goal at hand. Once you have achieved that, you will also have more confidence that you can achieve the next goal.

In practical terms, take the long-term goal and break it down into separate units, along with a realistic time frame for achieving each one. Even if you do not achieve a short-term goal within the planned time, do not worry, as you can adjust the timing overall and learn from the temporary setback. Think about what you have achieved instead of what you have not been able to achieve or what there is still to do. Keep reinforcing your commitment to achieving your ultimate goal.

Having a strong motive will help you to pursue your goal.

Endurance

Endurance is not just about keeping going without stopping. It is also about constantly picking yourself up off the floor when things go wrong. It's about having the ability to get up and try again.

PREPARATION

RELAXATION TECHNIQUE

- Put yourself in a comfortable position.
- Breathe slowly and easily.
- Think about your feet, and move your toes before letting them relax.
- Now think about first your lower legs and then your upper legs. Let them relax.
- Focus on your lower back, and let the muscles relax. Then do the same for your upper back.
- Focus on your fingers. Then focus on your forearms and upper arms. Focus next on your shoulders, letting them all relax as you think about them in turn.
- Then relax your neck and your jaw.
- If there is anywhere in your body where you still feel tension, focus on that. Let it relax.
- Lastly, focus on your breathing. Feel your stomach rise as you breathe in, and relax as you breathe out.
- Focus on pleasant thoughts and on relaxing.

Embrace vulnerability

Vulnerability is the awareness that you are only human and have limitations. Surprisingly, embracing vulnerability means that you may feel more confident in a challenging situation because you do not expect too much of yourself. You do not have to expect to feel confident all the time. You can accept yourself for who you are. You can also accept others.

Don't be surprised by feelings of nervousness.

Changing from negative to positive

You need to give yourself enough time to rest. Negative thoughts may lead to self-punishment, so remember to be kind to yourself. As needed, take time for a breather. Allow yourself a few moments to refocus. You will perform better if you give yourself time to calm down and refocus now and again. Relaxation is important. It allows your body and muscles to refuel so you can perform better.

DISTRACTIONS

Particularly in a disaster, there will be many unexpected things happening and plenty of distractions. However, being distracted is a choice. You do not have to let a distraction affect your mood or your ability to control a situation.

Practice dealing with small distractions to begin with, and see if you can maintain calmness and composure. This kind of practice may include making the choice to remain patient with a slow driver (as impatience may turn into road rage, which benefits no one). As you practice not allowing yourself to be distracted or overcome by unexpected or inconvenient events, you will increase your power to refocus and maintain your concentration, placing you in control of situations.

By controlling your natural emotional reactions to distractions, you can retain your focus. By not reacting to stressful situations, you can retain control and keep distractions, which are often quite small, in perspective. Constantly look for the positive in any situation, including those moments when distractions appear. Take a step back, and put distractions in perspective.

When dealing with a disaster, you can expect distractions of all kinds to be greater than usual. Try to let them bounce off you. Imagine them bouncing as far as possible. Make a commitment to act rather than react. Keep your focus on your plans and not on distractions or difficult personalities.

Elite soldiers learn to cope with distractions through intense and repetitive training regimes.

Accept your limitations

We cannot all perform at our best all of the time, even in conventional situations. When faced with a disaster, it is even less likely that we will perform at our best or have all the best solutions. Give yourself a break, and do the best you can in the circumstances, using the energy and resources that you have available. Then congratulate yourself on what you have been able to achieve. Doing the best you can is all that anyone can expect.

Do not confuse your value as a person with your performance in any situation, least of all a profoundly challenging one, such as a natural disaster or an accident.

RULE OF THREE

The rule of three is a thinking strategy used by the U.S. Marines. Using this strategy, you look at three options for a given situation and then carefully assess the merits and demerits of each one. The best option is the one you go for, and it is important that you follow through with that decision rather than have second thoughts.

WHAT TO CARRY AND TO WEAR

If you are faced with an emergency, such as a flood or wildfire, which forces you to abandon your home, you may have little time to think about what to take. If you live in an area that is liable to experience such threats, it is a good idea to think in advance about the clothing and equipment you would want to take with you. Also consider what you would need to carry the items. For example, having a large backpack, along with a smaller pack for emergency essentials, would be helpful.

Wearing the appropriate gear for the weather and climatic conditions can make all the difference when disaster unexpectedly strikes.

CLIMATE AND CONDITIONS

Most people have a tendency to overpack for the simple reason that they are not sure whether they will need certain items, so they pack the items just in case. More often than not, they don't need the things they questioned.

First, think carefully about the climate and conditions that you are likely to experience in your region, and then make a pile of clothing and equipment that you think you will need. When done, pare the pile down to the essentials.

Clothing

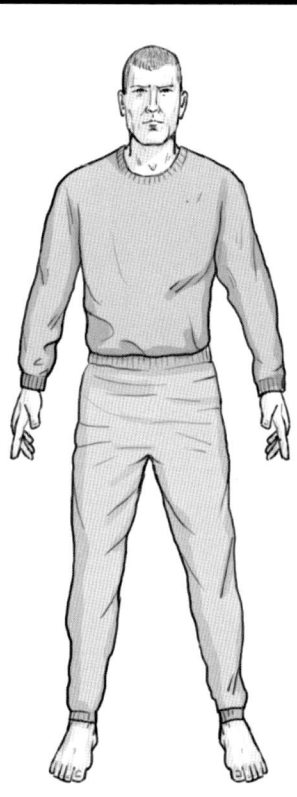

A base layer garment: This should be breathable and wicks sweat away: It is best to not use cotton garments, as they tend to absorb water and take a long time to dry. Choose either a manufactured material like polyester or a natural fiber like Merino wool. Merino is both comfortable and warm and has natural antibacterial properties, so it will not absorb body odor. It works efficiently even when damp and can absorb a lot of moisture without feeling wet.

A warm middle layer: Such as a long-sleeved or vest-style fleece, which is both warm and light to carry: There may be an option for zipping a fleece into your outer layer. Some soft-shell fleece layers have an element of weather protection so that they can be worn in moderately wet conditions without danger of soaking through or losing breathability. This means that you do not necessarily have to put on your shell jacket in light rain or drizzle. Choose the weight of fleece according to the likely temperature conditions. Select from lightweight to heavyweight.

Socks: Like other clothing, socks should be chosen to suit the climate. Wear finer socks in the summer, when your feet will expand and sweat more, and thicker ones for winter. Take a spare pair of dry socks to change into.

WHAT TO CARRY AND TO WEAR 47

A shell jacket: This will protect you from the worst of rain and wind: Make sure it is both fully waterproof and breathable, and ensure that the pockets suit your requirements. Some have lined pockets, which will help warm hands. Also think about the lengths that jackets come in, and select one based on the movements you will need to make while wearing it.

Waterproof trousers: These can be very handy to pull on in heavy rain or snow. They can keep the pants of your base layer dry. Waterproof trousers need to be easy to put on and remove, so versions with zip ankles may be a good choice.

Boots and shoes: Especially if you have to walk through areas that have experienced damage from earthquakes or floods, it is important to have sturdy footwear that will protect your feet and lower ankle as well as give you plenty of grip.

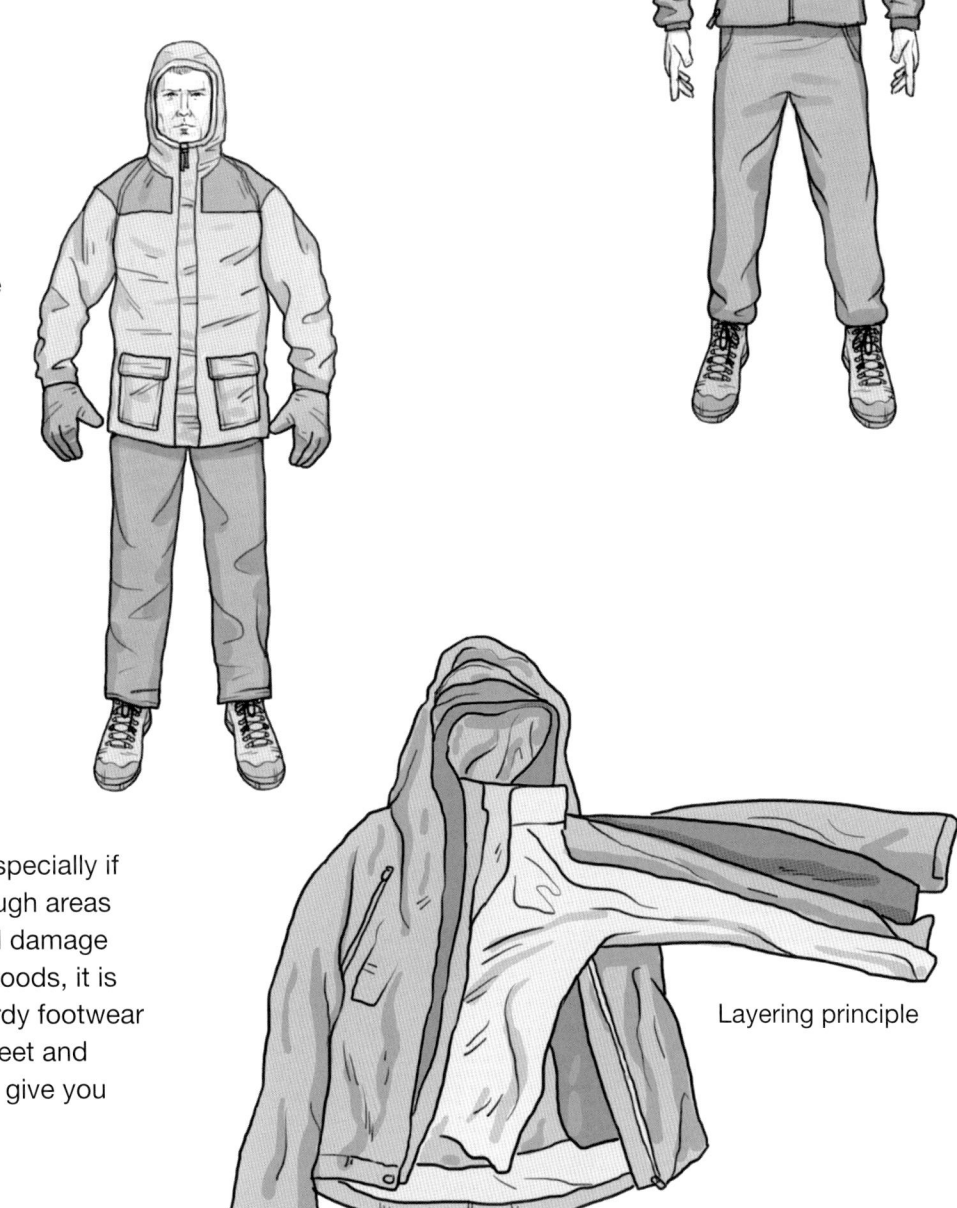

Layering principle

BACKPACK

Keep a backpack handy that is large enough to take your essentials, with a bit of room to spare. In order to minimize weight in your backpack, think of ways of taking the minimum equipment you require.

Small versions of shampoo, shaving foam, and toothpaste are available in many stores. Along with your emergency food, include chocolate or other favorite foods. Carry dried milk, coffee, and sugar in small packets.

If you have any hard items, such as cans of food or cooking stoves, make sure that they are stored toward the outside of the backpack and not against your back.

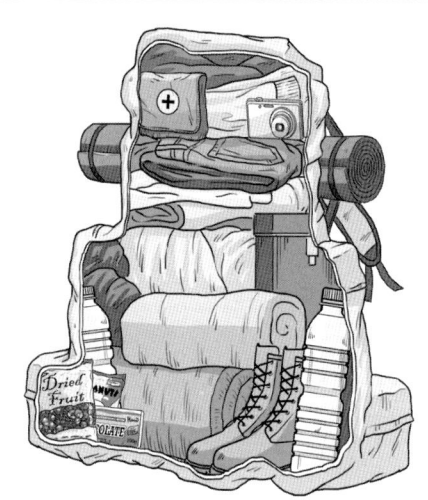

FIRST AID KIT

It is always a good idea to carry an emergency first aid kit. If there is a danger of your becoming separated from your backpack and other equipment, carry a first aid kit on your belt or in a jacket pocket.

Suggested contents of an emergency first aid kit:

- Waterproof bandages of various sizes
- Crepe bandage for supporting a twisted ankle or making a dressing
- Padded dressings to be placed on an open wound
- Cotton wool
- Medical tape
- Scissors
- Tweezers
- Antiseptic wipes
- Antiseptic cream/spray
- Iodine
- Thermometer
- Pain relief tablets, such as ibuprofen or aspirin
- Medicine for settling a queasy stomach

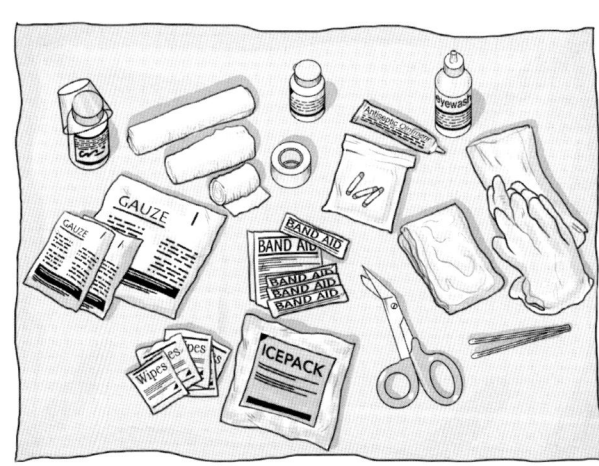

SURVIVAL KIT

Military personnel involved in operations with high risk of capture often carry survival equipment that will enable them to survive without access to their main equipment. In a military scenario, this may mean that soldiers dump their heavy backpacks in order to escape from enemy forces. In a civilian scenario, it may mean becoming separated from your main equipment after an accident or a natural disaster.

You can devise your own personal "bug out" kit that will provide you with some essentials to help make life more comfortable if you are away from home.

Here are some suggestions:

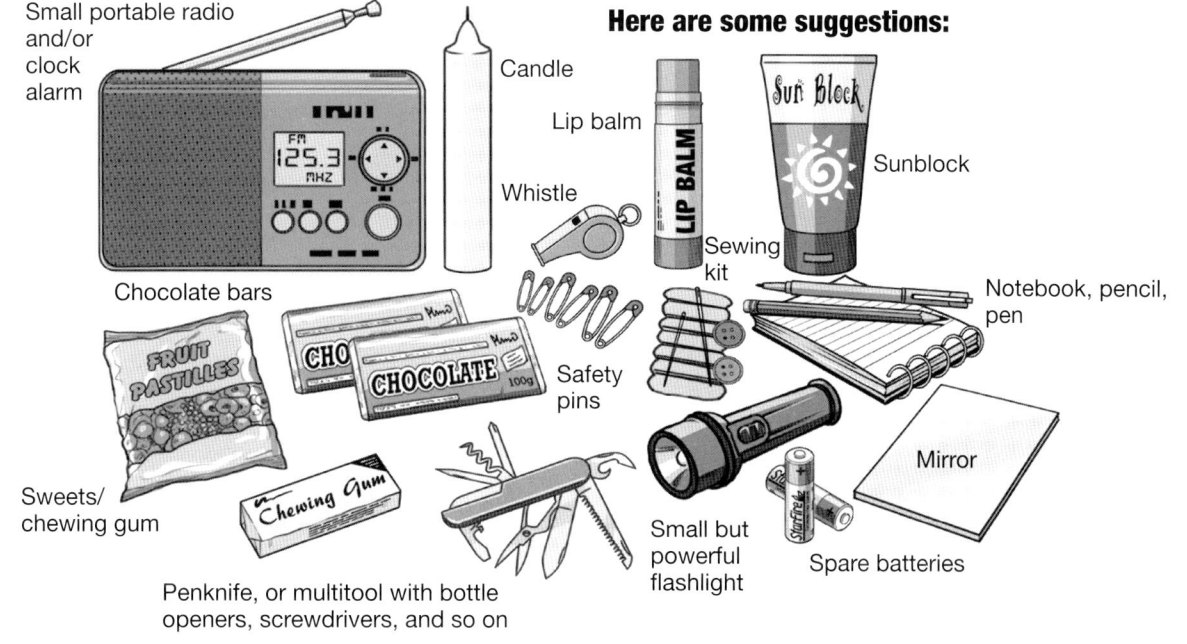

Packing essentials

Sleeping bags:
If you want to travel as light as possible, sleeping bags made with goose or eiderdown fillings are lighter and pack smaller. However, these natural materials take longer to dry when wet. If you are traveling in wet or snowbound areas, it is best to take a sleeping bag made with manmade materials such as Thinsulate.

Sleeping bag liner: This is a handy piece of equipment that you may wish to consider. It goes inside your sleeping bag, keeping the bag itself clean. It will absorb body odor and can be washed. It also has the potential to be used on its own in warmer climates or if you are sleeping in a hut or rescue center.

Waterproof bags: Keep some waterproof bags handy so that your clothes remain dry even if your backpack is soaked.

Water: Carrying enough water will be a priority in any environment. Make sure that you have enough capacity for it.

50 WHAT TO CARRY AND TO WEAR

NAVIGATION ESSENTIALS

The ability to navigate successfully will help you to cope with disasters that require you to find your way back to safety.

It may be impossible to access the Internet to get directions, so make sure you have a map with enough detail. A scale of 1:24,000 should be sufficient. On such a map, 1 inch represents 2,000 feet, and 1 centimeter represents 240 meters.

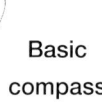

Basic compass

- Map case to protect maps, especially from rain
- A baseplate compass for use with a map
- A prismatic or marching compass for taking accurate bearings on features in the distance
- Map measurer for measuring distance on a map
- Pedometer for measuring how far you have traveled on the ground
- Tally counter for counting your paces

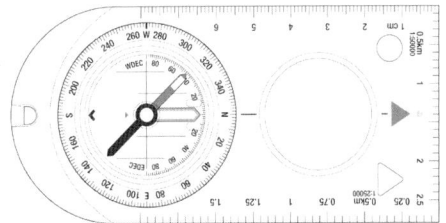

Baseplate compass

Prismatic compass

Other useful items

- Personal locator beacon (PLB) with global navigation satellite system (GNSS) in case you need to be rescued
- Head torch for walking at night
- Flashlight for reading maps
- Grease pencil to make markings on a map

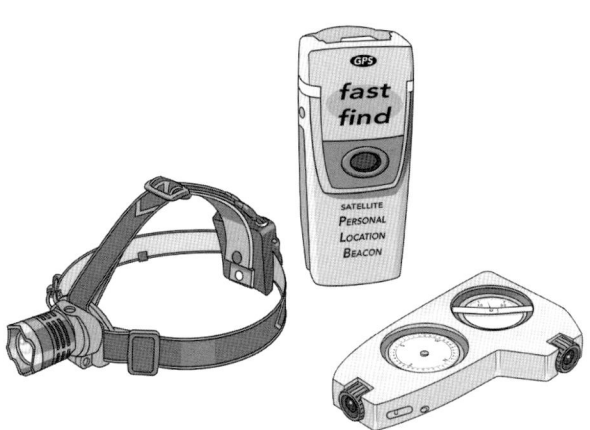

HOW TO TAKE A BEARING WITH A BASEPLATE COMPASS AND MAP

You should orient your map to the north so that the direction you are walking in is the same as the directions shown on the map.

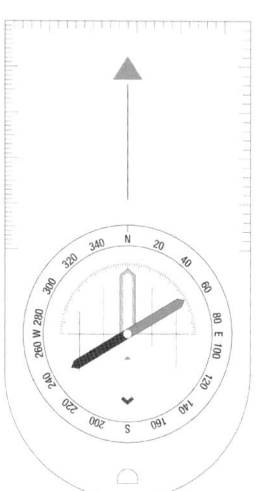

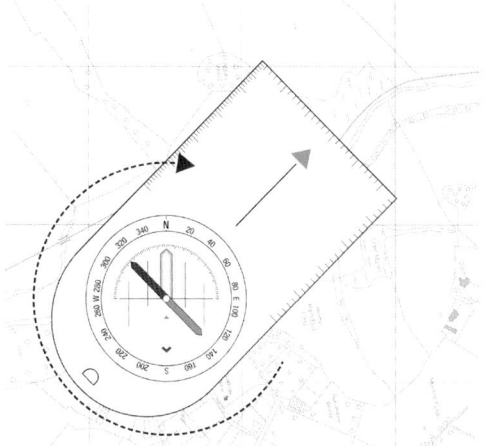

To take a bearing, place the compass edge along your current position and your destination.

Turn the compass housing so that the red arrow in the compass housing points north, parallel with the map meridians.

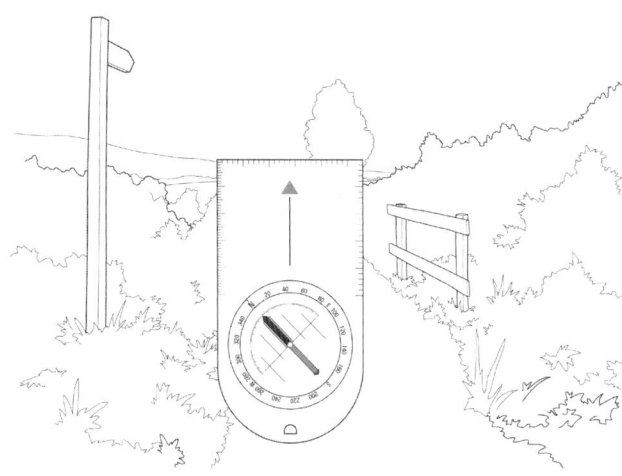

Then take the compass off the map and hold it horizontally. Turn yourself and the compass until the red end of the needle is inside the red north–south arrow. The direction of the travel arrow should now point toward your destination. Choose a landmark that lies on the line of travel to make it easier to follow.

ESSENTIALS FOR THE HOME

If your home is cut off, or if part of your house becomes inaccessible due to flooding or hurricane damage, you will need to have access to essential equipment, water, and food to keep you going.

Be aware of any warnings, and plan accordingly, particularly with regard to water and food. Plan to store enough water to keep your family going for at least three days, bearing in mind that each person should drink at least 0.5 gallons (2 l) of water per day. For a family of four people, that would be 6 gallons (24 l). If the weather is hot and humid, you will need more than that.

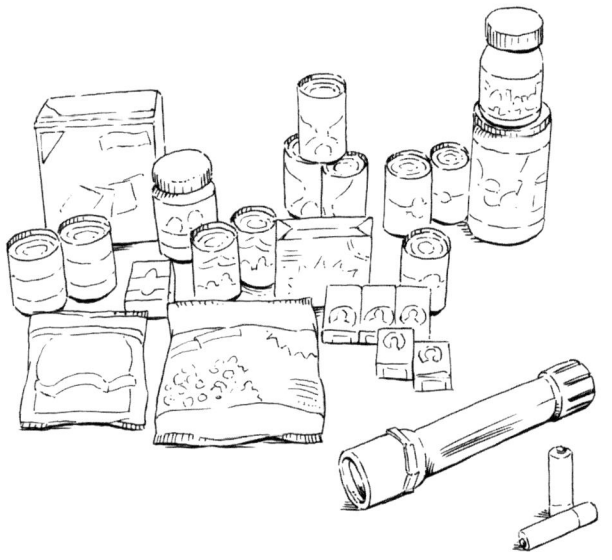

Keeping stores

- Store canned food in a safe place, and make sure that you have a can opener.
- Keep a stock of plates and mugs.
- Make sure you have enough spare toilet paper.
- Keep a plastic bucket with a lid.
- Make sure you have a roll of garbage bags.
- Keep a store of spare blankets and sleeping bags as well as sleeping mats or mattresses if you do not have access to beds.
- Acquire a home toolkit.
- Store a battery-operated radio and spare batteries to keep in touch with emergency broadcasts.
- Gather battery-powered storm lanterns.
- Have candles and matches.
- A family-sized first aid kit should include prescription medicines.
- Gather personal documents, including passports, insurance documents, and proof of address.
- Keep a cell phone and charger.
- Have duct tape.
- Include work gloves.
- Keep one change of clothing and footwear per person.
- Have rainwear for each family member.

BASIC DISASTER SUPPLIES KIT

After an emergency, you may need to survive on your own for several days. Being prepared means having your own food, water, and other supplies to last for at least 72 hours. A disaster supplies kit is a collection of basic items your household may need in the event of an emergency.

To assemble your kit, store items in airtight plastic bags and put your entire disaster supplies kit in one or two easy-to-carry containers such as plastic bins or a duffel bag.

A basic emergency supply kit could include the following recommended items:

- Water: One gallon of water per person per day for at least three days, for drinking and sanitation
- Food: At least a three-day supply of non-perishable food
- Battery-powered or hand crank radio and a NOAA Weather Radio with tone alert
- Flashlight
- First aid kit
- Extra batteries
- Whistle to signal for help
- Dust mask to help filter contaminated air and plastic sheeting and duct tape to shelter-in-place
- Moist towelettes, garbage bags, and plastic ties for personal sanitation
- Wrench or pliers to turn off utilities
- Manual can opener for food
- Local maps
- Cell phone with chargers and a backup battery

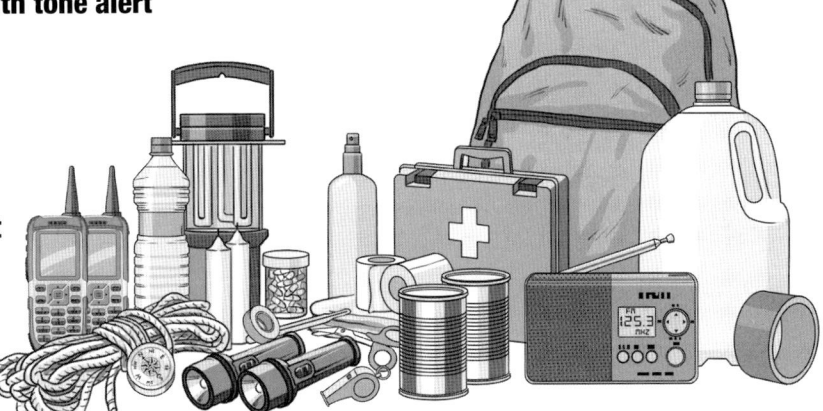

KEEPING SPARES

Depending on your circumstances and the age range of your family, you will need to plan to have spare supplies of the following:

- Diapers for very young children
- Prescription medication
- Infant formula/bottled milks
- Baby food in cans
- Paper or plastic cups, plates, knives, forks, spoons
- Can opener
- Sanitizing spray
- Moist wipes or wet towels
- Toilet paper
- Books, games, and puzzles
- Spare prescription and reading glasses
- Contact lens cases and cleaners/buffers

FLOODS AND TSUNAMIS

Floods are some of the most frequent and dangerous of all natural hazards. In the United States of America, no other natural disaster causes more death and destruction than floods. A tsunami is a catastrophic event that results from an earthquake, volcanic eruption, or landslide raising the ocean floor, creating waves that build up to enormous heights once they reach land. Tsunamis have caused terrible destruction and loss of life throughout history.

An earthquake measuring 9.0 magnitude hit Miyako City, northern Japan, on March 11, 2011. Here the tsunami caused by the earthquake breeches an embankment and floods a highway.

FLOODS

To some extent, floods can be predicted and controlled through the construction of dams, channels, and reservoirs, and by the management of floodplains. Natural features such as forests also have an important role in reducing the impact of floods.

When rivers overflow their banks, this can cause flooding, which is often the result of excessive rainfall. In some areas of the world, seasonal flooding can be beneficial to crops, such as in the Mississippi Valley in the American Midwest, or the Nile River Valley and the Tigris-Euphrates Valley in the Middle East. In these cases, rivers leave silt that makes the earth fertile for crops.

Uncontrolled flooding can cause massive damage and threat to life, though. Even a seemingly harmless occurrence such as a dam built by beavers can cause a river to burst its banks.

The ocean and seas can also cause flooding, due to surges. Tsunamis or large storms can bring large amounts of water on land.

A floodplain is nature's way of dealing with river flooding. Gradually the soil absorbs the water, and the river returns to its normal state. However, building developers are often tempted to build on floodplains, and the presence of concrete reduces the available area for natural ground absorption.

A truck drives through the flooded streets of Baton Rouge, La., after Hurricane Gustav struck the region in 2008.

Flood damage

Large bodies of water can move with the pressure of millions of tons and can carry away everything from cars to buildings. Water also erodes the soil so that even in cases where buildings are not crushed by the force of water their foundations may be eroded, causing them to subside or collapse.

Floods also leave potentially hazardous damage behind once they have receded. Drains can become mixed with floodwater, leading to diseases such as cholera. Floodwater can also become toxic due to contact with chemicals. Dangerous sharp objects can be left behind by floodwater, and floods can also create dangers with electric power lines.

MISSISSIPPI RIVER FLOOD

The Mississippi River is one of the longest rivers in North America and one of the mightiest rivers in the world. It covers a distance of about 2,320 miles (3,734 km). Its basin covers parts of 31 American states. The potential for such a river to flood is substantial, and this may be triggered by several factors, including heavy rain downpours, rapid snowmelt in spring, or early rains in the Great Plains.

In the summer of 1993, the Mississippi and its associated rivers such as the Missouri flooded simultaneously, breaking dams, floodwalls, and levies, and causing floods that covered 15 million acres (6 million hectares). Such floods are statistically calculated to have a 1 percent chance of happening in any given year.

Flash floods

Flash floods can be dangerous, hard to predict, and difficult to manage. As their name suggests, they can occur suddenly and with little warning due to a single event, such as a fierce storm with heavy rain or the melting of a glacier. Flash floods are particularly common in desert areas, where a thunderstorm can cause water to suddenly rush down canyons before the hard dry ground can absorb it.

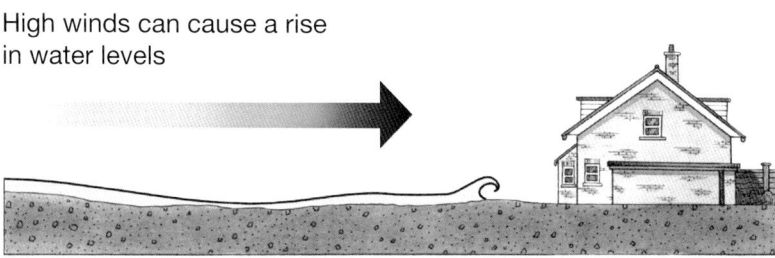

High winds can cause a rise in water levels

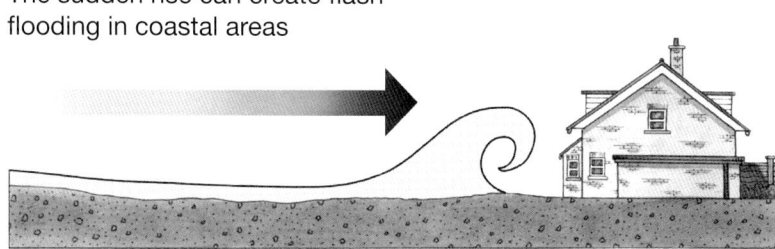

The sudden rise can create flash flooding in coastal areas

Global warming may be the cause of an increase of what might be called biblical flooding. Flash floods may be exacerbated in urban areas by the large amount of asphalt and concrete covering the ground.

Consider using gravel to create a driveway rather than concrete. Gravel will allow water to drain into the earth below, whereas it will skim quickly over concrete. Keep an eye out for blocked drains, either around your home or on local roads, and advise the authorities if necessary. It takes only a wad of leaves to block a drain, causing water to run over it rather than down and away.

ACTION IN A FLOOD

Keep abreast of local broadcasts and flood warnings if you live in a flood danger area. Check government websites to establish the level of danger. If a flood warning has been issued, give yourself plenty of time to prepare.

Inside your home, take up carpets if possible, and move as much furniture as you can to upper floors. Place furniture on bricks to minimize its contact with the floodwater. Place valuables on shelves. Turn off gas and electricity supplies.

Sandbags

Make sure that you get enough sandbags in good time to help protect your home. If you run out of traditional sandbags, use plastic bags or even pillowcases to make your own.

Place sandbags in front of doors, and build them up in a staggered way, like bricks, with the second layer covering the points between the bags on the first layer, and so on. Step on the bags, and stamp them down so that they mold together and form a seal.

Do not pile sandbags too high, as they may be in danger of toppling over with the force of the water against them. Consider hard flood barriers. Place sandbags in front of air vents.

Positioning sandbags

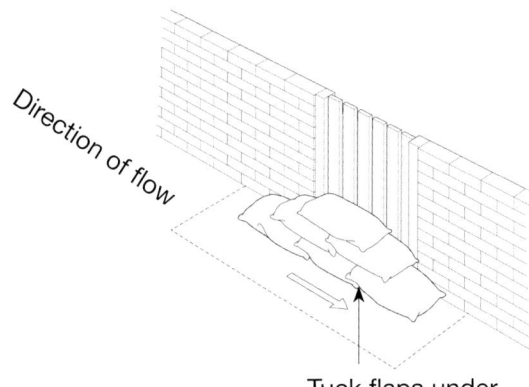

Pyramid Method
Ideal for sandbag protection more than three layers high.

Better Method
Lay plastic sheeting across the side of the sandbag wall on the water edge. Weigh down with additional sandbags.

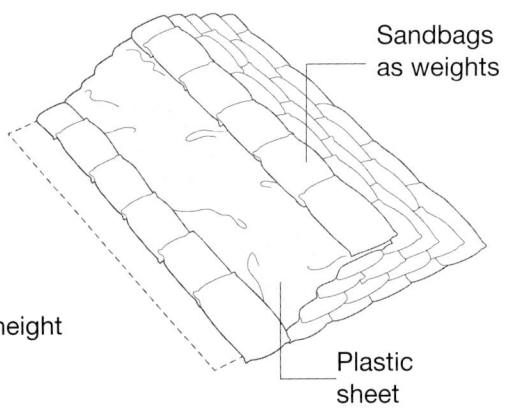

Yard

Create flood defenses in the yard and garden, based on the direction the water is likely to travel. If you have a garden wall that seals the property, make sure that you seal the gate area with sandbags or special defense systems.

The sandbag dyke provides excellent protection against rising floodwaters. Plastic sheeting will protect the sandbags from leakage.

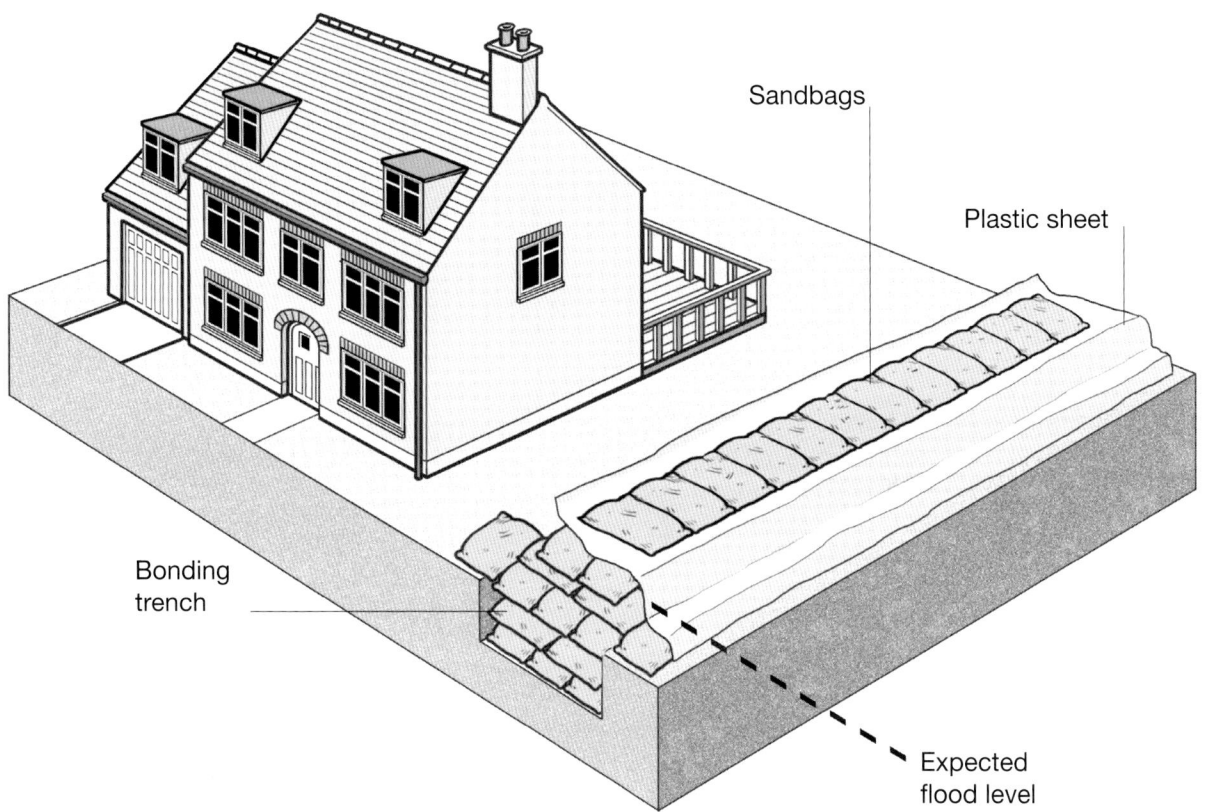

WATER

Fill bathtubs and sinks with clean water, and put aside plenty of bottles of drinking water. During the flood, try not to use municipal water for drinking, as it may be contaminated. Wait for clearance from the local authorities.

Car in a flood

When attempting to drive through water, keep the car in a low gear, and drive at a steady speed in order to avoid creating a bow wave and flooding the engine.

If your car is caught in a flood and the engine stalls, get away from the car, as it could be swept away. Keep the car facing the flow of water so as to minimize the force of water on the car and to prevent it from being turned over by the floodwater.

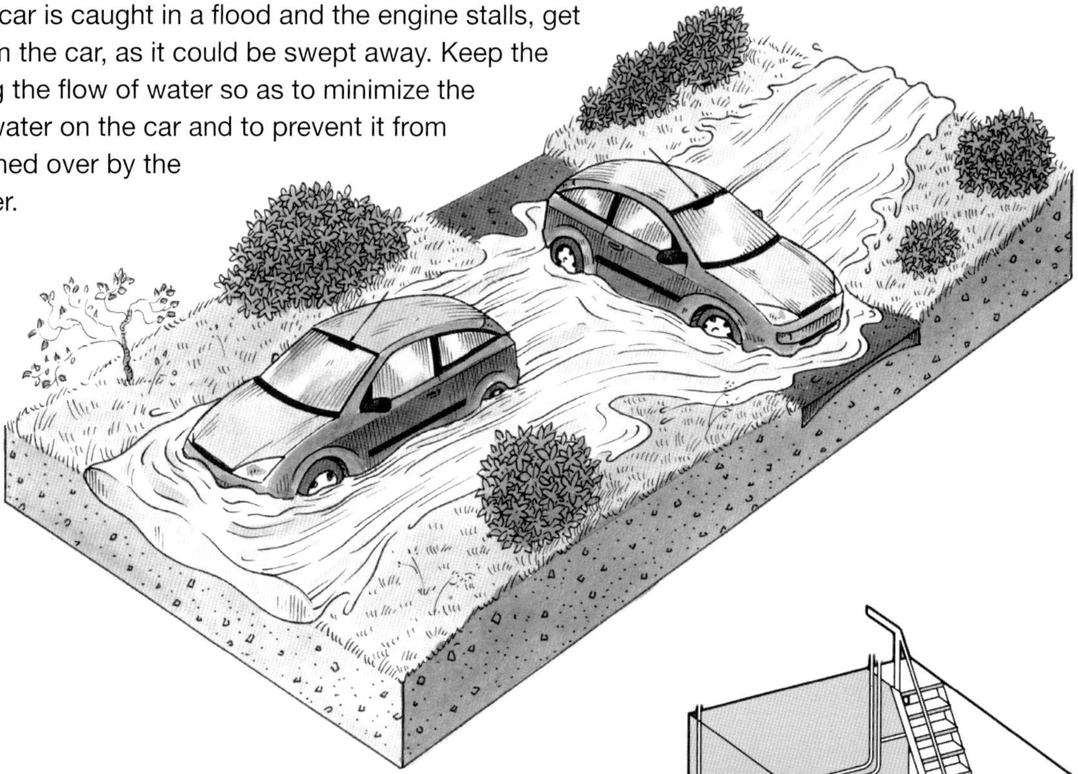

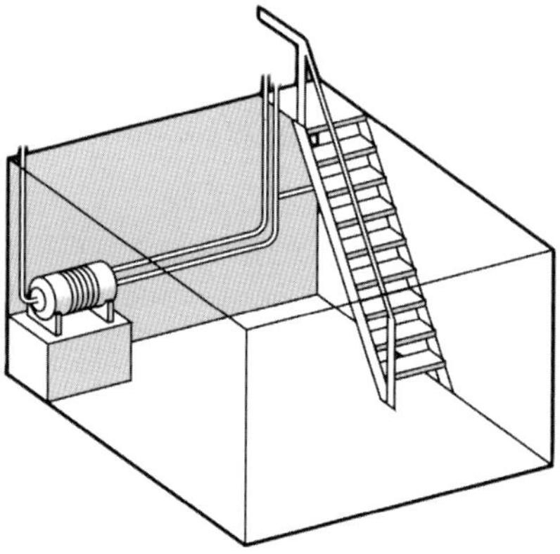

CLEAN UP

Avoid floodwater as far as possible, as it is likely to be contaminated. Once the floodwater has subsided, you will need to thoroughly clean and disinfect the areas of the house and furniture that have been in contact with the floodwater.

Basement flooding

If you live in an area prone to flooding, a good idea would be to buy a sump pump and fit it to your basement. This will drain out flood waters and control the flooding.

JAPAN 2011

On March 11, 2011 Masako Unoura and her aunt Noriko were driving to a meeting in Kesennuma, Miyagi Prefecture. Kesennuma is close to the epicenter of the earthquake that would occur that day, and large sections of the city would be destroyed by the tsunami that followed. Over 800 deaths were reported, with 1,196 missing.

As they drove, Masako and Noriko felt the tremors of the earthquake but continued driving. When they reached the building where the meeting was to be held, they were told that a huge tsunami was on its way and that they needed to get away immediately. They returned to their car and soon found themselves in a traffic gridlock.

As she could see water approaching, Masako realized that their best chance of survival was to get out of the car and find their way to high ground. Although unsure where to go, they were fortunate enough to bump into a coast guard who, seeing a wall of water approaching, told them to follow him. By scrambling over fences and walls and scaling buildings, they managed to get high enough onto the roof of a building to keep them out of the water that was swirling and rushing around them.

Masako's story demonstrates how quick thinking, determination, and a bit of luck can save lives. If a tsunami is approaching, there is no time to wait in traffic. You have to run for your life.

TSUNAMI

Tsunami waves, which can be relatively small in deep ocean areas, can travel at speeds of up to 500 miles per hour (805 kph), which makes it imperative that you act immediately once a tsunami warning is given.

As the waves reach the continental shelf, their speed decreases and their height increases. They can grow to about 100 feet (30 m) in under 15 minutes. Powerful surges of water can run onto the land, sweeping away everything in their path.

An earthquake-related tsunami is generated when the slip of tectonic plates at a plate boundary causes a massive water displacement, generating a huge wave that can travel hundreds of miles to strike land.

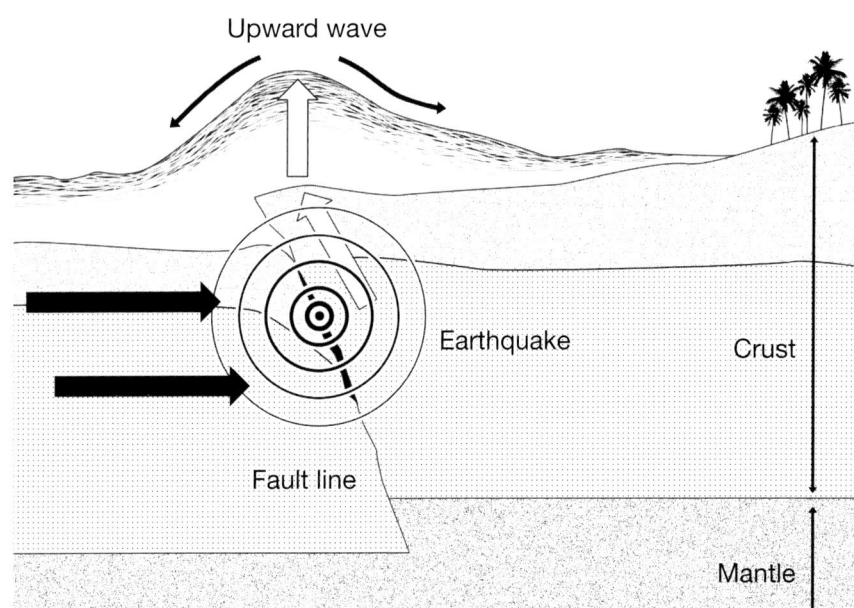

WARNING SIGNS

A tsunami may be visible as an approaching wave, but if it can be seen, there is very little time to avoid it. Another sign of a tsunami is seawater retreating from the shore, exposing areas that are usually underwater. The trough of an approaching wave is often the cause.

If you are traveling to an area that has previously been affected by tsunamis, familiarize yourself with the tsunami warning signs and the officially recommended escape routes. Walk the escape route with your family so that you are all familiar with it.

THAILAND 2004

On December 26, 2004, María Belón, a medical doctor, her husband Enrique Álvarez, and their three sons, Lucas, Tomás, and Simón, were spending the Christmas holiday at Khao Lak in Thailand. The family members were in and around the pool when the tsunami wave hit and swept them away.

María first grabbed for a tree but then heard Lucas screaming for help, so she let go and swam after him. At this point a second wave struck, dragging her over rough ground, during which she sustained serious injuries to her chest and leg. She and Lucas eventually managed to get to dry land, where she dressed her wounds with leaves. They managed to climb a tree for safety and were eventually rescued by local people who took María to a hospital with her son.

Enrique and the two other boys were also taken to a hospital, and they were eventually reunited with María and Lucas. The family's incredible story of survival was later dramatized in the movie *The Impossible*.

MOVE FAST

Do not attempt to gather together your possessions when there is a tsunami warning, as there is not enough time. Do not return to low-lying areas until you have received an official clearance from local authorities.

Tsunami response

The immediate action on a tsunami warning is to get to high ground, above the level of any wave or flooding. If you see or hear any signs of a tsunami, such as receding seawater or a large roar from the water, warn everyone around you, and try to contact someone in authority.

Be aware that there will be a large number of dangers following a tsunami, from damaged buildings and cars to broken glass and contaminated water. Keep clear of downed power lines, and be aware of loose bricks, concrete, or rubble falling from damaged buildings or bridges.

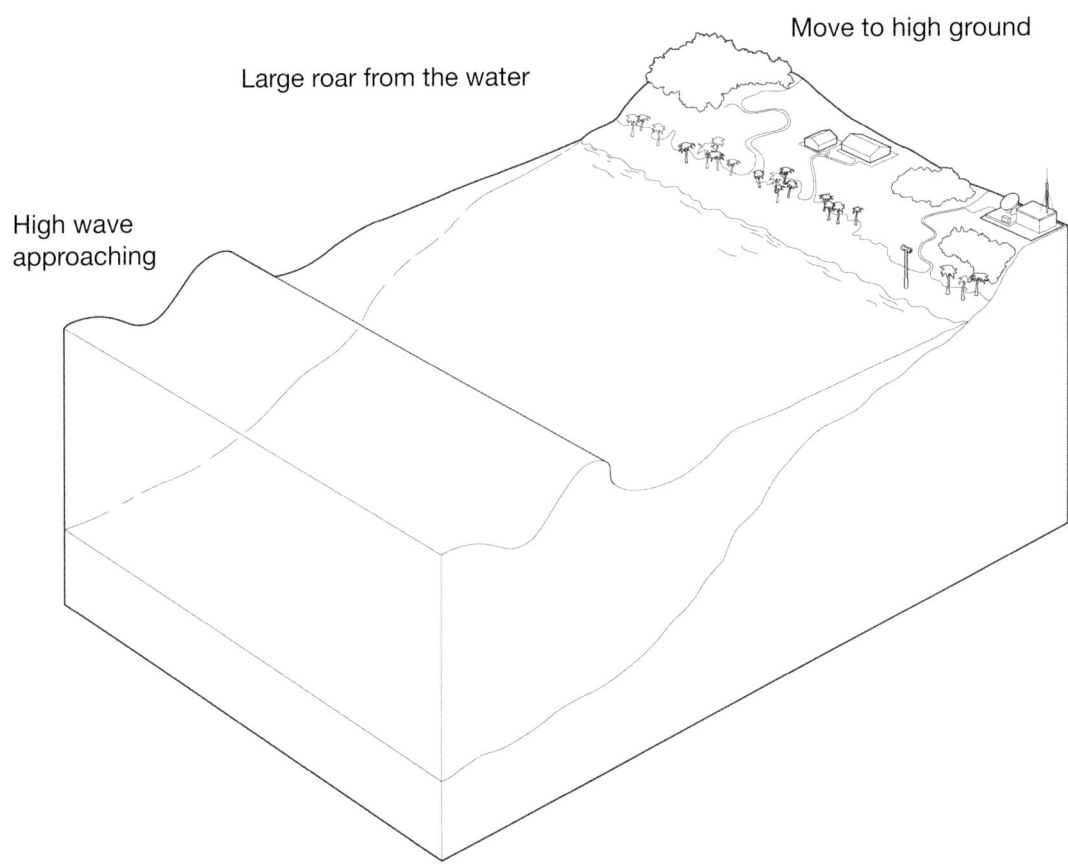

Devastating Tsunamis

Some of the world's most devastating tsunamis

Japan, northeast coast, March 11, 2011:

An earthquake of 9.0 magnitude created tsunami waves of up to 128 feet (39 m), which traveled at speeds of up to 497 miles per hour (800 kph). Sweeping over the east coast of Japan, the waves killed about 18,000 people and caused massive damage to towns and villages as well as to ports and industrial centers, traveling up to 6 miles (10 km) inland. These events also caused a nuclear emergency.

Sumatra, Indonesia, December 26, 2004:

This began with a 9.1 magnitude earthquake off the coast of Sumatra, where the fault line displaced the seafloor by 30 feet (9 m) horizontally above the rupture. The waves that hit the coast reached heights of 100 feet (30 m). Around 230,000 people were reported missing and presumed dead.

Sanriku, Japan, June 15, 1896:

A magnitude 7.6 earthquake off the coast of Japan created a tsunami wave that reached heights of 125 feet (38 m). The water swept the region of Sanriku, causing about 22,000 deaths.

Large coastal areas of southern India (shown here), Thailand, and Indonesia were devastated by the Indian Ocean tsunami in December 2004.

Chile, August 13, 1868:

An earthquake with a magnitude of about 8.5 occurred off the coast of Peru/Chile, creating tsunami waves of up to 52 feet (16 m) in height. About 25,000 people were killed.

Krakatoa, Indonesia, August 27, 1883:

When the Krakatoa caldera volcano self-destructed, tsunami waves of 135 feet (41 m) swept the region and, along with an earthquake, caused a death toll of nearly 40,000 people.

Lisbon, Portugal, November 1, 1755:

A magnitude 8.5 earthquake caused tsunami waves of up to 65 feet (20 m) high to sweep the coast of Portugal and southern Spain. The earthquake and tsunami caused about 60,000 deaths in Lisbon and devastated the city.

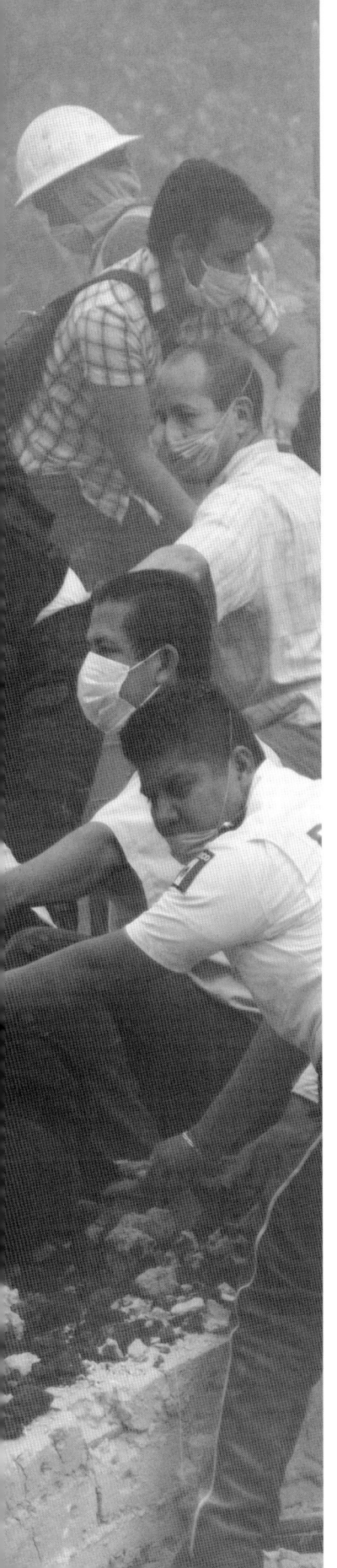

EARTHQUAKES AND VOLCANOES

Earthquakes are usually caused when rock masses near geological fault lines grind against each other, releasing seismic waves. A volcano is an event where molten underground rock, accompanied by gases from Earth's hot core, burst through the crust of the planet, often with hugely destructive force.

First responders rescue people trapped in rubble following an earthquake in Mexico City in September 2017.

EARTHQUAKES

The margins of Earth's tectonic plates are the areas where earthquakes most frequently occur. One of the world's most high-risk zones is the Pacific Ring of Fire, a horseshoe-shaped area that includes many small islands in the Pacific Ocean, as well as Japan, the Philippines, South America, and Alaska.

Preparing the home

If you live in an earthquake danger zone, take precautions with the internal fittings of your home, such as bolting bookcases with wall studs as well as securing any other cupboards or wardrobes that may come loose.

Identify a safe area in each room of the house, such as a sturdy table or desk, where you can seek refuge. You should have an emergency kit available.

If possible, you should turn off your gas and water lines before an earthquake, in case pipes are broken.

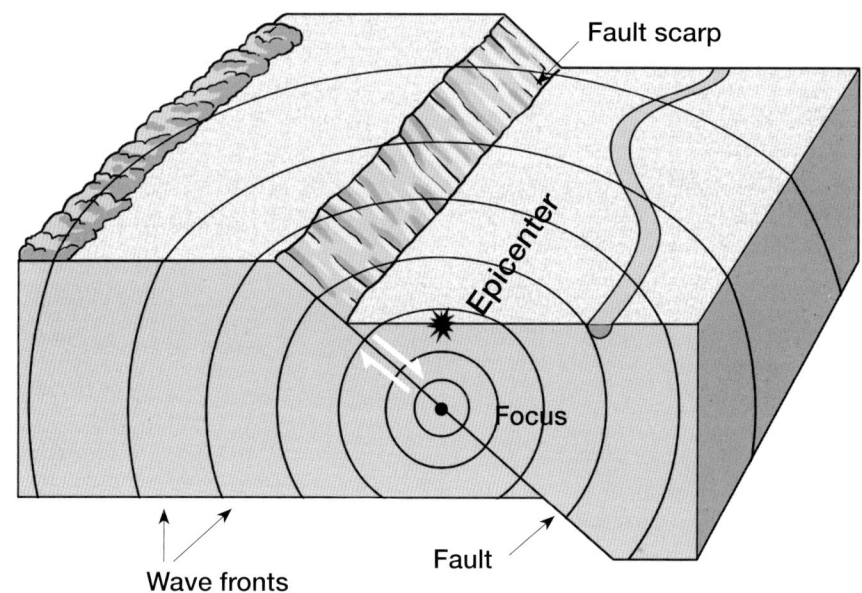

Seismic waves radiate from the focus of an earthquake

STAY PUT

If you are in a building during an earthquake, do not be tempted to run outside, as you may be exposed to falling masonry, glass, or other hazards. It is not advisable to seek shelter in cellars or tunnels during an earthquake, as exits may become blocked.

EARTHQUAKES AND VOLCANOES

What to do

In a building
Once the shaking of the earthquake begins, get under a table or another protection and hold on. When the shaking stops, you can come out from the secure area, but be careful around any furniture or shelves that may be loose.

Keep away from windows during an earthquake, as there is a strong risk of shattered glass.

If you need to leave a building after an earthquake, use the stairs rather than the elevator. However, if you smell gas, you will need to get out of the building as soon as possible. Before you leave the building, check the area for any visible dangers.

Outside
If you are outside during an earthquake, get away from buildings, trees, lampposts, and power lines. Drop to the ground, and keep low until the earthquake subsides. Injuries in earthquakes often occur when people move around and either fall over or get hit by falling debris or objects.

In a car
If you are in a car when an earthquake starts, slow down and drive to a clear area if possible, away from buildings or trees. Stay in the car until the shaking stops. Avoid bridges or overpasses.

Anatomy of an earthquake

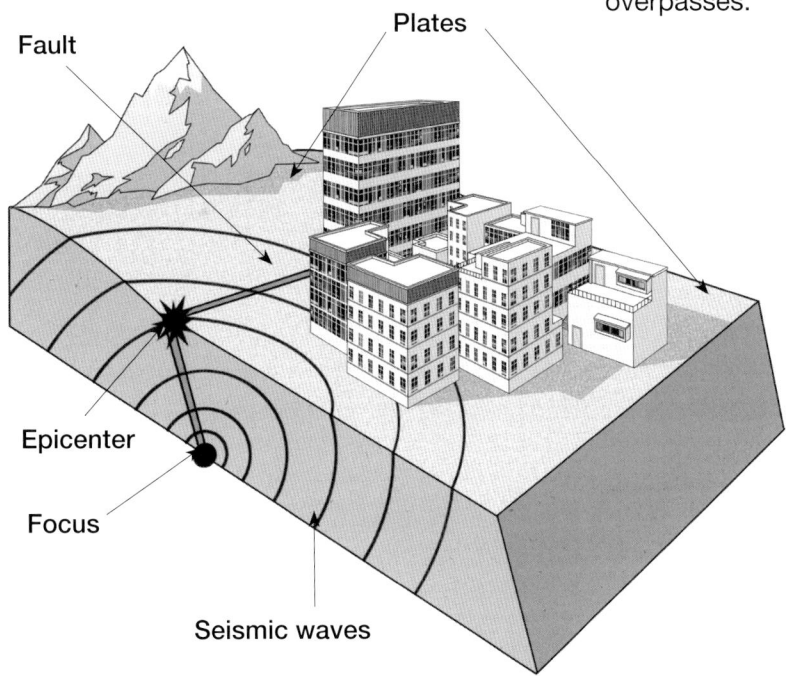

After the Earthquake

During and after an earthquake, beware of secondary effects, such as landslides if you live near hills, or tsunamis if you are near the coast. Fire is also a common post-earthquake phenomenon. Earthquakes often lead to aftershocks that can continue for hours, days, weeks, or even months.

After an earthquake, there may be multiple dangers, including broken gas pipes, downed power lines, and damaged drains. Keep clear of any structures that may have been weakened during the earthquake and which may be liable to collapse.

Weakened structures may be in and around your own home. Your chimney may have been weakened. Shingles or tiles may fall off your roof. You will need to have your house checked inside and outside later, especially if you can see obvious cracks in walls or ceilings. Take care when opening wardrobes and cupboards, as loose objects may have shifted.

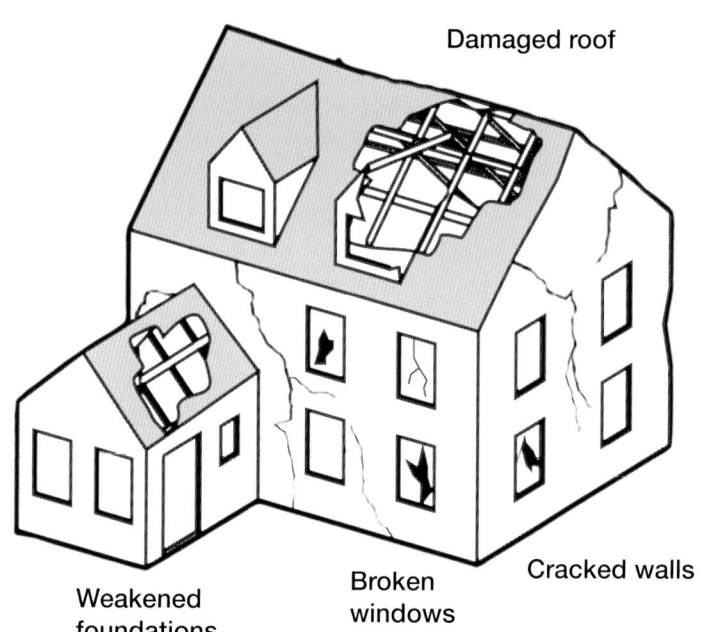

Damaged roof

Weakened foundations

Broken windows

Cracked walls

PHONE AND MEDIA

- **Save phone calls for emergencies.**
- **Once safe, monitor local news reports via battery operated radio, television, social media, and cell phone text alerts for emergency information and instructions.**

TRUE STORY

On May 18, 1980, Mount St. Helens experienced an earthquake of magnitude 5.1, which caused a landslide on the north face, followed by an explosive blast of ash and stone from the volcano. These were followed by pyroclastic flows and mudflows. Simultaneously, there was a blast out of the top of the volcano of gas and ash that rose as high as 16 miles (26 km) into the air.

Camping by a river 30 miles (48 km) from the mountain were Venus Dergan and Roald Reitan. They heard a warning siren from the nearby town of Toutle but did not know what it meant.

As water from the river started rushing toward them, they ripped down their tent and climbed into their car. What they did not know was that a mass of hot mud was heading down the river toward them as well.

The car would not start, so they climbed on the roof. The vehicle was soon swept away by the mudflow. Dergan and Reitan were carried with it, but as the river of water quadrupled in size, they were thrown from the top. Reitan managed to get hold of Dergan and was able to pull her onto a log. They were taken about 1 mile (1.6 km) downstream before a helicopter picked them up.

Smoke and ash billow from the peak of Mount St. Helen, Washington. This volcano is well known for its ash explosions.

VOLCANOES

Volcanoes can have many side effects, including causing earthquakes, tsunamis, and mudflows. Magma may flow down the side of a volcano and into populated areas, causing immediate danger to life and property.

Sometimes volcanoes may explode, sending gas and ash hundreds of feet or meters into the air, along with solid pieces of rock.

A pyroclastic flow on a volcano may travel more than 60 miles per hour (100 kph), and the gas may reach temperatures of 1,100°F to 1,300°F (593°C to 704°C).

The gas clouds emitted from a volcano can include carbon dioxide, carbon monoxide, hydrogen sulfide, and sulfur dioxide. These gases can be fatal if inhaled.

This building has become buried by lava flow from Mount Etna on the island of Sicily.

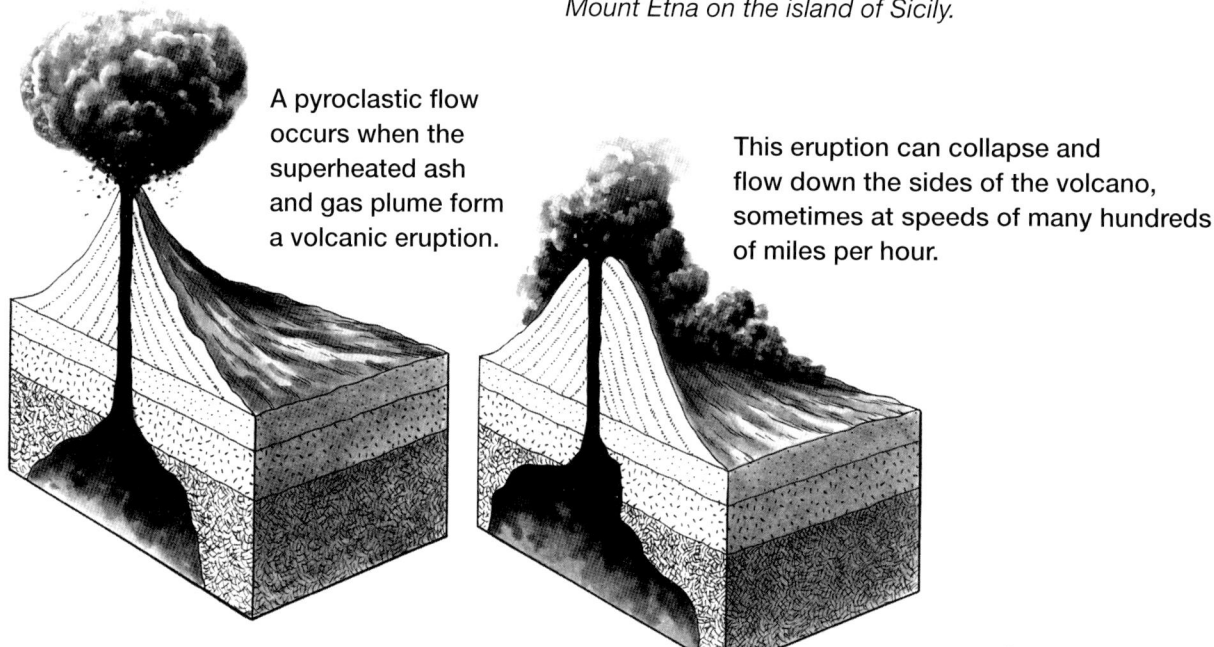

A pyroclastic flow occurs when the superheated ash and gas plume form a volcanic eruption.

This eruption can collapse and flow down the sides of the volcano, sometimes at speeds of many hundreds of miles per hour.

EARTHQUAKES AND VOLCANOES   73

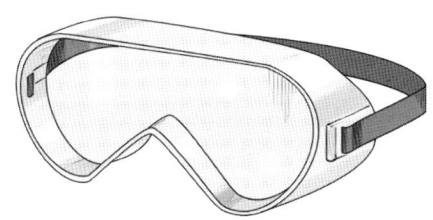

Safety goggles

Safety

There are about 50 volcanic eruptions of various kinds around the world every year. It may be the case, therefore, that you may travel to an area where there is volcanic activity.

If you are staying indoors, close windows and doors, and block chimneys. Block air vents and any other holes that might allow ash into the house.

Volcanic ash may present itself in the air, so make sure that you have goggles and a protection mask available. You may also need a flashlight. If you are exposed to ash and do not have access to a face mask, hold a damp cloth over your face. If there is a danger of flying volcanic projectiles, such as rocks or pieces of metal, wear a hard hat or keep in a sheltered area.

WARNING SIGNS

Be aware of the warning signs from the volcano itself, such as rumblings, steam, gas, and sulfurous smells. Volcanoes often provide early warnings of any explosions, so do not ignore these signs. Get expert advice if you are unsure.

Plan your escape route so that you can get away quickly. Make sure that there is enough fuel in your vehicle. However, volcanic ash can damage vehicle engines, so consider the option that you may need to get away on foot.

If there is a dangerous magma flow, do not stay in low-lying areas. Get away and find higher ground. Keep close to the radio and listen for reports and instructions about what to do and where to go.

FACEMASKS

Protection masks can help you avoid ingesting volcanic ash after an explosion. Industry standard facemasks are close-fitting and provide effective respiratory protection. A surgical facemask can also be used if closely fitted, as can a scooter mask designed for road travel. A simple healthcare mask will offer some limited protection.

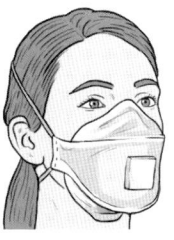

Industry facemask

Surgical mask

Scooter mask

Healthcare mask

LOMBOK VOLCANO EARTHQUAKE

Mount Rinjani, located on the Indonesian island of Lombok, is at 12,224 feet (3,726 m) the second highest volcano in Indonesia. Located on the volatile Pacific Ring of Fire, it presents at least two dangers. One is the ever-present risk of earthquakes due to the movement of tectonic plates in the region, and another is that the earthquakes might trigger a volcanic eruption.

Mount Rinjani, an active volcano, erupted on September 27, 2016. Though no earthquake was reported that September, a 6.4 magnitude earthquake took place in July 2018 on Lombok, triggering landslides that caused casualties among local residents and hikers visiting the popular tourist spot. About 16 people were killed, and over 330 were injured.

Indonesian military personnel and rescuers evacuate wounded from the island of Lombok.

Coastal dangers

The mixing of hot lava and cold seawater may in itself cause steam-driven explosions, which can hurl hot rocks 3 feet (1 m) in size both inland and out to sea.

Super-heated steam plume

Lack of awareness by those visiting the sites of natural volcanic phenomena, such as the active volcanoes Kilauea, in the U.S. state of Hawaii, or Cotopaxi, in the country of Ecuador, can lead to serious injury and death, especially when potentially dangerous phenomena are assumed to be benign. A steam plume, for example, may look like ordinary steam, but is acidic and also carries tiny shards of volcanic glass.

Hot lava from Mount Kilauea, Hawaii, flows down into the seas as waves crash along the coast of the volcanic island.

Hot lava

Where a volcano is located near the sea, the lava may flow into the water, where it will eventually cool. However, lava flowing into the sea creates an unstable lava delta, which may collapse unexpectedly, due to the extra weight on the rock structure below or due to an underwater landslide.

Water passing over a hot lava delta may also be temporarily super-heated. Anyone who is hit by the waves may be severely scalded or killed. In addition, the reactions may create an acidic steam that can be dangerous. It may cause skin and eye irritations. The wind may blow this cloud plume over a wider area, causing widespread air quality dangers.

MEASURING SCALES

Richter scale

Invented by Charles F. Richter in 1935, the Richter magnitude scale is a measurement of the height of the largest seismic wave produced by an earthquake, calibrated on a seismograph. Since then, the science of earthquake measurement has continued to develop. Modern technology can sense earthquakes that early seismographs were unable to detect.

Magnitude	Category	Effects
1.0–2.9	Micro	Recorded on local instruments but not felt by people
3.0–3.9	Minor	No damage but felt by people
4.0–4.9	Light	Some objects broken; felt by everyone
5.0–5.9	Moderate	Some damage to weak buildings
6.0–6.9	Strong	Some damage in populated areas
7.0–7.9	Major	Serious damage over a large area and loss of life
8.0 and higher	Great	Severe destruction and loss of life over a wide area

The Mercali scale

Developed in the late 1800s and early 1900s, the modified Mercali intensity scale is a representation of the effects of an earthquake. It is a measurement of what people can detect, as well as their responses.

I.	Felt by almost no one.
II.	Felt by very few people.
III.	Tremor noticed.
IV.	Felt indoors by many.
V.	Felt by almost everyone. Trees and poles swaying.
VI.	Felt by everyone. Furniture moved. Slight damage.
VII.	Considerable damage to poorly built structures.
VIII.	Specially designed structures damaged; others collapse.
IX.	All buildings considerably damaged. Cracks in ground.
X.	Many structures destroyed. Ground badly cracked.
XI.	All structures fall. Bridges wrecked. Wide cracks in the ground.
XII.	Total destruction.

EARTHQUAKES AND VOLCANOES

WORST EARTHQUAKES IN HISTORY

Below are a list of the most destructive earthquakes in history, listed by magnitude.

	Magnitude	Location	Name	Date
1.	9.5	Bio-Bio, Chile	Valdivia Earthquake	05-22-1960
2.	9.2	Southern Alaska	1964 Great Alaska Earthquake, Prince William Sound Earthquake, Good Friday Earthquake	03-27-1964
3.	9.1	Off the West Coast of Northern Sumatra	Sumatra–Andaman Earthquake, 2004 Sumatra Earthquake and Tsunami, Indian Ocean Earthquake	12-26-2004
4.	9.1	Near the East Coast of Honshu, Japan	2011 Tohoku Earthquake, Great East Japan Earthquake	03-11-2011
5.	9.0	Off the East Coast of the Kamchatka Peninsula, Russia	Kamchatka Earthquake	11-04-1952
6.	8.8	Offshore Bio-Bio, Chile	Maule Earthquake, 2010 Chile Earthquake	02-27-2010
7.	8.8	Near the Coast of Ecuador	1906 Ecuador–Colombia Earthquake	01-31-1906
8.	8.7	Rat Islands, Aleutian Islands, Alaska	Rat Islands Earthquake	02-04-1965
9.	8.6	Eastern Xizang-India Border Region	Assam–Tibet Earthquake	08-15-1950
10.	8.6 and 8.2	Off the West Coast of Northern Sumatra	Indian Ocean Earthquakes	04-11-2012

A man and his elephant sort through the wreckage of the city of Banda Aceh, Sumatra, following the earthquake and tsunami of December 26, 2004.

FIRES

Wildfires are conflagrations that consume brush, trees, and other vegetation. Some wildfires are natural occurrences, with causes such as lightning, volcanic eruptions, and dry climatic conditions. However, humans cause most fires; the source is often carelessness, such as when a cigarette is dropped in dry grass or when a campfire is not properly extinguished. Many wildfires can be traced to sparks from power lines and other equipment. Some fires get started through acts of arson.

In this aerial view taken from a helicopter, fire and smoke engulf the forests near Myrtle Beach, South Carolina, 2009.

DETECTION

Outdoors, flames may travel at speeds of more than 6 miles per hour (10 kph) in forests, and 14 miles per hour (22 kph) in grasslands. Wildfires are prone to starting in dry areas where there is also high wind.

Wind and vertical convection can send fiery embers far in front of a wildfire's front. The flames can leap over firebreaks or other barriers, such as roads or rivers.

Fires may be spotted from lookout towers as well as by ground or aerial patrols. However, it can be difficult to detect the start of a fire, so human observation is increasingly backed up by technology, such as camera detectors and satellites.

This satellite view shows the smoke from a wildfire in Idaho.

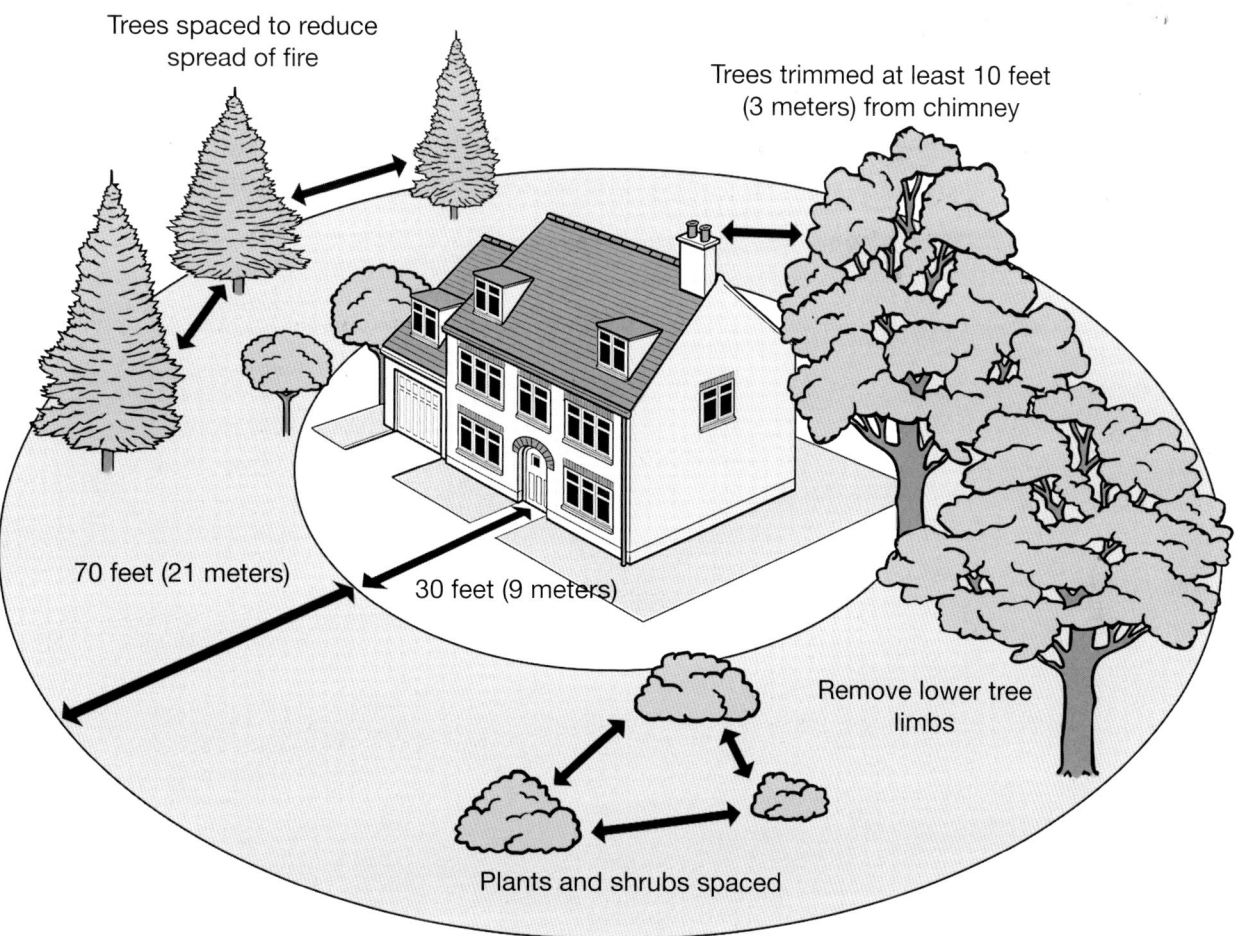

Safety zone

There are about 10,000 new wildfires each year in the United States, 99 percent of which are contained. Wildfires that get out of control are almost always resolved by changes in the weather rather than fire suppression.

If you live in or near a dry forested area, officials recommend that you create a safety zone around your home. In the state of California, for example, officials recommend that property owners clear 100 feet (30 m) of defensible space. Leave little for a wildfire to burn.

Keep tree branches at least 10 feet (3 m) from chimneys and other trees. Remove dry foliage from gutters or anywhere near the house. Keep grass within 100 feet (30 m) of buildings mowed. Assure that plants beneath trees and power lines are removed. If propane gas tanks are in use, they should be 25 feet (7.6 m) from buildings, and plants around the tanks should be cleared.

RESPONSE

If a fire has started in the vicinity, follow orders. Ensure that your car has enough fuel to get away, bearing in mind that gas stations may be closed or have long lines. Take an emergency pack, including plenty of water.

Agree on communication procedures and meeting points with family members, if they are away from home. Turn off gas or any other combustible fuel supplies before leaving. Create defenses if time allows, but if told to evacuate, do so as fast as possible.

- Prune tree branches 10 feet (3 m) from the ground.
- Remove flammables from the yard, such as cushions, lawnmowers, and woodpiles.

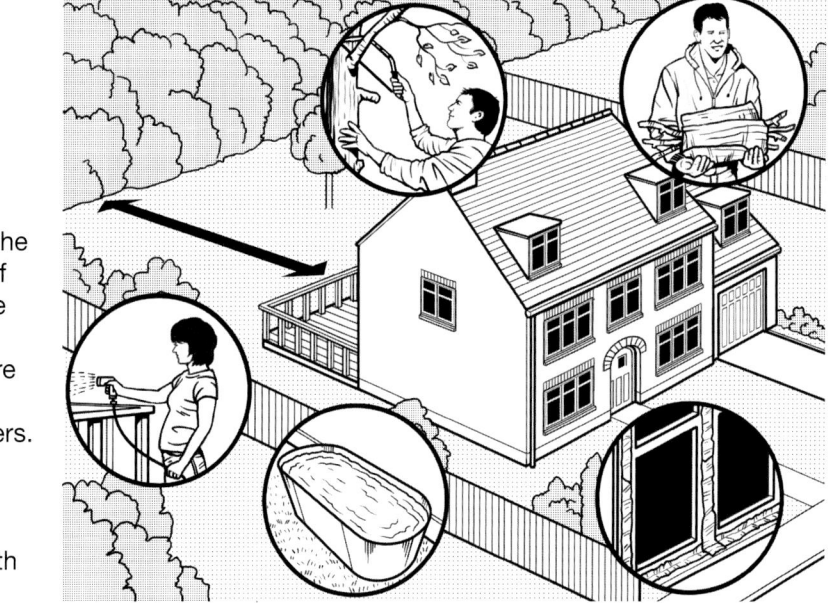

- Hose down the yard and roof to reduce the chance that they catch fire from wind-carried embers.
- Fill bathtubs and sinks with cold water.
- Cover windows with plywood.
- Cover vents with mesh screens to prevent embers from blowing in.

If trapped inside your home, turn on lights so rescuers in smoky conditions can see the house. Call 911. Close doors and windows, but keep them unlocked.

Minimize smoke by placing duct tape over vents. Stay away from outside walls and windows. Take flammable materials such as curtains off the windows.

FIVE Ps

If there is a risk that you may be evacuated due to fire, prepare essential items to take with you, following the five Ps:

1. People—your family and, if necessary, pets
2. Prescriptions—including medicines and other necessities, such as batteries, power cords, eyeglasses, and hearing aids
3. Papers—including vital documents, such as passports or other forms of ID
4. Personal needs—clothes, water, food, cash, phones, and chargers
5. Priceless items—jewelry, special photos, and other valuables

Any vital items that cannot be immediately moved should be stored in a fireproof and waterproof box for later recovery.

LONG-TERM PREPARATION

Official advice from the U.S. Federal Emergency Management Agency (FEMA) includes the following:

- **Sign up for your community's warning system. The Emergency Alert System (EAS) and National Oceanic and Atmospheric Administration (NOAA) Weather Radio (NWR) also provide emergency alerts.**
- **Know your community's evacuation routes, and find several ways to leave the area. Drive the evacuation routes. Find shelter locations. Have a plan for pets and livestock.**
- **Gather emergency supplies, including N95 respirator masks that filter out particles in the air you breathe. Keep in mind each person's specific needs, including medication. Don't forget the needs of pets.**
- **Keep important documents in a fireproof safe. Create password-protected digital copies.**
- **Use fire-resistant materials to build, renovate, or make repairs.**
- **Have an outdoor water source with a hose that can reach any area of your property.**
- **Create a safety zone free of flammable materials around the home.**
- **Review insurance coverage to make sure it is enough to replace your property.**

HOME ESCAPE PLANS

Install smoke alarms on each floor of your house. Smoke alarms should be fitted as centrally as possible, at least 12 inches (30 cm) away from any light source.

Run through escape plans with your family so that everyone knows where to go if the smoke alarm sounds. Everyone must get out as fast as possible.

Make sure that your house keys are easily available so that you can unlock the door in dark and smoky conditions. Install escape ladders in upper-floor windows if needed. Make sure that keys for window locks are available. Place fire extinguishers on each landing or in bedrooms as well as in the garage.

Home security devices

Your home should include a variety of safety sensors, ranging from flood sensors in the basement to smoke and heat sensors in the upper floors of the house.

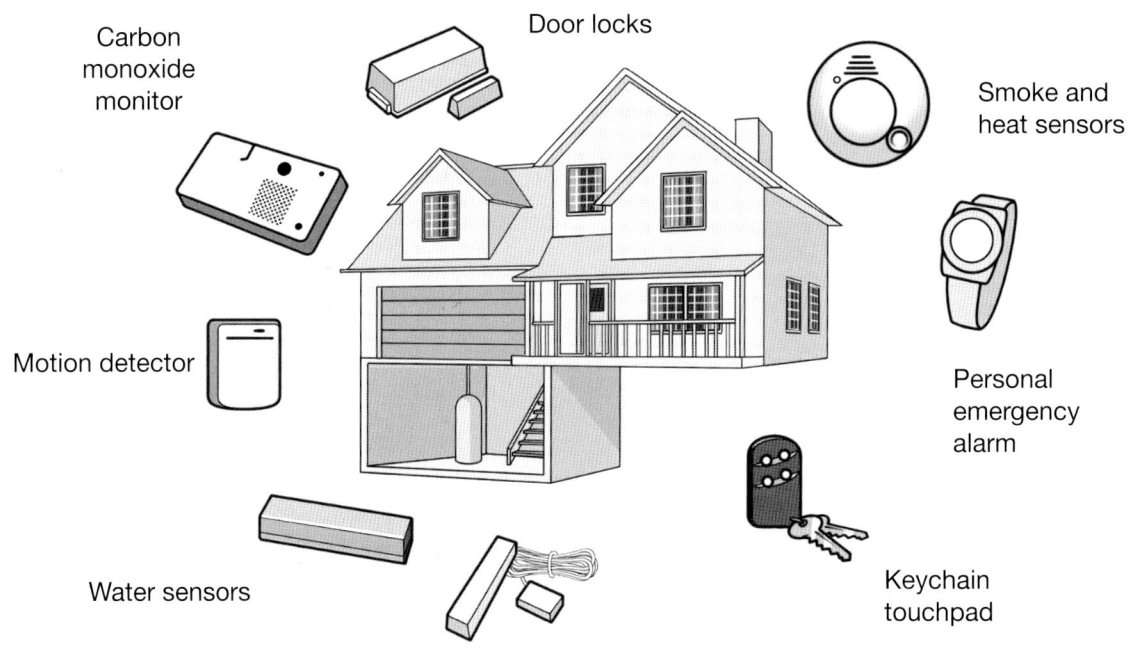

Carbon monoxide monitor

Door locks

Smoke and heat sensors

Motion detector

Personal emergency alarm

Water sensors

Keychain touchpad

Freeze sensors

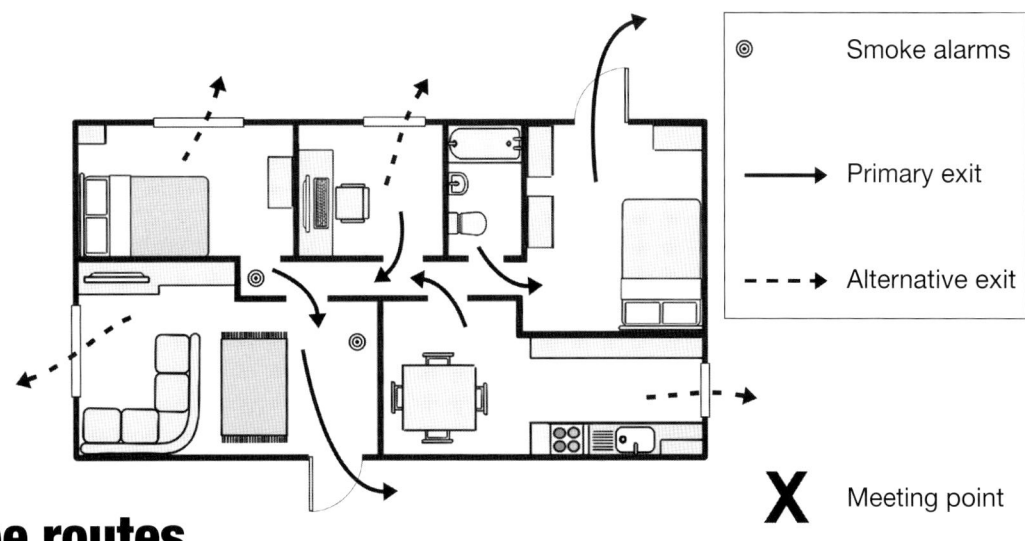

Escape routes

Plan escape routes carefully, and look out for any potential hazards or obstacles that may be difficult to handle in the dark. Child safety bars or gates, for example, could cause a problem if people are rushing down the stairs in the dark. If you need to jump out of a first-floor window, make sure the ground below does not have stakes or any other sharp objects that may cause injuries. Plan more than one escape route, taking into account different parts of the house that may be affected by fire.

BLACK SATURDAY

On February 7, 2009, a major wildfire started in the Shire of Murrindini in the Australian state of Victoria. It followed an unprecedented heat wave, with temperatures soaring above 109°F (43°C). That day, a series of fires burned across the state, igniting one of the worst conflagrations in Australia's history. Now called the Black Saturday bushfires, the disaster claimed 173 lives and injured hundreds more.

On that day, Jenna Pritchett and her partner Josh Fairbridge were picnicking by the Murrindini River with their two young children. After smelling smoke, they tried driving away but a wall of flame was approaching. There was no escape.

Forest rangers who arrived on the scene were shocked to see the family in such a dangerous area. The threat of flames and smoke was growing, and the effect of the smoke's toxins on the children's fragile lungs was likely to be devastating. The forest rangers put the family into their own 4x4 vehicle and drove it into the river. In the water, they were relatively safe from the flames, and the effect of the smoke was minimized.

Safety in apartments and condos

If you live in an apartment or a condo, your safety plan will differ from that of someone living in a single house. Call your local emergency services number if a fire starts, and give details of your address, apartment number, and the best way to reach it.

Apartment fire doors are designed to hold out against smoke and flames for between 30 and 60 minutes. If you open your door, you may be exposed to smoke and flame, and also create channels for the fire to breathe. If a fire occurs in another part of the building, it is sometimes best to stay in your own rooms. Move immediately if directly affected by heat or smoke.

Flames and smoke burst from an apartment building.

Get out, and stay out

If you live in a single-family home, your priority when faced with fire is to call emergency services and get out immediately. The longer you fight the fire on your own, the longer the delay in emergency services' reaching it. The delay also increases the time for the fire to take hold, increasing risk.

When moving around the house in a fire, try to stay as close as possible to the floor to minimize the amount of smoke you breathe in. If you come to a closed door, place the back of your hand against the door to feel whether it is hot. If it is, it is better not to open the door.

STOP, DROP, AND ROLL

If your clothes catch fire, do not run, as it will fan the flames. Fall to the ground, and roll over. If you can, roll in a heavy blanket or carpet or even better a fire blanket.

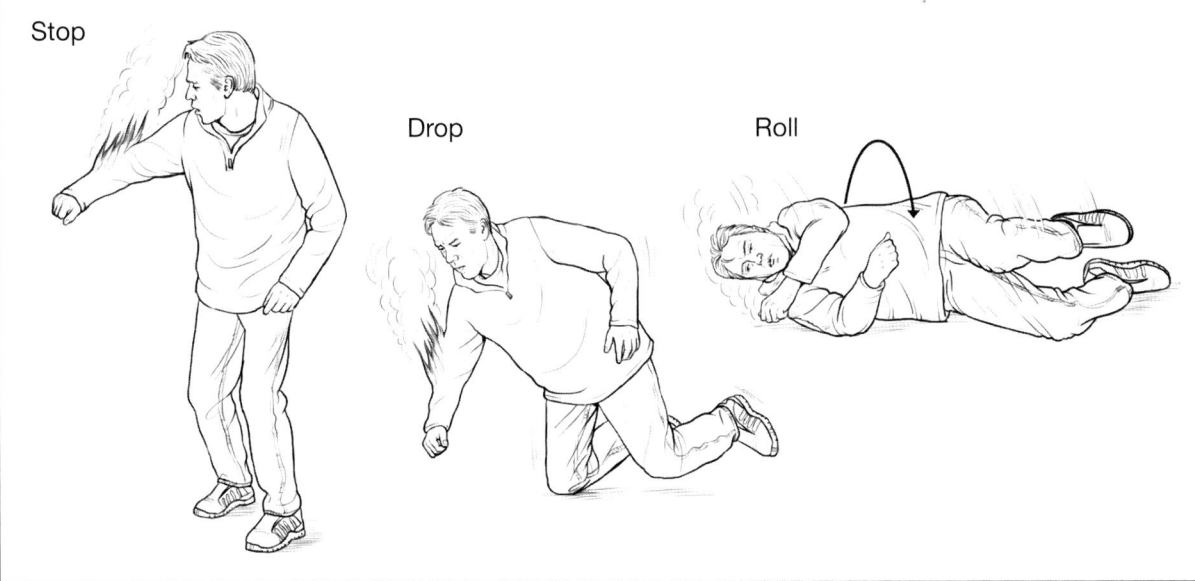

Too hot in the kitchen

There is a 60 percent chance that any home fire will start in the kitchen. Because kitchens are often full of steam and sometimes smoke, it is more effective to install a heat alarm in a kitchen rather than a smoke alarm.

To minimize dangers, do not leave the kitchen when food is still cooking because food can overheat rapidly. Keep the kitchen and especially the cooking area clean. Wipe off grease that could catch fire. Make sure everything on the stovetop is turned off after cooking. Clean the toaster regularly, as crumbs can ignite if overheated.

Fires on the stove can be smothered (above) with a wet cloth (far right).

OUTDOOR REFUGE

If you are in immediate danger, try to find a body of water to take refuge in, such as a river or a lake. Alternatively, try to find a clearing out of reach of the fire or in a rocky area clear of vegetation.

If you cannot find an area to escape to, scrape a hole in the ground, and cover yourself with earth. Breathe the air close to the ground to avoid inhaling smoke.

After a fire has passed through, beware of any areas where ash may still be hot. Trees that have been badly scorched may still be dangerous, especially if their roots have been burned.

CAMPFIRE SAFETY

Before building a campfire, clear grass, wood, leaves, and twigs in an area 10 feet (3 m) around the site. Dig a pit about 1 foot (0.3 m) deep. Place rocks around the pit.

Build a campfire of choice over the pit, including fires classified as tepee, log cabin, lean-to, or council.

Do not leave the fire unattended or let it grow too large. Plan for the fire to burn down to ash before leaving it.

When done, pour enough water on the fire to drown out embers. Alternatively, cover the embers with earth or sand to extinguish them. Do not leave embers on exposed pieces of wood. The campfire should be cool before you leave.

FORT McMURRAY WILDFIRE

On May 1, 2016, a wildfire that initially covered only 2 acres (1 ha) quickly got out of control and threatened the town of Fort McMurray, in Alberta, Canada. More than 80,000 people were evacuated. The flames destroyed about a tenth of the buildings.

The large evacuation inevitably led to massive traffic jams on roads in and around the city. Airlifts were set up to take the most vulnerable citizens to safety, and the police organized convoys to get the remaining people out. The fire also threatened major oil and gas installations in the region, some of which had to be shut down.

Firefighters were brought in from other Canadian regions, and a specialist team also arrived from South Africa. The fire was declared officially under control on July 5, after the arrival of rainy weather.

A wildfire burns behind abandoned vehicles on Alberta Highway 63, Fort McMurray, Alberta, Canada, May 2016.

Health risks from smoke

Smoke from a wildfire contains a number of elements that are dangerous to humans, including carbon monoxide, nitrogen oxide, organic chemicals, and particulate matter, which is made up of dust and liquid droplets. Particulate matter can cause or exacerbate conditions such as asthma or bronchitis.

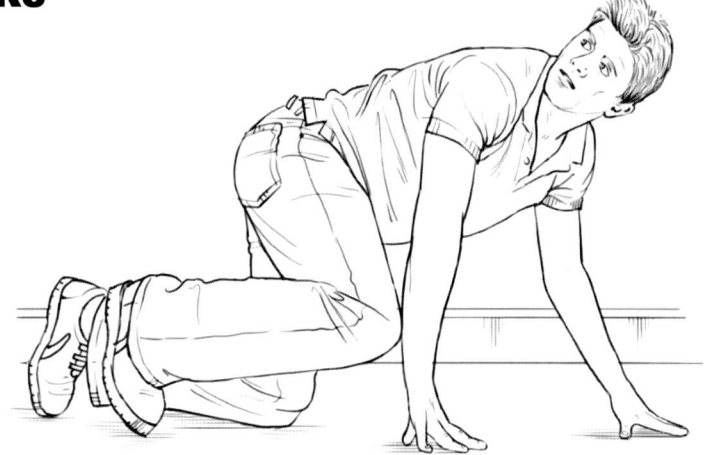

Practice makes perfect

In a crisis situation, practice and training is a great help, as it allows you to respond automatically. If you have practiced your escape routes and methods, you are more likely to get to safety quickly in an emergency. Do not bother about what you might be able to salvage: you don't have time.

If you go through a door, close it behind you, unless someone else needs to come through.

If someone has stayed in the building and fire services have arrived, it is better for the professionals to perform the rescue than for you to risk serious injury attempting to help.

If you are trapped in the house and cannot get out, gather any remaining family members or friends into one room. Seal the door gaps as much as possible to reduce the amount of smoke coming into the room.

A mattress can be an effective way to seal a door against smoke coming into a room.

WILDFIRE WYOMING

On July 18, 2006, flames trapped firefighter Lathan Johnson and his team during a major wildfire in Shoshone National Forest, Wyoming. The team had to use all their training that day. It was afternoon, and the most dangerous wildfire conditions were present: hot sun, low relative humidity, and high winds.

After turning a corner on a trail, the team faced a plume of smoke. It was ripping through dried-out trees and approaching fast. There was no time to outrun the flames, so they pulled out their aluminum fire shelters, as they were trained to do. They unzipped the cases, shook the foil shelters open, stepped in, and pulled the protection over their heads. Then they lay with their faces close to the ground, where the air would remain relatively clear.

The fire hit them. Although it raged around them for five minutes or so, the reflective shelters turned the heat away from their bodies, and after a while they were able to climb out to continue firefighting. Then another wave of fire approached, and they were forced back into their shelters. This time it was worse. Lathan had to wiggle to knock hot embers away as they fell on his shelter.

After about 45 minutes, it was safe for the firefighters to emerge again. A team member had become separated, so they searched for her. She had deployed her shelter in a rocky stream. Despite exposure to the fire wave, she had survived, too.

Wildfires have a rapid forward rate of spread (FROS) when burning through dense forests and brush. They can move up to 14 miles per hour (22 km per hour) in grasslands.

STORMS

Storms are disturbances of Earth's atmosphere. There are many types of storm, and their effects can vary from torrential rains and high winds, which can cause temporary local inconveniences, to devastating hurricanes and tornadoes. Some storms can cause national disasters. Whatever type of storm you may face, preparation is key to coming through safely and with minimum damage. It is important to react promptly and intelligently to public safety warnings.

In 2008, Hurricane Ike caused terrible devastation across the Caribbean, especially in Cuba and parts of Texas.

TORNADOES

Tornadoes are pillars of wind circulating at very high speeds. They often occur in spring and summer in the middle latitudes, where warm tropical air and cold polar air meet.

Though tornadoes occur all over the world, the most violent and dangerous tornadoes tend to occur in the central United States, particularly the western areas of the southern Great Plains. Another area prone to violent tornadoes stretches from the state of Iowa through Illinois and Indiana, including parts of Wisconsin and Michigan, to northern Kentucky.

Tornado activity tends to move gradually westward and then northward as spring gives way to summer. Tornadoes are often associated with thunderstorms that develop when cold and warm air meet. The most violent storms have a tendency to occur in late afternoon and evening, due to the heating of Earth's surface.

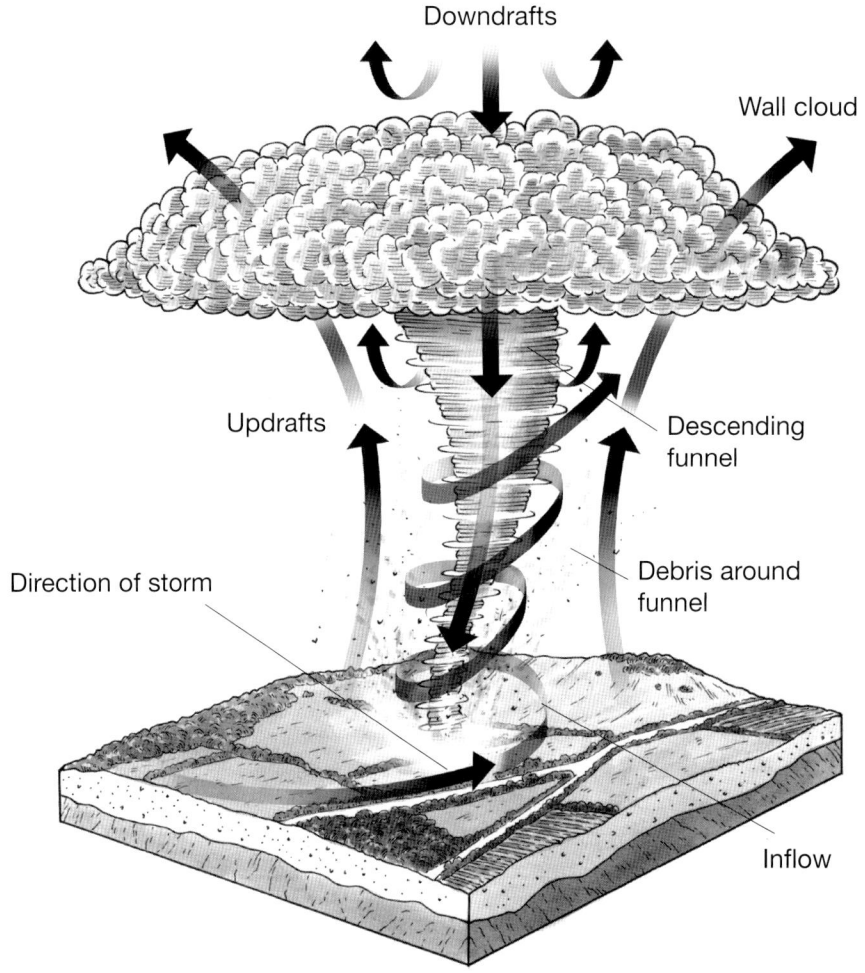

Tornado watch and warning

Using advanced equipment, including radars and satellites, forecasters can now identify the wind patterns likely to foster a tornado, and issue warnings a few hours in advance of a tornado's formation. A tornado warning is made to the public when a tornado has been identified visually or has been found on weather radar. Tornado warnings have reduced the number of fatalities associated with these storms.

The major dangers of a tornado include flying debris. In some instances, people are thrown to the ground. Occasionally, a tornado will lift people and drop them to the ground from a great height. The effects of a tornado on a building are often devastating. Air traveling at high speeds over a building creates forces that pull upward and outward. Once the air enters a building through broken doors or windows, it produces an explosive force that can rip a building apart in seconds.

Tornado survival

Ashley was 28 years old and living with her parents in Florida on February 22, 1998, when there was an unexpected event. Florida is outside Tornado Alley, the tornado-prone area in the U.S. states of Texas, Oklahoma, Kansas, and Nebraska. Although Ashley had done safety training at school in the event of hurricanes or tornadoes, a tornado was not expected.

On that Saturday, a storm began at about 11 p.m. There were seven tornadoes in the area, and the most dangerous headed in their direction. The power went out, after which Ashley and her family began to notice repetitive lightning. They gathered in a hallway, as they had no other internal rooms, and prepared to sit it out. The tornado came closer, and as the pressure grew, the house shook and then exploded. Everything went blank as Ashley and her family were sucked out of their house and dumped unceremoniously into a nearby creek.

The next thing she knew, Ashley heard her father calling her name as she was being pulled out of the water. All around were debris, smashed trees, and downed power lines. They went to a neighbor's house, and air medics were flown in. Ashley had sustained a deep wound to her leg and was taken to a hospital.

The wound on Ashley's leg was complex and took a long time to heal, leaving a large scar. She also suffered from Post Traumatic Stress Disorder (PTSD), anxiety, and memory loss. Although Ashley carries a physical scar on her leg, the mental scars of PTSD have been more enduring. She strongly recommends counseling for those who have experienced the trauma of a natural disaster.

Tornado safety precautions

A basement or cellar is a good place to shelter. If there is no basement, identify a small room, preferably with no windows. Otherwise, find shelter under a strong table to be protected from flying debris and glass. Use mattresses, thick blankets, or coats, to cover yourself.

Crouch down, shielding your head and neck with your arms. Keep well clear of windows. If you are in a mobile home or similar building with a weak structure, it is best to try to seek shelter in the basement of a sturdy building nearby. Alternatively, take refuge in a ditch or some other protected area.

If you are caught in the open by a tornado, keep low on the ground or find shelter in a ditch or drain. Try to hold onto a solid object, such as a post or tree stump, to prevent being rolled along by the wind. If you are in a car when a tornado is approaching, it is best to get out of the car and seek shelter as described above. Tornadoes can be powerful enough to roll cars over and even lift them off the ground and drop them.

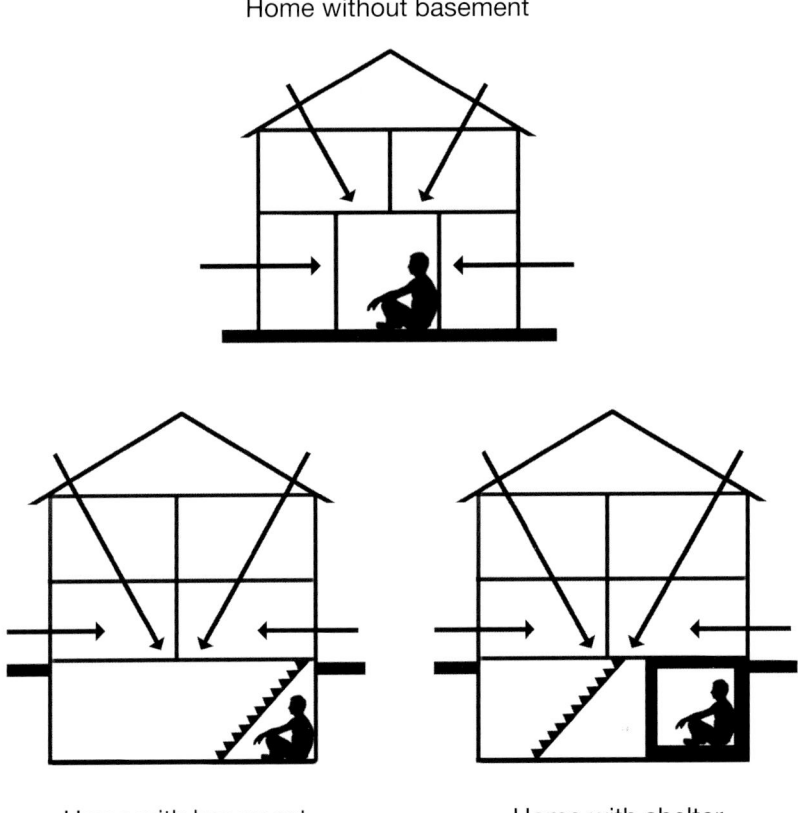

Home without basement

Home with basementHome with shelter

TROPICAL CYCLONES, TYPHOONS, AND HURRICANES

Tropical cyclones, typhoons, and hurricanes are similar kinds of storm. They tend to be called typhoons in eastern Asia, cyclones in central southern Asia, and hurricanes in the North Atlantic and Eastern Pacific.

These storms originate over warm tropical oceans, when warm air rises and starts to rotate intensively. A tropical cyclone will continue to rotate as long as it is over warm water. Apart from generating intense rain, this kind of storm may also have the effect of sucking up seawater to create a storm surge. A surge may raise the level of the ocean by 20 feet (6 m). Sea surges may have catastrophic effects when they reach land.

Tropical cyclones and similar storms circulate counterclockwise in the Northern Hemisphere and clockwise in the Southern Hemisphere. Typically they are up to 6 miles (10 km) high and about 350 miles (563 km) wide. They travel at speeds between 15 and 40 miles per hour (24 and 64 kph). They can travel up to 400 miles (644 km) a day for a distance of about 3,000 miles (4,828 km) in total before they die out.

The center of the storm, known as the eye, is a relatively calm area in which air subsides. The edge of the eye, known as the eyewall, is the fiercest and most dangerous part of the storm, with winds circulating at the highest speeds.

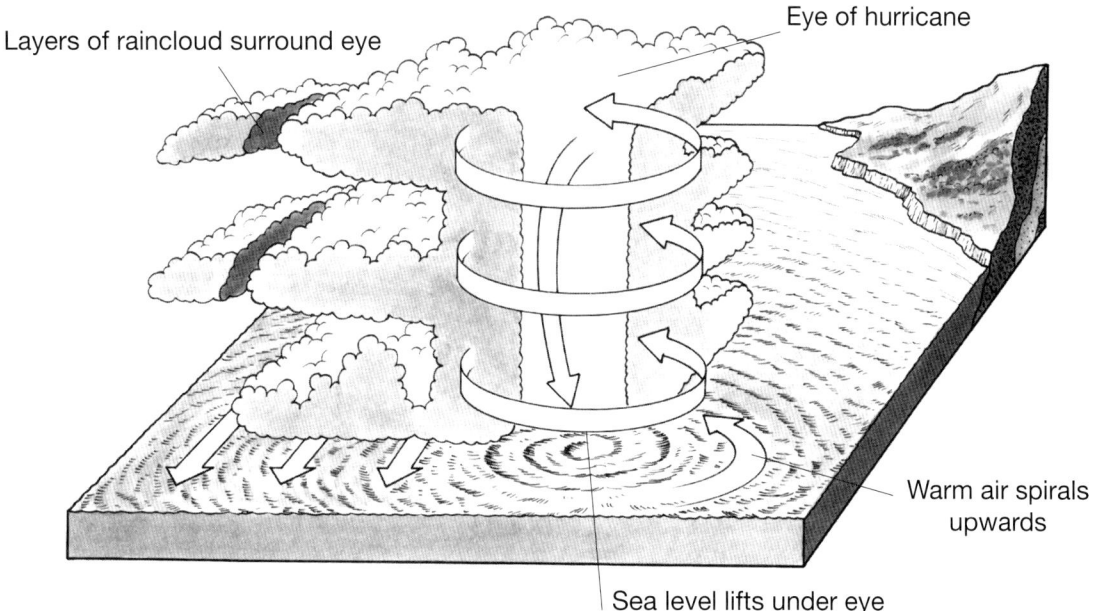

Layers of raincloud surround eye
Eye of hurricane
Warm air spirals upwards
Sea level lifts under eye

DANGERS ASSOCIATED WITH TROPICAL CYCLONES

STORM SURGE: Water rising by several feet or meters can cause severe flooding and damage.

HIGH SEAS: Strong winds caused by such a storm can rise to about 49 feet (15 m) and are a danger to vessels, especially smaller craft.

HEAVY RAIN: Massive rainfall can cause flooding inland from where the storm strikes.

TORNADOES: Dangerous concentrations of spinning air from the storm can create havoc.

HIGH WINDS: Winds around 150 miles per hour (241 kph) with gusts up to 200 miles per hour (322 kph) are categorized as high.

A tornado forms over Oklahoma, creating a dangerous funnel of spinning air.

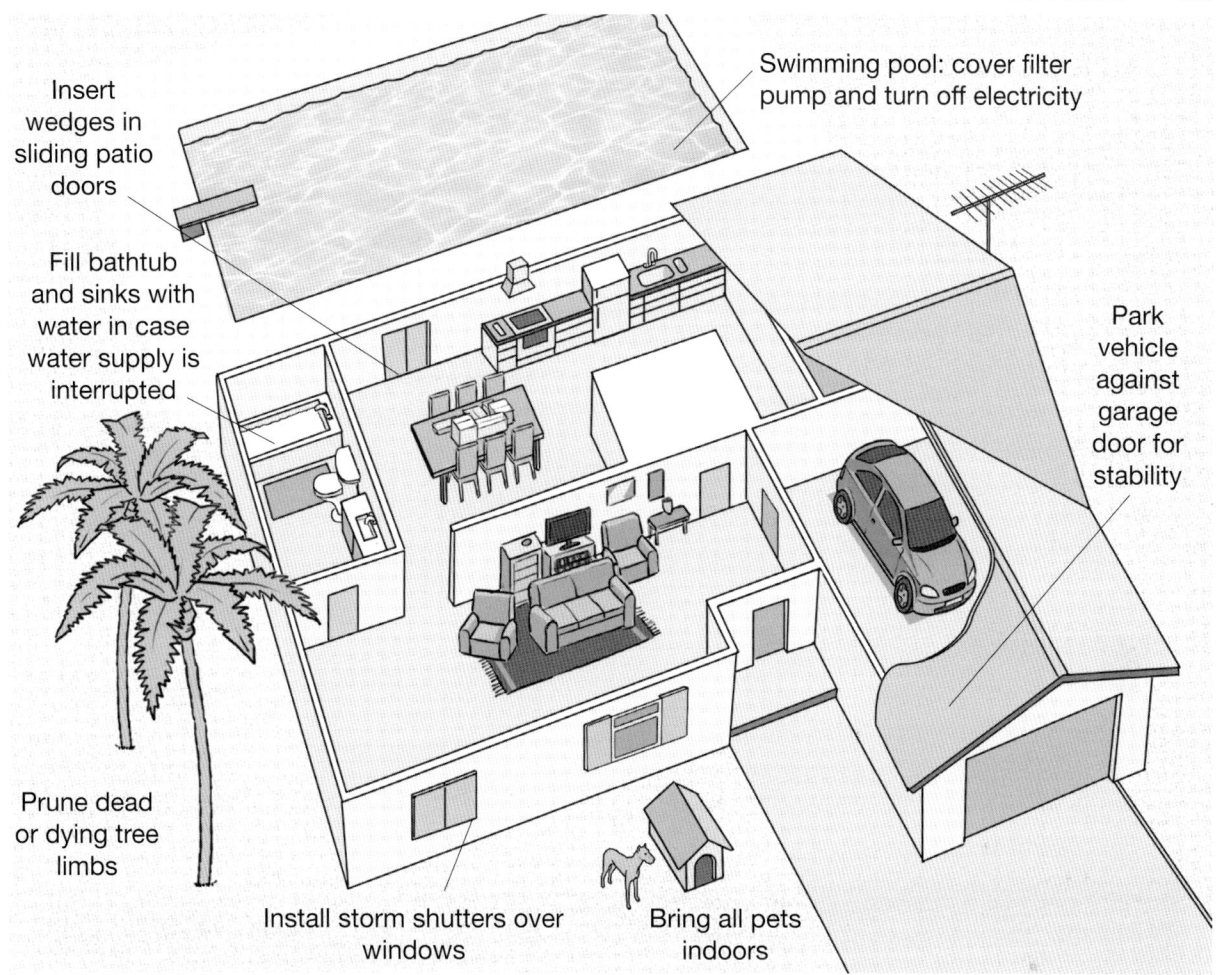

Hurricane safety

A hurricane is often a national emergency that can lead to the displacement of hundreds and sometimes thousands of people. If you live in a hurricane danger area, listen to local radio and television or alert stations for warnings, advisories, and updates.

Make yourself familiar with evacuation procedures, bearing in mind that thousands of people may be on the road at the same time. Find out if there is an emergency shelter run by an organization such as the Red Cross. A shelter will provide a safe harbor, food and water, mental health services, and other support.

Make sure you have a full tank of gas in case you are ordered to evacuate the area. Take inside anything that could be picked up by the wind, such as lawn chairs or tables. In case of a flood, move valuable items or furniture upstairs. Turn off utilities if advised to do so. Make sure that all doors and windows are securely closed. Secure hurricane shutters if you have them. Otherwise, use plywood to cover windows and doors.

Avoid contact with floodwater if possible, whether on foot or in a vehicle. Keep away from beaches and other coastal areas as well as from riverbanks.

FEMA HURRICANE PREPARATION ADVICE

- To begin preparing, you should build an emergency kit and make a family communications plan.

- Know your surroundings. Learn the elevation of your property and whether the land is prone to flooding. This will help you know how your property will be affected if tidal flooding or storm surges are forecasted.

- Identify levees and dams in your area, and determine whether they pose a hazard.

- Learn community hurricane evacuation routes and how to find higher ground. Determine where you would go and how you would get there if needed.

- Make plans to secure your property. Cover all windows. Permanent storm shutters offer the best protection. A second option is to board up windows with 5/8-inch (16-mm) marine plywood, cut to fit and ready to install. Tape does not prevent windows from breaking.

- Install straps or additional clips to securely fasten your roof to its supporting structure. This will reduce roof damage.

- Be sure trees and shrubs around your home are well trimmed, so they are more wind resistant.

- Clear loose and clogged rain gutters and downspouts.

- Reinforce your garage doors; if wind enters a garage it can cause dangerous and expensive structural damage.

- Plan to bring in all outdoor furniture, decorations, garbage cans, and anything else not tied down.

- Determine how and where to secure your boat if you have one.

- Install a generator for emergencies.

- If in a high-rise building, be prepared to take shelter on or below the tenth floor.

- Consider building a safe room.

STORMS 101

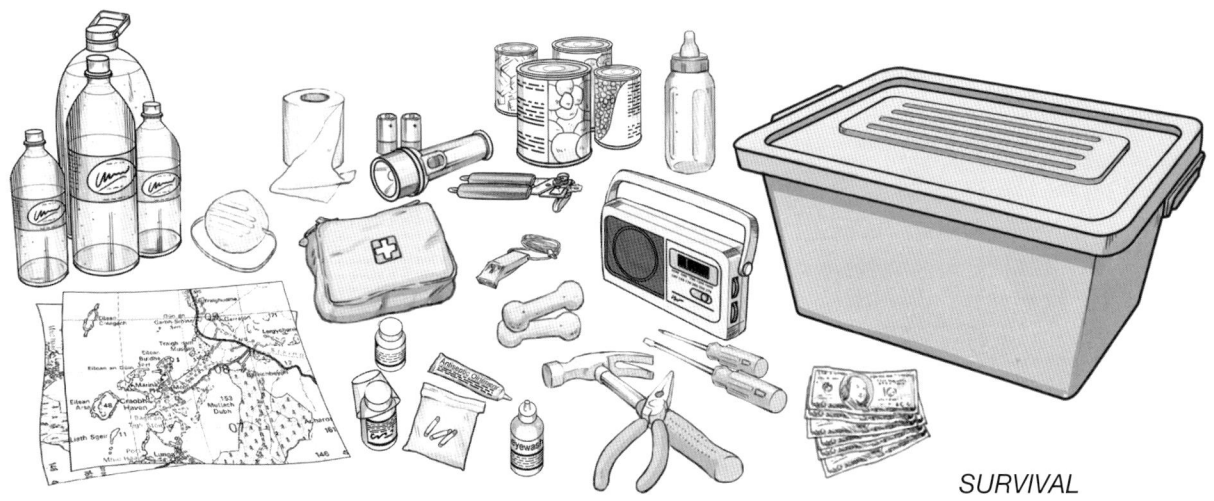

SURVIVAL ESSENTIALS
Ensure you have enough water, food, medical supplies, tools, a map, and medicines to survive a period where infrastructure and power may be cut off.

Hurricane countdown

36-hour warning: Tune to the latest broadcasts on television or radio. If necessary, replenish the emergency supply kit. Make sure you have enough food and water to last at least three days.

Check that communication methods used with family and friends are working. Text is usually best. Make sure that family members understand the evacuation plan. Make sure that each member of the family can reach for essential equipment to leave at short notice.

Ensure that your car is filled with gas and ready to go. Check the vehicle's emergency kit.

18-to-36-hour warning: Make any preparations in and around your home, such as trimming loose branches from trees or taking in or tying down loose garden equipment. Close storm shutters on windows, or use fitted plywood.

6-to-18-hour warning: Keep a check on emergency broadcasts. Charge cell phones and any other electrical equipment.

6-hour warning: Find out whether the instructions from authorities are to evacuate or not. Secure storm shutters, and keep away from windows. Turn fridges and freezers to the coldest setting in case power is lost, so food will stay cooler for longer.

HURRICANE KATRINA

Hurricane Katrina began as a powerful tropical cyclone over the Bahamas and then struck the southeastern coast of the United States in August of 2005. Hurricane Katrina proved to be the third-most-intense hurricane to hit the U.S. mainland and the costliest natural disaster in U.S. history.

When Hurricane Katrina approached Miami, Florida, it was rated as a category 1 hurricane. However, by the time it spilled into the Gulf of Mexico, it was boosted by the warm waters into category 3, with winds of 115 miles per hour (185 kph). It then moved north toward Louisiana and the Mississippi Sound, becoming a category 5 hurricane on August 28, with winds of around 160 miles per hour (257 kph). The accompanying storm surge reached heights of 26 feet (8 m), smashing into homes and other structures along the coast.

Although not directly in the path of the storm, New Orleans, Louisiana, was to suffer a secondary effect. Torrential rain, along with storm surge on the coast, caused flooding that overwhelmed the city's protective levies. In the end, 80 percent of New Orleans was underwater. Although 1.2 million people evacuated the city under

orders from the mayor on August 28, many thousands remained. Many had to be rescued while emergency services were constrained by the flooding. National Guard troops were deployed on September 2 to rescue survivors and to distribute food and water.

More than 1,800 people died as a result of Hurricane Katrina. The financial damage was more than $160 billion.

U.S. military heavy equipment operators help local authorities with search and rescue efforts along the coast of Mississippi following the damage caused by Hurricane Katrina in 2005.

FEMA ADVICE ON HOW TO SURVIVE DURING A HURRICANE

- If told to evacuate, do so immediately. Do not drive around barricades.
- If sheltering during high winds, go to a FEMA safe room, an ICC 500 storm shelter, or a small interior room or hallway on the lowest floor that is windowless and not subject to flooding.
- If trapped in a building by flooding, go to the highest level. Do not climb into a closed attic. You may become trapped by rising floodwater.
- Listen for current emergency information and instructions.
- Use a generator or any gasoline-powered machinery ONLY outdoors and away from windows.
- Do not walk, swim, or drive through floodwaters. Turn around. Don't drown! Just 6 inches (15 cm) of fast-moving water can knock you down, and 1 foot (30 cm) of moving water can sweep your vehicle away.
- Stay off bridges over fast-moving water.

HOMEMADE BUNKER

For committed "Preppers," a homemade bunker forms the ultimate survival retreat. Fully stocked with months of survival supplies, and often reinforced to withstand even nuclear blasts, such a bunker can be the safest and best option to survive hurricanes, tornadoes, earthquakes, terrorist attacks, civil strife, or radioactive fallout. Buried underneath the property, it includes features such as periscope viewing, blast-proof outer doors, and plentiful storage shelving for food and survival equipment.

    Ideally, the walls of the shelter should be built from reinforced concrete or bricks, with plastic vapour barriers against them to protect against damp. The entire bunker needs to be covered with at least 1.2m (4ft) of soil, which acts as a barrier against wind, blast and radioactivity. Ensure a good system of ventilation. You can make manual ventilator systems that pump in outside air, with one-way valves that close against blast waves, hurricanes, or tornadoes, but open as necessary when you pump air into the bunker. Also ensure that you have proper sanitation and running water.

WINTER STORMS

Blizzards are fairly regular winter events in many parts of the world. They involve winds of 35 miles per hour (56 kph) or more, accompanied by considerable amounts of snow, and they last for three or more hours.

Some of the most severe blizzards occur in the snowbelt of the United States, which extends across the Great Lakes region from Minnesota to Maine. Major cities are affected, including New York City, Detroit, and Milwaukee. Blizzards in the United States tend to be more severe than those in Europe.

One of the many dangers of a blizzard is the wind chill factor. This is a combination of low temperatures and high winds. In the U.S. Midwest, the wind chill factor can be −60°F (−51°C) during a blizzard. This presents a danger of frostbite or hypothermia.

Strong winds and heavy snow can cause power outages and freezing pipes. This means that you may not have power or gas for heating your home.

Driving during a blizzard or heavy snowstorm is dangerous for many reasons, including black ice, low visibility, and possible mechanical breakdown.

Preparing for severe winter weather

Check doors and windows for weatherproof fittings such as draft blockers. Consider installing extra blinds or placing plastic coverings over windows to provide extra insulation. Assess your heating equipment and fuel supplies, whether gas, electricity, coal, or wood. Get extra supplies of wood or coal if you have a fireplace or stove. Do not overheat your home, and do isolate unused rooms.

During cold conditions, wear layers of warm, loose clothing, but take care not to overheat. Drink warm fluids such as soup. Alternatively, drink juice and water. Do not drink too many caffeinated beverages, as caffeine can accelerate hypothermia and cause dehydration. Avoid alcohol, which disrupts the body's heat management system. A taste of whisky or brandy may feel warm as you swallow it, but alcohol inflames the blood vessels on the surface of your skin, causing you to lose more heat.

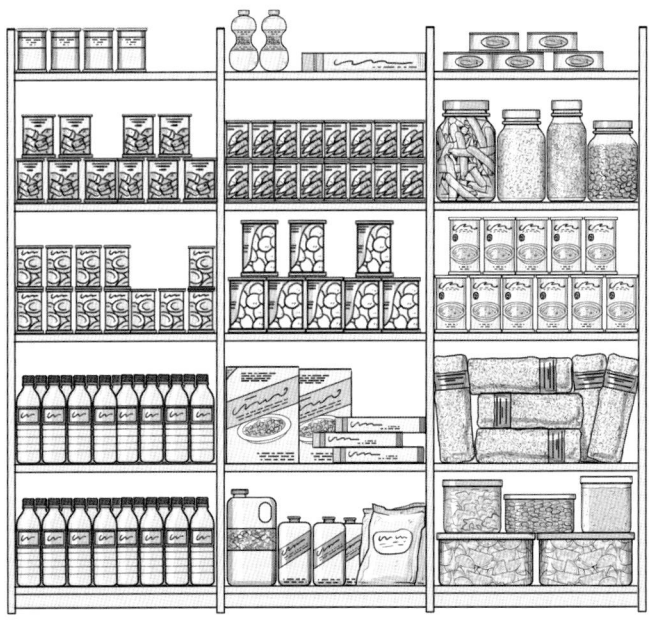

Food storage

Ensure you have stockpiled enough water and dried and canned food to last you and your family at least a week.

FEMA ADVICE ON WINTER STORM PREPARATION

- **Know your area's risk for winter storms.** Extreme winter weather can leave communities without utilities or other services for long periods of time.
- **Prepare your home to keep out the cold** with insulation, caulking, and weather stripping. Learn how to keep pipes from freezing. Install and test smoke alarms and carbon monoxide detectors with battery backups.
- **Pay attention to weather reports and warnings of freezing weather and winter storms.** Sign up for your community's warning system. The Emergency Alert System (EAS) and National Oceanic and Atmospheric Administration (NOAA) Weather Radio (NWR) provide emergency alerts.
- **Gather supplies in case you need to stay home for several days without power.** Keep in mind each person's specific needs, including medication. Do not forget the needs of pets. Have extra batteries for radios and flashlights.
- **Create an emergency supply kit for your car.** Include jumper cables, sand, a flashlight, warm clothes, blankets, bottled water, and nonperishable snacks. Keep the gas tank full.
- **Learn the signs of, and basic treatments for, frostbite and hypothermia.**

If you are outside in extreme cold

Wear appropriate clothing in layers. Wear mittens and a hat, as the body loses a disproportionate amount of heat through the head if the rest of the body is covered. Keep dry both from external moisture in snow or sleet but also from body sweat. Do not wear too much clothing if you are going to work in the snow, such as clearing paths and driveways. Wear waterproof shoes or boots, and consider adding crampons for walking in deep snow or on ice.

The heart has to work harder in cold conditions, so be careful not to strain yourself when working outdoors. Protect your mouth from cold air, and do not take deep breaths, as the cold air may damage your lungs.

DRIVING IN BLIZZARDS

How you drive in blizzard conditions will depend on the type of vehicle and on fittings such as tire chains. Make sure that you have emergency supplies on board and warm blankets in case you get stranded.

Vehicle stranded in snow

Do not get out of your vehicle unless you can see a source of help within 100 yards (91 m). In blizzard conditions, you could get lost if you move too far from your car. Tie something bright to the radio antenna, or put something bright on the roof.

Do not keep the engine running, or you will run out of fuel. Turn the engine on for 10-minute spells every hour, and run the car heater. Keep one window slightly open to allow circulation of air. Turn on the inside light of your vehicle when the engine is running. Do not leave vehicle lights on when the engine is off, as you will run down the vehicle battery.

If there is more than one person in the car, keep close together in order to preserve warmth. Wake each other up periodically so that each person can increase his or her body temperature and circulation. Make sure that passengers eat and drink regularly to maintain energy.

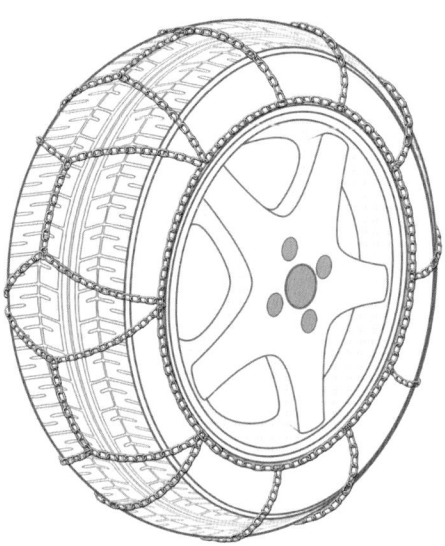

Tire chains

Fit tire chains to your vehicle's wheels if you intend to drive in snowy conditions. Learn how to fit snow chains before the emergency occurs, as the process can be tricky, even in good weather. After fitting the chains, drive a short distance then stop and check they haven't loosened. If they have, tighten them up.

PREPARING YOUR VEHICLE FOR A WINTER STORM

It is a good idea to have your car serviced before the winter season. Check that you have the right amount of antifreeze in your engine. Add cold-resistant windshield washer fluid to the fill line on the reservoir where it's held.

Keep windshield defroster equipment, such as scrapers and liquid sprays. Think of buying winter tires if you have long-term snow in your area. Fit snow chains to standard tires if necessary. Keep traction mats in case you get stuck. Also keep an emergency kit in the car.

EMERGENCY KIT FOR THE CAR

- Flashlights and spare batteries
- Tire chains and traction mats
- Shovel
- Sand
- Jumper cables
- Can opener
- Fruit and nuts
- Drinking water
- Sleeping bags
- Blankets
- Matches
- Tool set
- Rain gear
- Coffee can and candle

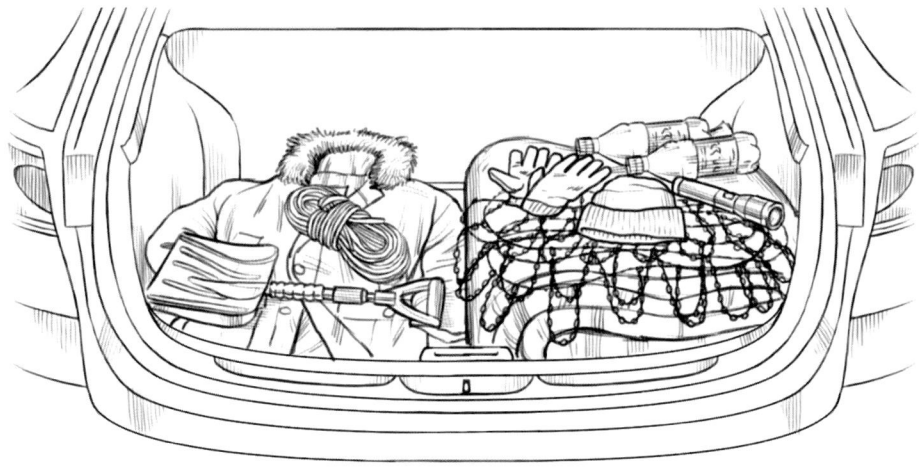

ELECTRICAL STORMS

Electrical storms are the result of high electric fields within clouds and also between thunderstorm clouds in different locations. Depending on the altitude and temperature, positive and negative charges are generated.

This can lead to electrical discharges in the form of lightning, which can move from a cloud to the air, within a cloud, between separate clouds, and from a cloud to the ground. Aircraft can also trigger lightning, and sometimes tall structures on the ground will attract the charge.

Most lightning occurs over land in the afternoon, when the sun has warmed Earth. In the Northern Hemisphere, most lightning occurs between May and September, and in the Southern Hemisphere, between November and March.

Lightning strikes near a camping site close to Las Vegas, Nevada.

Geomagnetic storms

Geomagnetic, magnetic, or solar storms are caused by massive eruptions from the outer layer of the sun, also known as the corona. The eruptions throw out plasma consisting of protons and electrons. Traveling at speeds of up to 1,200 miles per second (1,931 kps), the plasma can reach Earth's magnetosphere in 24 to 72 hours. The effect is normally visible at Earth's poles as an auroral display.

The effects on Earth itself are usually fairly minimal, though the intensification of magnetic fields can sometimes interfere with global positioning system (GPS) devices, cell phones, and satellite television. As they are farther out in space, satellites can be directly affected by solar particles traveling at high speed.

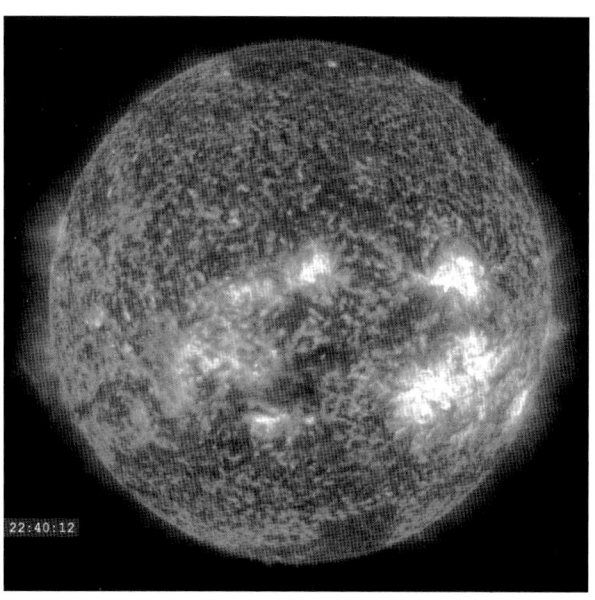

A major solar eruption is shown in progress in 2003.

RECOGNIZING CLOUDS

If you learn to read the clouds correctly, you will be in a better position to take evasive action to avoid rain and thunderstorms. Generally, if clouds move lower and darken, then bad weather is likely.

Bad weather clouds

Cirrostratus: These are high transparent clouds, which sometimes form a halo effect around the sun. They do not carry rain but can indicate that bad weather is on the way.

Nimbostratus clouds: These appear in thick layers and are likely to bring long-lasting rain or snow.

Stratus clouds: These white or gray clouds are normally at a low level and can produce either drizzle or snow.

Cumulonimbus: These tall clouds often form an anvil-shaped head. They are a clear warning of potential extreme weather, including torrential rain or thunderstorms.

Changeable clouds

Stratocumulus: These clouds hang at a low level and sometimes have gaps between them. Although they do not often produce rain, they can indicate a change in the weather.

Altostratus: These are high clouds that look like white sheets. They are usually an indication of an imminent weather change.

Cumulus: These fluffy clouds can be good or bad news, depending on the spacing between them. Separated like fluffy cotton wool, they tend to be a sign of good weather. Bunched together, however, they can bring rain showers or snow.

Good weather clouds

In general, high clouds mean good weather.

Cirrus: Sometimes known as mare's tails, these long spandrels of cloud normally indicate good weather.

Cirrocumulus: These clouds have a patchy appearance and are normally a sign of good weather.

Altocumulus: These fluffy clouds high in the sky mainly mean good weather.

Types of cloud

Clouds are formed by large masses of condensing water vapor. They are classified based on their altitude and shape. Fair-weather clouds tend to be higher and white. Low, black clouds clustered together indicate imminent storms. Many rain-producing cumulonimbus clouds can reach the top of the troposphere.

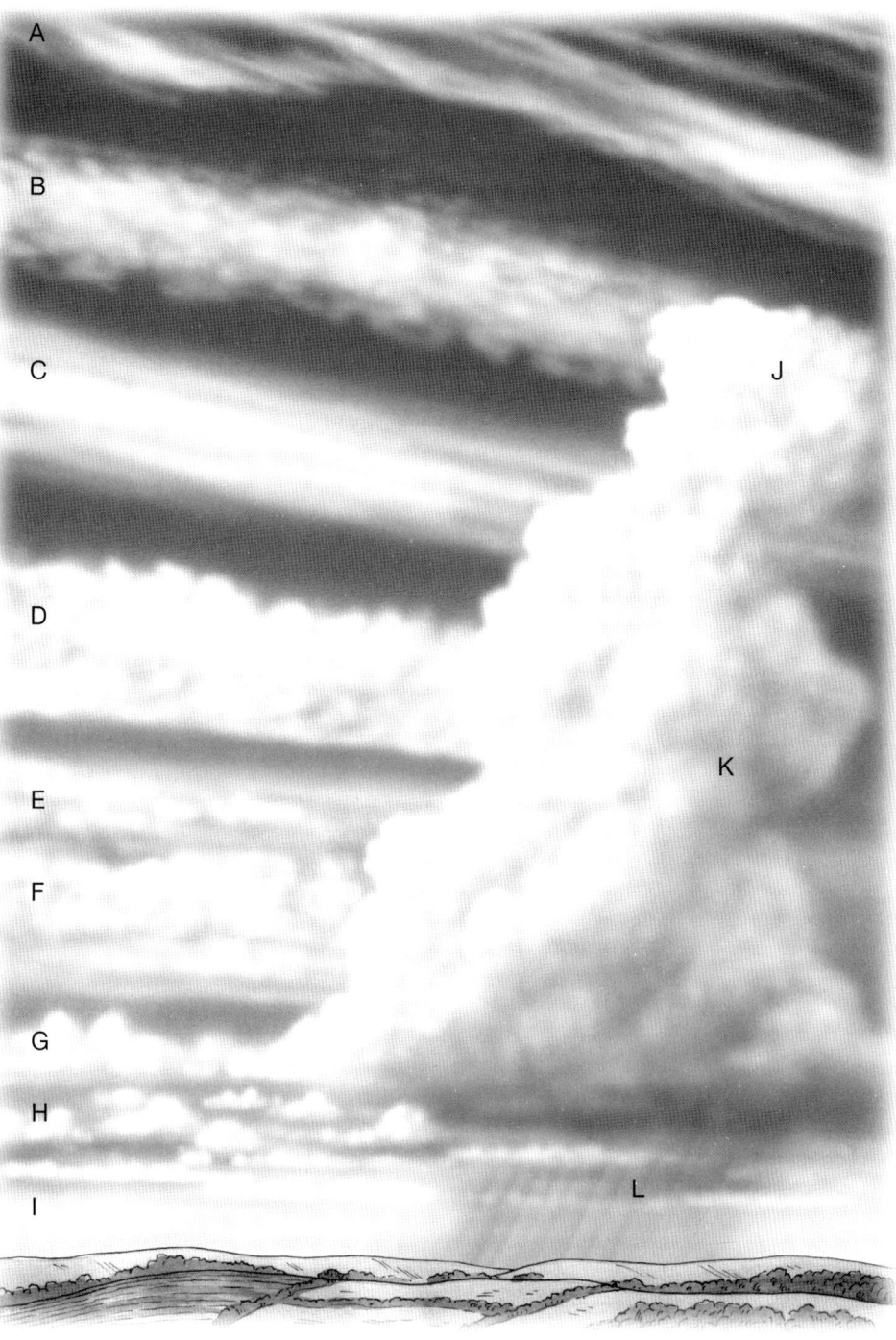

- A. Cirrus
- B. Cirrocumulus
- C. Cirrostratus
- D. Altocumulus
- E. Altostratus
- F. Stratocumulus
- G. Nimbostratus
- H. Cumulus
- I. Stratus
- J. Anvil Head
- K. Cumulonimbus
- L. Rain, hail and squall winds

HEAT WAVES AND DROUGHTS

A heat wave is a prolonged period of above-average temperatures. If high levels of humidity accompany the heat wave, it can lead to dangerous conditions for people, such as heat cramps, exhaustion, and heatstroke. A heat wave can occur when high pressure is persistent over a particular area. Urban areas can be riskier during a heat wave, as concrete and asphalt tend to store heat during the day and release it at night, creating higher nighttime temperatures.

This farmland in Australia has been turned into a cracked desert landscape by a prolonged drought.

DROUGHT

Drought is caused by lack of rain for an extended period, leading to water shortages, low reservoir supplies, reduction of groundwater, and dry soil. There are a variety of strategies you can deploy to cope with drought conditions.

Some areas of the world experience permanent drought conditions, and any vegetation has to be supported by irrigation schemes. Occasional cloudbursts provide only temporary relief and do not change the underlying conditions.

Droughts can be caused by changes in atmospheric circulation patterns, which can prevent storms from occurring in certain regions. Climate patterns, such as variables in ocean warming and cooling, can also contribute to drought.

Plants in areas of permanent drought adapt to their conditions. Cacti have developed efficient water storage while minimizing evaporation through their spiky leaves. For example, the yucca plant has a complex root system, which seeks out any available moisture.

If a drought takes place in an area accustomed to regular rainfall, the plants will not be able to adapt and will eventually die.

Other side effects of a drought may include soil erosion and wildfires, due to the intensely dry conditions and atmospheric conditions such as lightning.

Road surfaces and rail tracks can also be damaged when heat is extreme.

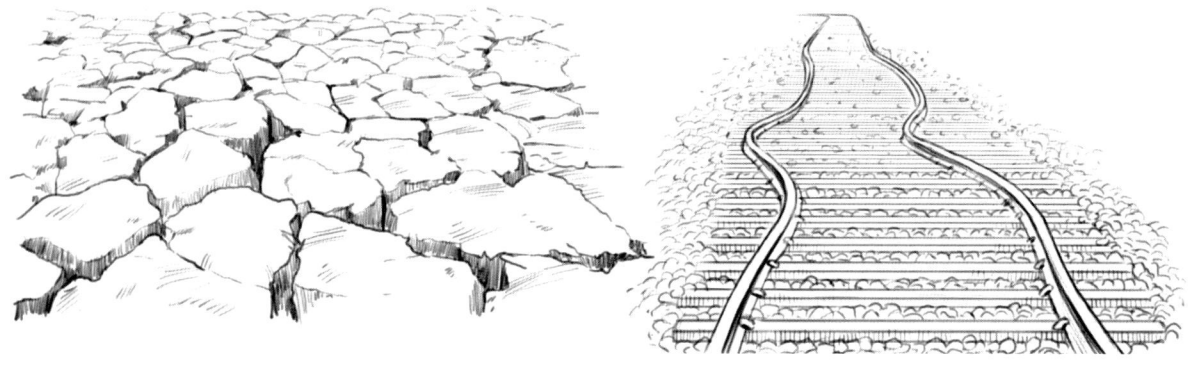

PREPARING FOR DROUGHT

Water supplies are critical in a disaster situation. Some emergency water can be found in toilet cisterns and water tanks (as long as no chemicals are added), and you should fill the bathtub and sink at the first sign of danger.

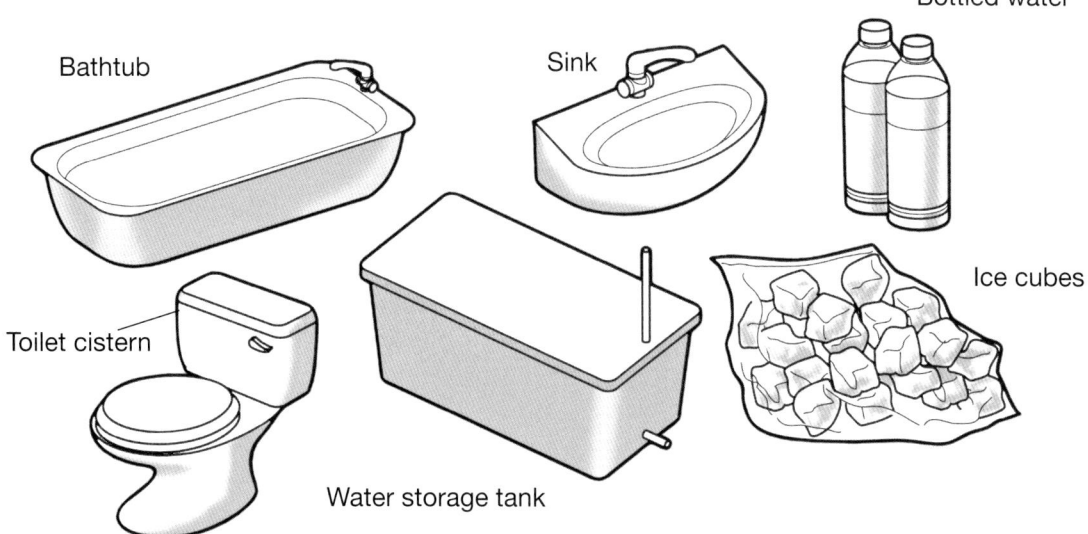

Bathtub
Sink
Bottled water
Toilet cistern
Water storage tank
Ice cubes

Storage

Keep an eye on the weather forecast, and if there is going to be a long period of unusually hot and dry weather, try to store as much water as possible.

Install rain barrels that feed off the gutter system around your home. Around 500 gallons (1,893 l) of water may run off the roof of a typical house during a 1-inch (3-cm) rainfall.

Water conservation

OUTSIDE

Conserve water when carrying out tasks outdoors. Put off washing the car, and wash only essential parts, such as the windshield and windows. Water plants with a watering can, preferably with water taken from a rain barrel, rather than running the hose. Leave the lawn to fend for itself. Grass is good at recovering after a dry spell. Place mulch in flowerbeds to preserve moisture and to keep weeds down.

INSIDE

Inside, you can store water in the fridge for drinking, rather than running the tap each time you want a drink. The tap does not need to run while washing dishes. Wash vegetables in a bowl of water rather than under a running tap. Use the leftover water to water the plants.

Put the washing machine and dishwasher on economy cycles. If you have a dehumidifier, use it to collect water for watering plants. Repair any dripping taps by replacing the internal washers, which may have become worn. Place a jug or bottle of water in the toilet tank to reduce the volume of water used for flushing. Use pebbles to weigh the jug down. Take a short shower in preference to filling the bathtub.

FEMA ADVICE ON HOW TO SURVIVE DURING A HEAT WAVE

- Never leave a person or an animal alone inside a vehicle on a warm day.

- Find places with air conditioners. Libraries, shopping malls, and community centers can provide a cool place to take a break from the heat.

- If outside, find shade. Wear a hat wide enough to protect your face.

- Wear loose, lightweight, light-colored clothing.

- Drink plenty of fluids to stay hydrated. If you or someone you care for is on a special diet, ask a doctor how best to accommodate it.

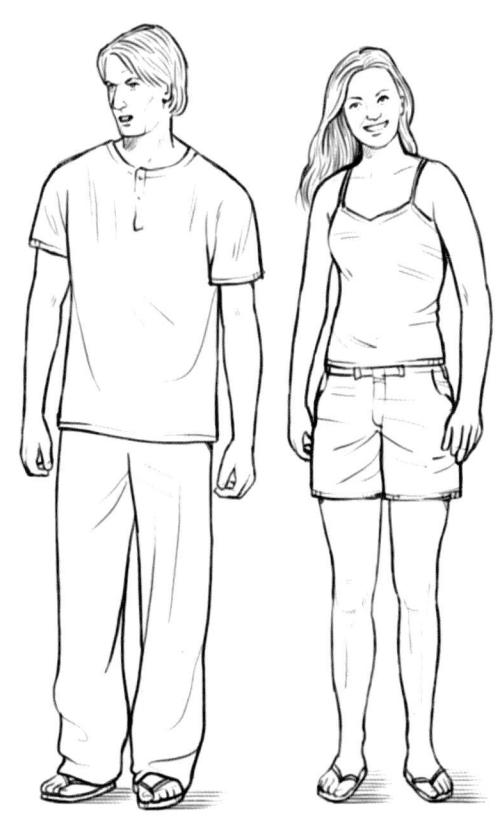

- Do not use electric fans when the temperature outside is over 95°F (35°C), as this could increase the risk of related illness. Fans create airflow and a false sense of comfort but do not reduce body temperature.*

- Avoid high-energy activities.

- Check family, neighbors, and yourself for signs of heat-related illness.

* When a fan evaporates sweat, the blood is no longer being cooled; increased blood temperature in the brain can be very dangerous and cause major medical issues.

CAUTION

Never leave children or pets alone in cars during a heat wave. Keep drinking water regularly. Do not wait to feel thirsty. Wear loose, lightweight clothing.

U.S. Army medics assist a woman who passed out from heatstroke in Zacapa, Guatemala, 2014.

HEAT EXHAUSTION

Heat exhaustion is caused by increased blood flow to the skin after periods of hard work in the sun. This reduces the amount of blood available to vital organs, which may cause a form of shock. If the sufferer continues to be exposed to heat, he or she may suffer from heatstroke. Heat exhaustion may be caused by long exposure to heat, by working in hot environments, or by too much exposure to direct sunlight.

SYMPTOMS: Skin may appear pale, ashen, or even flushed, and it may feel cool and clammy. Other symptoms include dizziness, weakness, exhaustion, and headache.

TREATMENT: Move the sufferer to a cool, shaded area, where there is circulating air. Use a fan, if available. Remove clothing, and apply damp, cool cloths to cool the body. If the person is able to drink, offer sports drinks or juice to restore electrolyte balance. Also provide water, which should be drunk regularly in small quantities.

HEATSTROKE

Heatstroke or sunstroke: This is when the body's temperature control system stops working. The body temperature continues to rise, which can cause brain damage and death. Heatstroke is more dangerous than heat exhaustion and can be life-threatening.

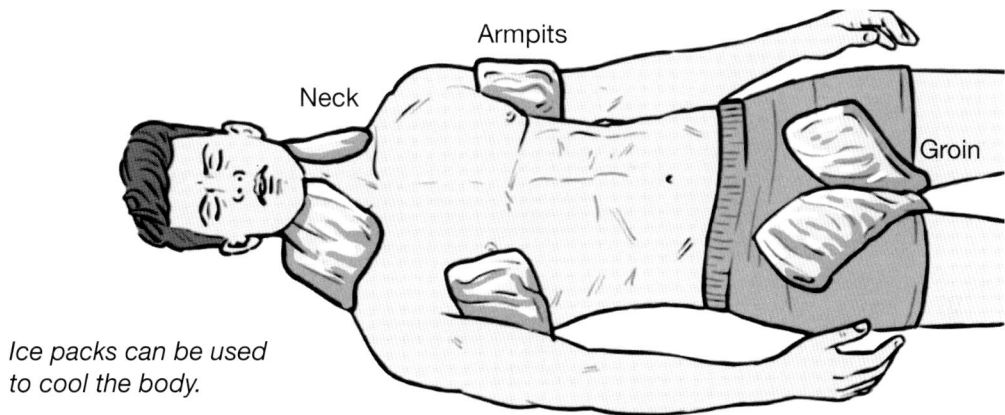

Ice packs can be used to cool the body.

SYMPTOMS: These include red skin (either dry or clammy); very high body temperature; rapid, weak pulse; rapid, shallow breathing; vomiting; and confusion.

TREATMENT: Call your national emergency number immediately for care. Immerse the patient in cold water, taking care not to leave the patient, as he or she might lose consciousness. Alternatively, spray the patient with cold water. Use towels soaked in iced water to sponge the patient's body. Place bags of ice around his or her joints. These rapid cooling methods should continue for at least 20 minutes.

Submerging the forearms in cold water has the effect of cooling the entire body through cooling blood circulation.

FEMA ADVICE ON TREATING HEAT-RELATED ILLNESSES

Know the signs of heat-related illness and ways to respond to it.

HEAT CRAMPS

- **Signs:** Muscle pains or spasms in the stomach, arms, or legs
- **Actions:** Go to a cooler location. Remove excess clothing. Take sips of cool sports drinks with salt and sugar. Get medical help if cramps last more than an hour.

HEAT EXHAUSTION

- **Signs:** Heavy sweating, paleness, muscle cramps, tiredness, weakness, dizziness, headache, nausea or vomiting, fainting
- **Actions:** Go to an air-conditioned place; lie down. Loosen or remove clothing. Take a cool bath. Take sips of sports drinks with salt and sugar. Get medical help if symptoms worsen or last more than an hour.

HEATSTROKE

- **Signs:** Extremely high body temperature of above 103°F (39°C), taken orally; red, hot, and dry skin with no sweat; rapid, strong pulse; dizziness; confusion; unconsciousness
- **Actions:** Call 911, or go to a hospital immediately. Cool down with whatever methods are available until medical help arrives.

HEAT WAVES AND DROUGHTS   123

FINDING WATER

If away from normal sources of water, for example, in a remote area after an accident, it is important to find alternative water sources if supplies are low. More often than not, it will be key to purify the water found, often by boiling it.

You can plan for these kinds of challenges by obtaining a straw-style water filter, a device that uses sunlight to clean water, or some disinfecting tablets. You can also learn how to make a solar still.

Deserts

In desert areas, you may find wells that people have made. If not, identify areas where it looks like water has run in the past, and then probe, especially in bends where any streaming water would have been most concentrated. Dig down until you find moist sand or earth. The Bushmen peoples of the Kalahari insert a tube made from the stem of a bush with a soft core. They then pack sand around it and suck on the tube to extract moisture from the ground. An alternative method is to place wet mud or sand in a cloth and wring out the drops of water into a container. Then allow the sediment to settle at the bottom before drinking.

ROCKY AREAS

Even in dry regions, water may collect in rocky areas, such as cliffs or outcrops. Caves may also be a good source of water. Do not go too far into caves in case you lose your way. If you cannot see clearly into outcrops, probe with a stick in case dangerous insects or reptiles are present. If you find brackish water that looks unpalatable, try to find the source, where water may be clearer.

Plants with water

There are many types of plant that store water, particularly in hot and arid environments. For example, it may be possible to extract water by cutting through a barrel cactus, if you mash the pulp inside. Just beware that some cacti are poisonous, especially the multiarmed variety found in the Arizona desert. Most cacti have aggressive spikes as well as smaller furry ones that can stick in the flesh and cause sores.

Date palms are a source of water. These plants are found in North America in the U.S. state of California, as well as parts of Africa and Asia. Cut a palm branch at the base, and collect the liquid that oozes out. The baobab tree, found in Africa, Madagascar, and parts of Australia, is another source. You will need a strong knife to cut into the trunk and extract the water inside. Prickly pears' liquid can be squeezed from its fruit or lobes. These plants are found in the United States, Mexico, and certain countries in South America. The saxaul plant, found in arid areas of Asia, holds water in its bark. Strip off the bark, and squeeze it.

The roots of some plants in arid areas hold moisture. Cut the roots and try to extract the water through pulping or sucking. When extracting water from plants, beware of any plant with milky sap. It is likely to be poisonous and should be avoided.

You can extract water from some types of vine, but avoid those with milky sap. When extracting water from a safe vine, first reach up and cut a notch high up the stem. This will prevent the plant from drawing water back in. Then cut through the vine at the base, and let the water drip out into a container.

Rainwater and dew

Rain is an excellent source of drinkable water, and you should plan ahead to make sure that you could catch it if needed. Keep an eye on the movements of clouds and recognize those that mean rain.

Tarps and plastic sheeting are useful for catching rain. If you do not have such items, you can use large leaves to direct water into a container. Cotton absorbs water, so if cotton clothing or similar materials are clean, you can set them out and then wring water into a container.

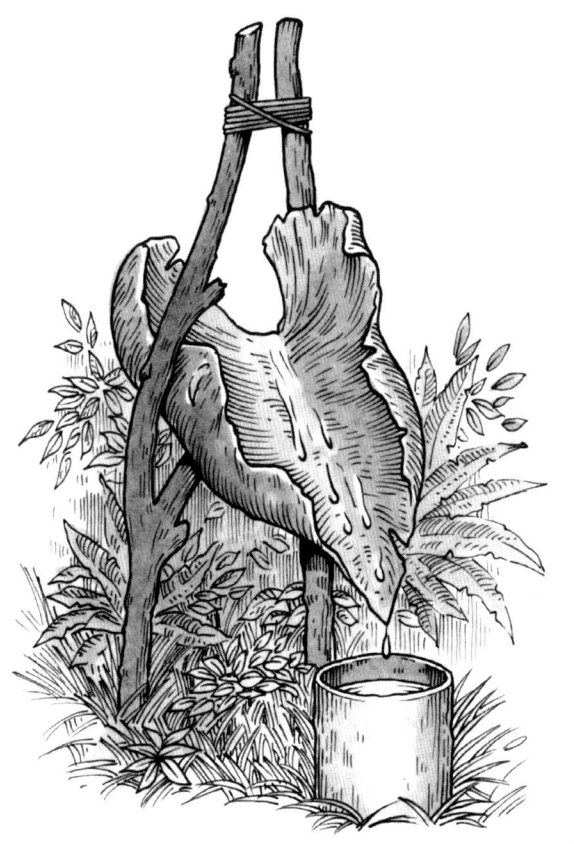

ANIMALS AND WATER

Animals need water, too, and if observed, they may lead you to water sources. Grazing animals will often head toward water at dawn and dusk. In areas where carnivores prey on such animals, you may need to be careful. There may be dangerous predators nearby. Likewise, carnivores such as alligators may be in the water.

Condensation

Creating condensation is another way of collecting water. Tie a plastic bag around a branch and its leaves or a leafy plant. As water evaporates from the leaves, it produces condensation in the bag.

No sweat

The more you sweat, the more valuable water is lost from your body, which then needs to be replaced to avoid dehydration. To reduce sweat, reduce your level of activity in heat if water supplies are limited. Also minimize your level of exposure to the sun.

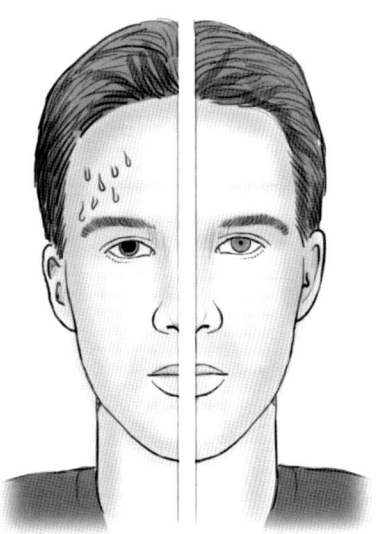

Sweat test

Fit people tend to sweat more than less fit people, as the body tends to develop more sweat glands in response to regular exercise as a way of managing body temperature efficiently.

SOLAR STILL

- Dig a hole approximately 3 feet (1 m) across and 2 feet (0.6 m) deep in an unshaded spot. Place a container, such as a plastic cup, into the bottom.
- Place a plastic sheet over the hole, and anchor its edges. Make sure the sheet does not touch the bottom. The sheet should droop but clear the container.
- Put a fist-sized stone in the center of the sheet above the container.
- Water should condense on the underside of the sheet and drip into the container. Within 24 hours, there should be about a pint of water in the container.

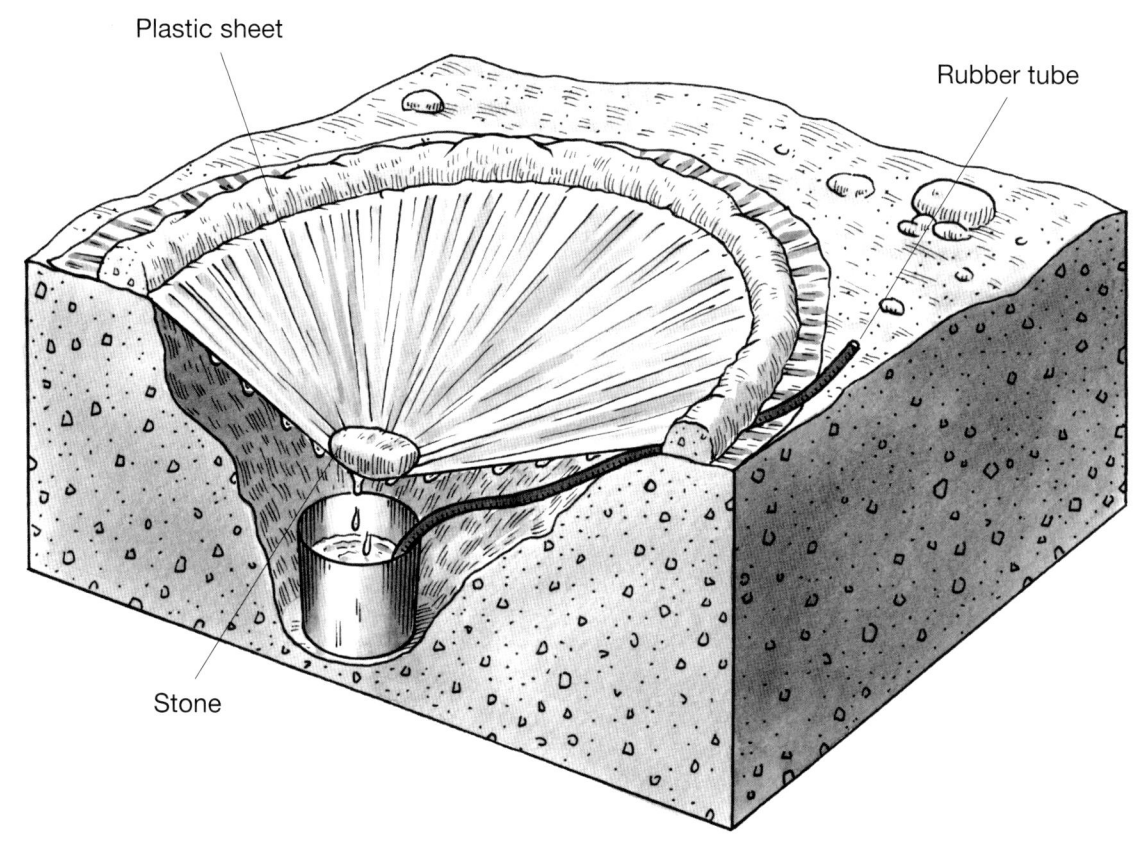

SIGNS OF DEHYDRATION

1–5 PERCENT BODY FLUID LOSS:

Flushed skin, lack of appetite, impatience, dizziness

6–10 PERCENT BODY FLUID LOSS:

Dizziness, headache, difficulty walking, labored breathing

11–20 PERCENT BODY FLUID LOSS:

Delirium, dim vision, difficulty swallowing, deafness, numbness

Loss of water through sweating is proportional to body weight. Someone who weighs about 180 pounds (13 stones) running or walking in a temperature of about 50°F (10°C) will need to drink about 5 fluid ounces (148 ml) of water for every 1 mile (1.6 km) that person runs or walks. When walking in the desert in a temperature of 100°F (38°C) water is lost through sweat at the rate of about two pints per hour.

Thirst is not an accurate way to judge your water requirements. A fuzzy feeling in the head or dark urine is a better indicator of a need for water.

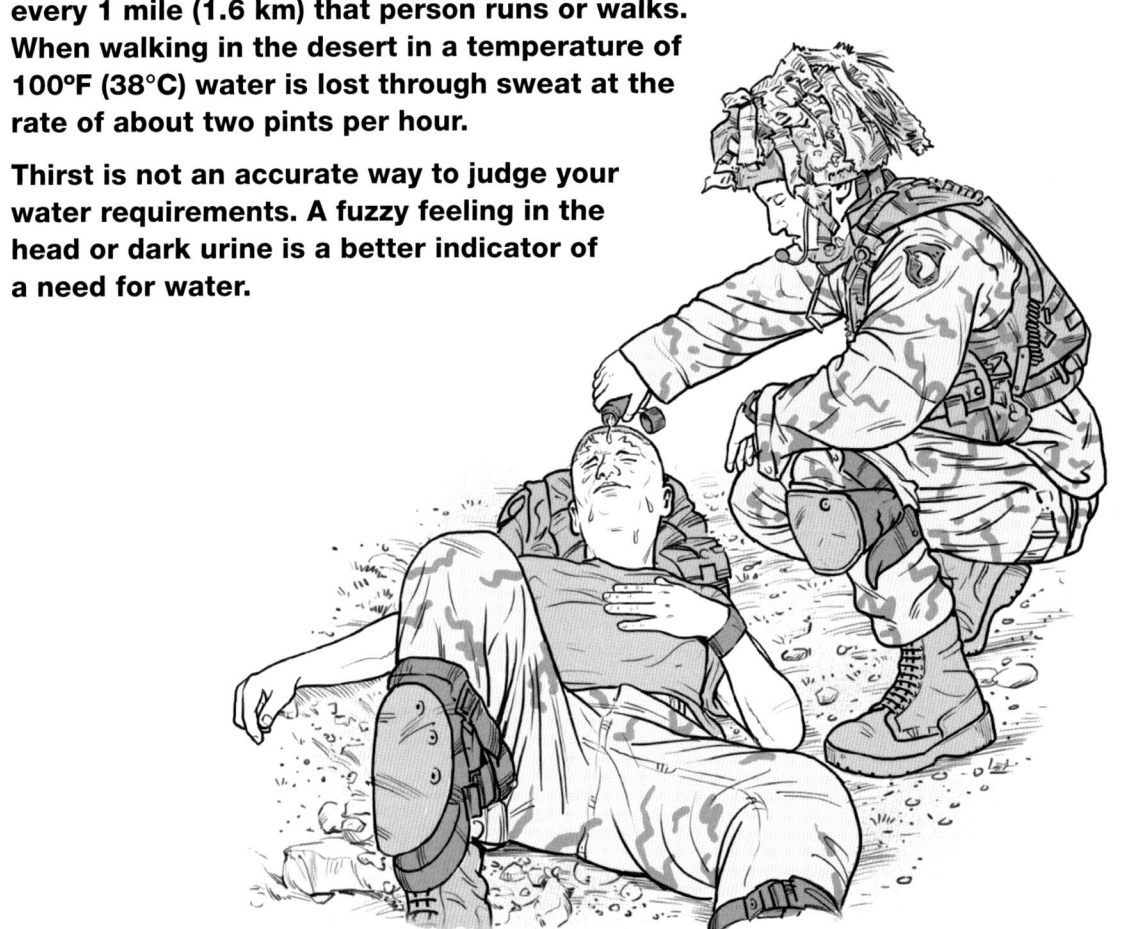

DESERT SURVIVAL

Deserts have very low rainfall, and therefore plant and animal life are also limited. If you are ever stranded in a desert, the main priorities are finding water, building a shelter, getting out of the sun, preserving energy, finding food, and being rescued.

Though most deserts have rain for 15 to 20 days annually, some have no rain for years, so it requires considerable skill to survive in a desert environment. It is important to wear loose-fitting clothing that allows cool air to circulate near the body. It is smart to cover the skin as far as possible to reduce the risk of sunburn.

Possible sources of heat gain in the desert

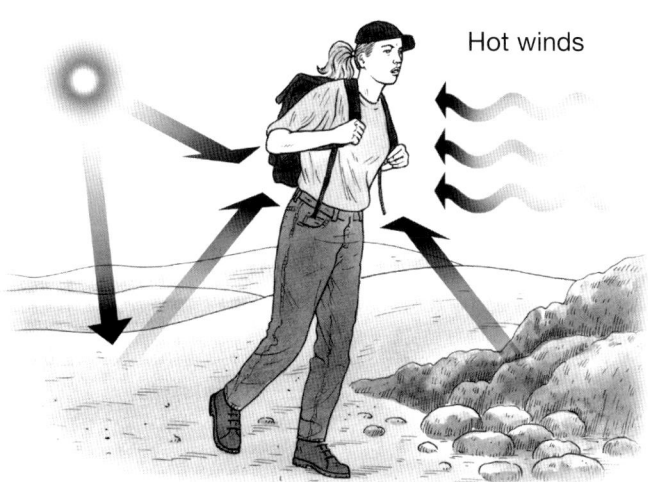

Direct rays from the sun

Hot winds

Reflective heat

Protective head gear

Protecting the head and neck is important. Wear a wide-brimmed hat to shade head and neck. The Arab-style keffiyeh also provides excellent all-around protection for head, face, eyes, and neck. When the end of the keffiyeh is rolled under the face, it helps to protect eyes from the reflected glare from the desert floor.

SHELTERS

It is best to build a shelter during the cool of the evening and to improvise during the day with a temporary shelter made from a tarp.

SIMPLE TARP SHELTER:

Find two upright poles, or cut two branches. Push them into the ground about 8 feet (2.4 m) apart. Use rocks for support if necessary, or run supporting string to a peg in the ground. Stretch string or rope between the two poles, and tie it there. Drape a tarp or other protective cover over the string, and secure it to the ground with pegs.

ASYMMETRICAL TARP SHELTER:

Lash two poles together to make an A-frame. Rest a pole on the top of the A-frame, and let it run to the ground, leaving enough space for you to lie under it. Drape a tarp or cover over the leaning pole, and weigh it down at the sides with rocks.

HEAT WAVES AND DROUGHTS 131

WEIGHTED TARP SHELTER (1):

Find two upright poles, or cut two branches. Push them into the ground about 8 feet (2.4 m) apart. Use rocks for support if necessary, or run supporting string to a peg in the ground. Stretch string or rope between the two poles, and tie it there. Place part of the tarp under your sleeping bag area, and pass the rest over the top of the horizontal string. Then attach the ends to pegs.

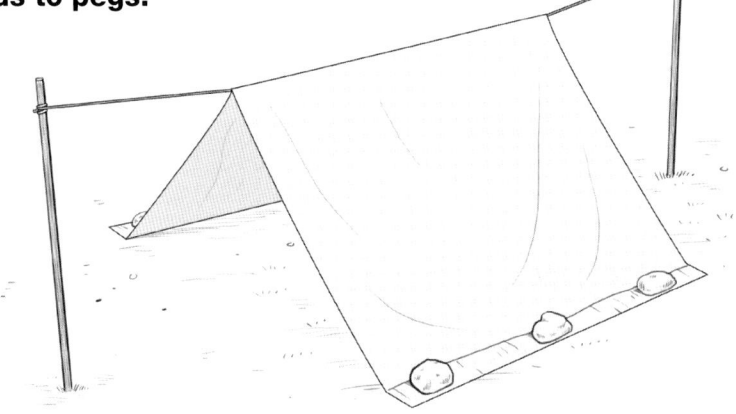

WEIGHTED TARP SHELTER (2):

An alternative weighted tarp shelter can be constructed by using four poles and two supporting ropes. This will create a larger shelter capable of accommodating more than one person.

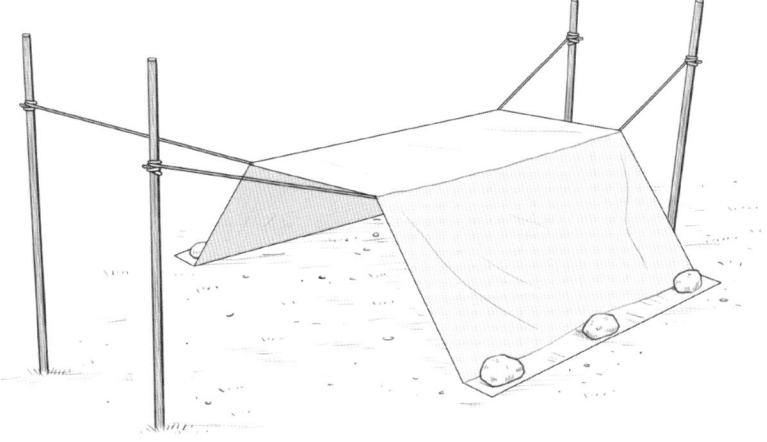

SHELTERS CONTINUED

UNDERGROUND SHELTER

This shelter is protective by getting you out of the wind. Find a depression in the ground that gives you enough space to lie down with room to spare, or alternatively dig a trench about 2 feet (0.6 m) deep. Pile sand and rocks around the edges.

Place a poncho over the area, and weigh it down with rocks or sandbags. If you have another poncho, lay it over the sandbags, and weigh it down to create a double layer to provide better insulation from the sun.

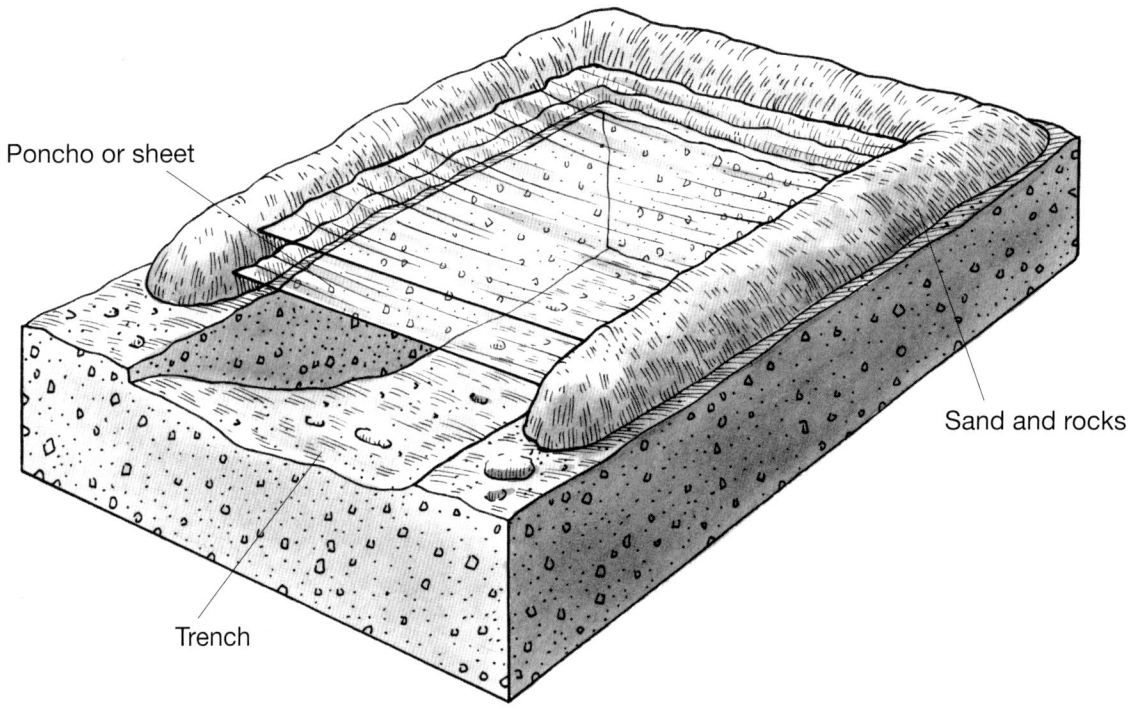

Poncho or sheet

Sand and rocks

Trench

GROUND SHELTER

This shelter will provide more ventilation than an underground shelter. The construction is similar to that of an underground shelter but without a trench. Fill sandbags, and place them at the four corners of the area you will shelter in. Place a poncho or tarp across the area, and weigh it down with sandbags or rocks. You can create a double layer if you have two.

HEAT WAVES AND DROUGHTS 133

IMPROVISED SHELTER

If there are enough rocks or wood available, pile them together to create a windbreak as well as shade. If there is vegetation available, use that to create a roof. Alternatively, weigh down a tarp or poncho to create a sheltered area.

If there are any rocky areas nearby, search for a cave, or build around a recessed area to maximize its protective qualities. Use a poncho or some other material to make a roof.

DUST AND SANDSTORMS

A desert sandstorm, or haboob, is a formidable and dangerous event. They can be 10,000 feet (3,048 m) high and last for days. A sandstorm carries sand particles in strong winds.

If a sandstorm is approaching, seek shelter as soon as possible behind a large object such as a boulder. This will help to protect from the flying sand particles. Do not lie in a gully or ditch, as you may be hit by a flash flood. Stay close to the ground, protecting your head with your arms or with a backpack. Cover eyes, nose, and mouth. To avoid getting buried in the sand, move regularly from side to side to displace the sand.

LANDSLIDES, AVALANCHES, AND CAVING

Landslides are masses of rock, earth, or debris that fall off or slide down slopes, pulled by the force of gravity. Possible triggers include heavy rain or melting snow, which reduces the cohesive strength of earth, clay, and sand. Deforestation can contribute to the instability of Earth's surface, as tree roots help to hold earth in place. Forest fires can contribute to landslides by devastating tree cover and undergrowth. Earthquakes, volcanoes, and explosions set off by humans can also create landslides.

Powder snow avalanches can be hundreds of feet high and descend at remarkable speeds.

TYPES OF LANDSLIDE

Landslides can be caused by a wide range of factors, including earthquakes, severe rain, wildfires, or deforestation. They are categorized both by the method of movement as well as their composition.

Falls happen when masses break off suddenly. A topple occurs when a mass pivots before falling. Slides occur when materials slide on sloped surfaces. A spread is a movement that takes along soft materials beneath the moving surface. Flows make a flowing movement. For example, a rockfall features rocks breaking off along a line of weakness. A debris flow is a mix of soil, rock, and other matter that flows with water.

FEMA ADVICE ON LANDSLIDE WARNING SIGNS

- Changes occur in the landscape, such as a difference in stormwater drainage, especially where runoff converges; slight land movements; slides; or flows.
- Doors or windows stick or jam for the first time.
- New cracks appear in plaster, tile, brick, or foundations.
- Outside walls, walks, or stairs begin pulling away from a building.
- Slowly developing, widening cracks appear on the ground or on paved areas, such as streets or driveways.
- Underground utility lines break.
- Bulging ground appears at the base of a slope.
- Water breaks through the ground surface in new locations.
- Fences, retaining walls, utility poles, or trees tilt or move.
- A faint rumbling sound increases in volume as a landslide nears.
- The ground slopes downward in one direction and may begin shifting in that direction underfoot.
- Unusual sounds, such as trees cracking or boulders knocking together, might indicate moving debris.
- Collapsed pavement, mud, fallen rocks, or other indications of possible debris flow can be seen when driving. Embankments along roadsides are particularly susceptible to landslides.

LANDSLIDES, AVALANCHES, AND CAVING 137

Triggers

The best way to avoid a landslide is to be aware of potential dangers and also of triggers, such as heavy rain or wind. Listen for any unusual sounds, such as trees creaking or rocks crashing together. Notice if there is an increase in sediment in rivers. If you are in a danger area, evacuate as soon as possible.

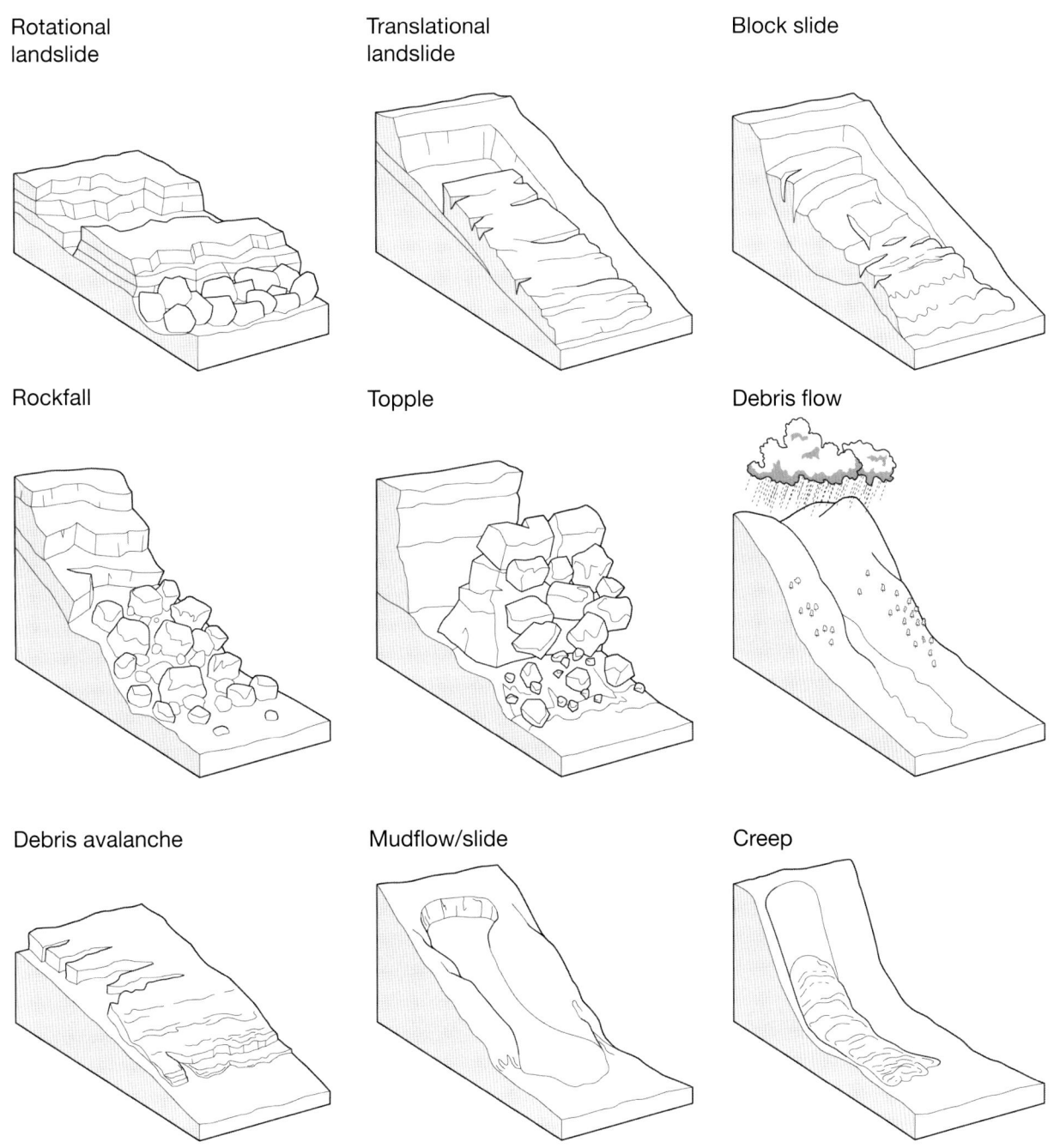

Rotational landslide

Translational landslide

Block slide

Rockfall

Topple

Debris flow

Debris avalanche

Mudflow/slide

Creep

FEMA SAFETY ADVICE REGARDING LANDSLIDES

- During severe storms, stay alert and awake. Many deaths from landslides occur while people are sleeping.
- Listen to local news on a battery-powered radio for warnings of heavy rainfall.
- Listen for unusual sounds that might indicate moving debris, such as trees cracking or boulders knocking together.
- Move away from the path of a landslide or debris flow as quickly as possible. The danger from a mudflow increases near stream channels and with prolonged heavy rains. Mudflows can move faster than you can walk or run. Look upstream before crossing a bridge, and do not cross the bridge if a mudflow is approaching.
- Avoid river valleys and low-lying areas.
- If you are near a stream or channel, be alert for any sudden increase or decrease in water flow, and notice whether the water changes from clear to muddy. Such changes may mean there is a debris flow upstream, so prepare to move quickly.
- Curl into a tight ball, and protect your head if escape is not possible.

A landslide has caused a supporting wall to collapse across a mountain road.

LANDSLIDES, AVALANCHES, AND CAVING 139

AVALANCHES

Avalanches are masses of snow, either wet or dry, which move fast down a slope. They are regular occurrences in mountainous regions, and the best way to survive them is to avoid them.

Check beforehand

Before setting out in the mountains, check for recent avalanche activity, and if there has been a slide, find out what kind it was. Look out for signs that suggest the snow is wet and unstable, such as cracks in the snow surface or rolling balls of snow.

THREE As FOR AVOIDING AVALANCHES

ANGLE: Avoid slopes with angles of more than 25 degrees.

ASPECTS: Look for dangers, such as strong sunlight or strong winds.

ALTITUDE: Check recent bulletins for altitude-related warnings.

Look to see how much snow cover there is. Feel the snow. Is it light or compacted? Listen for any squeaking or whumping sounds, which indicate that snow is moving or under strain.

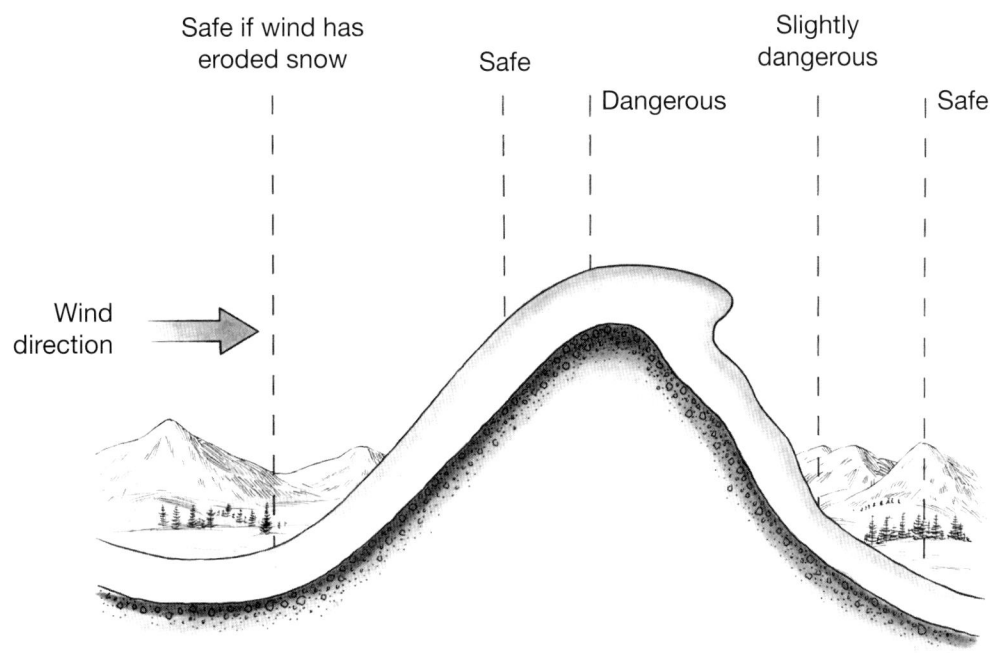

Slab avalanche

This is the most powerful and destructive form of avalanche. It looks like an enormous plate of snow sliding downward. A slab avalanche, which can cause widespread damage, often occurs on a slope with an incline between 30 and 50 degrees. Slab avalanches are less likely to happen where there are trees or rocky outcroppings, as these tend to anchor snow.

Slab avalanches often occur after heavy snowfall accompanied by strong wind. Higher temperatures and rainfall can also lead to this kind of disaster.

Other avalanche types

In a glide avalanche, the snowpack falls in one piece, moving like a glacier. Icefalls are falling blocks of ice. These and other forms of avalanche are identified by their behavior and how they are formed.

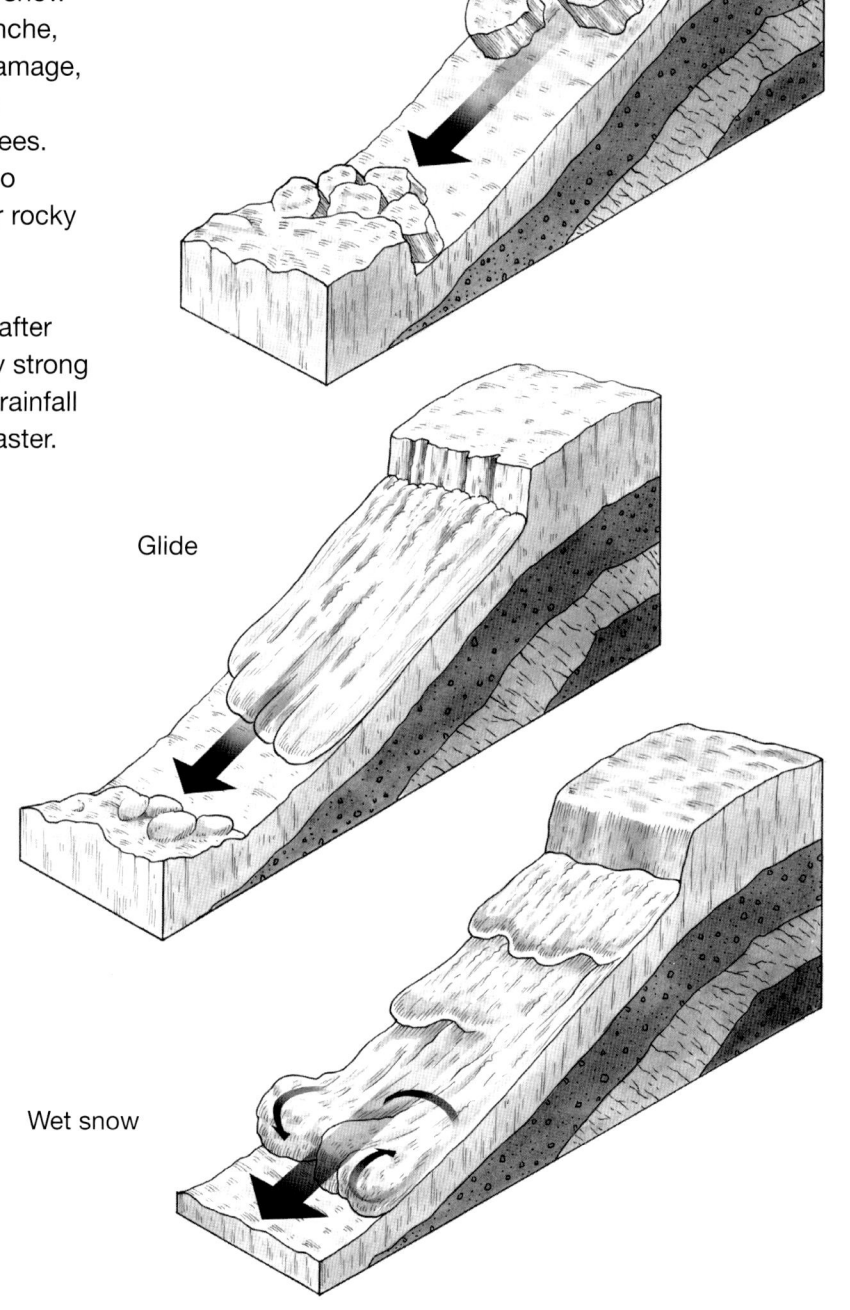

Triggers

If snow is liable to avalanche, it only needs a small trigger to set it off. The majority of avalanche victims, more than 90 percent, cause the avalanche that they are caught up in. The trigger is often a skier or snowboarder. However, natural triggers include falling cornices, fresh snowfall, or snow deposited by wind.

LANDSLIDES, AVALANCHES, AND CAVING 141

Avoiding avalanches

If you need to cross a potentially dangerous slope, cross it as high as possible and keep close to any rocky outcroppings or trees that you can use for protection.

Staying roped

If you are crossing an area with other people, stay roped together, allowing about 50 feet (15 m) of rope between each person, so you do not necessarily fall together. When crossing a slope, take a slope meter, so you can work out the gradient of the slope and the potential for danger.

FEMA ADVICE ON AVALANCHE AVOIDANCE

- Learn about local avalanche risk.
- Sign up for alerts from a U.S. Forest Service Avalanche Center near you. Your community may also have a local warning system on which you can rely.
- Learn the signs of an avalanche and how to use safety and rescue equipment.
- Receive first aid training to recognize and treat suffocation, hypothermia, traumatic injury, and shock. Learn how to use safety and rescue equipment.
- Travel with a guide who knows locations to avoid. Always travel in pairs.
- Follow avalanche warnings on roads. Roads may be closed, or vehicles may be advised not to stop on the roadside.
- Avoid risky areas, such as slopes steeper than 30 degrees or areas under steep slopes.
- Know the signs of increased danger, including recent avalanches and cracks across slopes.
- Wear a helmet to help reduce head injuries and to create air pockets.
- Wear an avalanche beacon to help rescuers locate you.
- Use an avalanche air bag that may help you from being completely buried.
- Carry a collapsible avalanche probe and a small shovel to help rescue others.

AVALANCHE SAFETY EQUIPMENT

AVALANCHE TRANSCEIVER
The avalanche transceiver, also called an avalanche beacon, sends out a regular signal that can be picked up by other transceivers. It will increase your chance of survival by shortening the time it takes rescuers to get to you. Make sure that you and companions have practiced location techniques, or better still, attend a professional training course. If buried by snow, it can help if one's training can take over.

Wear the transceiver close to the body and preferably under a jacket, so it does not get ripped off in a fall. Make sure that the transceiver batteries are working before setting out, and make sure that the equipment is turned on.

SNOW PROBE
The snow probe is designed to help find avalanche victims in an area where a strong signal has been found. This tool comes in sections, which can be assembled by pulling on a string or cable. The probe also helps a rescuer assess the depth of the snow.

A skier checks her avalanche transceiver.

SHOVEL

Once you have located an avalanche victim, you want to dig the victim out as fast as possible to increase the chances of survival. Carry a sturdy collapsible shovel at all times in an avalanche area, and make sure that it is easily accessible.

AVALANCHE AIR BAG BACKPACK

When deployed during an avalanche, a pack increases chances of survival. The pack adds volume to your body, which helps you rise to the top of rolling debris.

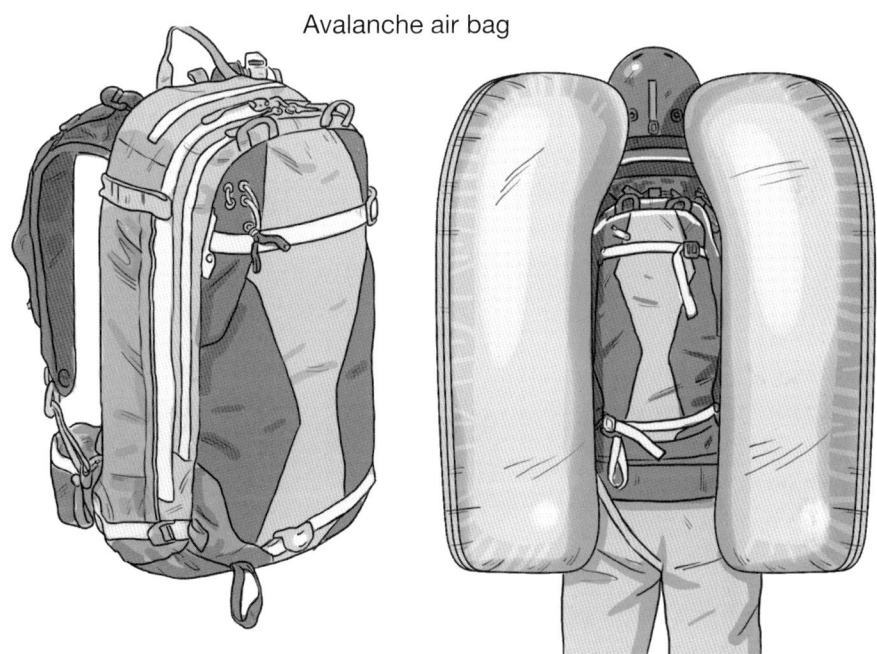

Avalanche air bag

BREATHING TUBE

A breathing tube is designed to maintain access to valuable oxygen when caught in snow. It draws air from other parts of the snowpack.

SKI HELMET

This can provide additional protection to your head against falls when skiing or from avalanche debris.

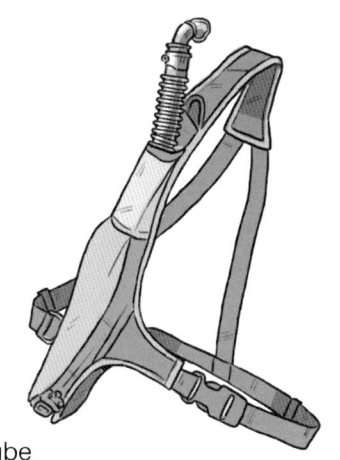

Breathing tube

What to do if caught in an avalanche

If approached by an avalanche while skiing or snowboarding, try to pick up speed heading downhill, and then steer toward the side of the avalanche and out of harm's way. If there is a boulder or tree to shelter behind, try that. If you have an avalanche air bag, pull the operating toggle if you think you are going to get caught.

Swim!

If carried along by an avalanche, use a strong swimming motion to keep as near to the surface as possible. As the snow begins to slow down, adopt a feet-down, head-up position. Punch one arm strongly toward the surface, and use the other to create a breathing space in front of your face. Do so by touching your opposite shoulder with your hand.

POLAR SURVIVAL

In polar regions, the experience of extreme cold can be made worse by factors such as windchill, a measure of how quickly a body loses heat. The sun can stay below the level of the horizon for several months. During this period, the main source of warmth is warmer air flowing from the south.

Environment

Vegetation is usually tundra or northern forest, though there is a distinct tree line beyond which trees cannot grow. Animals in polar regions include polar bear, seals, and penguins. There are caribou, arctic weasels, arctic hares, lemmings, arctic wolves, arctic foxes, gyrfalcons, ptarmigans, skuas, and snowy owls.

Northern forests in countries such as Canada and Russia are home to numerous animals and a source of food for the skilled survivalist. In polar regions, food can be found in summer along the coast or in streams, rivers, and lakes. The available seafood includes various fish as well as clams, crawfish, mussels, snails, and crabs. Seabirds can be eaten, too. Hunting in lower latitudes features tundra animals, such as musk, reindeer, arctic hares, caribou, and lemmings.

TEMPERATURE FACTORS

Arctic winter temperatures vary widely, with a mean around 20°F (–7°C) in the coldest month. Mean temperatures in summer are around 50°F (10°C). In the Antarctic summer, the interior temperature is typically between –4°F and –31°F (–20°C and –35°C).

Windchill can significantly exacerbate the low temperature conditions.

Wind Speed	Windchill
11 mph (18 kph)	17°F (–8°C)
22 mph (35 kph)	5°F (–15°C)
34 mph (55 kph)	–1°F (–18°C)
44 mph (71 kph)	–3°F (–19°C)

Clothing

Specialist clothing is essential in polar regions. Dress in layers, and include a windproof layer as an outer shell. Fur linings on hoods help to prevent your breath from freezing on your face.

Footwear

Plan your footwear according to what you plan to do. Waterproof leather or canvas boots with rubber soles and an insulated liner are designed to keep feet and lower legs warm and dry. Wear three layers of socks inside boots. Try to dust off as much snow as possible before entering a shelter or getting into a sleeping bag.

Stay dry

Make sure that you do not overheat when doing anything physical, as this can create cold sweat. Clothing should be kept as clean and as dry as possible. Keep the clothing fairly loose, so air can circulate. The hood and cuffs should be tightly fastened in harsh weather, but should be loosened when you are walking or working.

LANDSLIDES, AVALANCHES, AND CAVING 147

Finding Water

Although it is important to wear plenty of clothing to keep warm, the combination of heavy clothing and dry polar air can dehydrate a body very quickly.

Remember to keep drinking regularly. You should be able to get water during summer months from streams, lakes, or ponds. In winter, melt ice. When looking for ice to melt, choose rounded ice with a bluish tinge, as this will be more palatable.

When filling a water bottle, allow some space in case the water freezes. Keep the water bottle close to the body to reduce the likelihood of its freezing.

Melting ice

The improvised melting device below is good for turning large blocks of ice into drinking water.

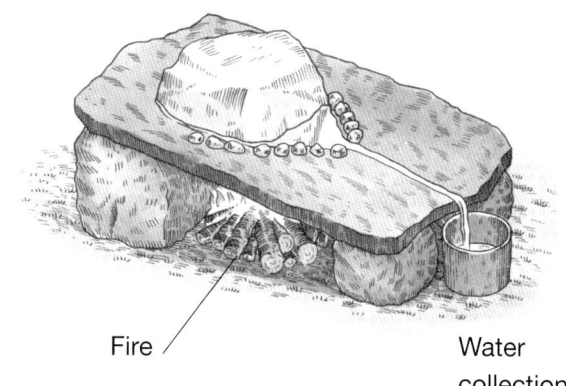

Block of ice

Fire

Water collection

Making improvised snowshoes

Snowshoes are essential if you have to move through very deep, soft snow. Take care that none of the bindings cut into the flesh of your ankle or lower leg.

• Take a sapling and bend into a horse shoe shape

• Fit cross-members

• Shape into a frame and tie the ends

POLAR SHELTERS

It is vital to keep out of the wind as much as possible in polar regions. If sheltering from a blizzard, look for a natural area of shelter, and then assure that snowdrifts do not bury it. Keep an eye out for caves, overhanging rock shelves, fallen trees, or spruce trees. You can dig to the base of a spruce, and its overhanging branches can serve as a natural canopy.

Dome shelter

For a more straightforward shelter, consider the molded dome shelter. You can fill a tarp with any material, including bark, twigs, and foliage, to create a ball large enough to form living space. On a firm surface, you can cover the ball with snow to make a dome. Once the snow is hardened and will not collapse, you can carefully pull out the tarp and contents, which will leave an interior living space. If building a dome, however, be sure to create at least one ventilation hole to have enough oxygen when sheltering.

Pile up a thick layer of snow on a large mound of brush material

Once the snow has hardened, remove the brush

Tie up a bundle of brush with a sheet to act as a door

Igloo

If you have more time and energy, a range of more elaborate shelters can be erected. Some require cutting tools. The best-known polar shelter is the igloo, but do not underestimate the amount of time it takes to plan and build an igloo, using snow blocks.

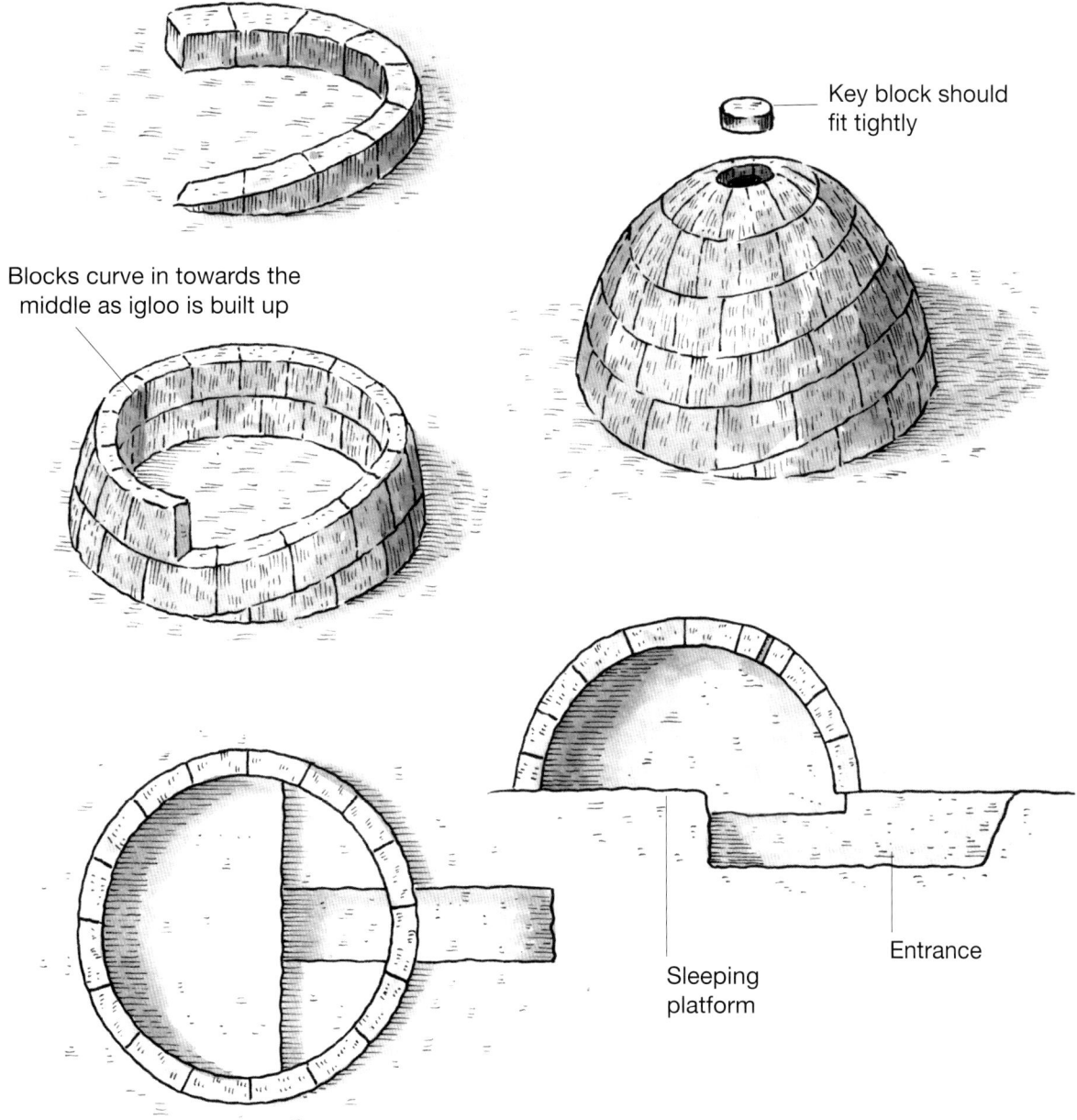

Blocks curve in towards the middle as igloo is built up

Key block should fit tightly

Sleeping platform

Entrance

MOUNTAIN SURVIVAL

The conditions you will experience in high mountain regions are similar to those in polar regions, including low temperatures aggravated by a severe windchill factor. The steep terrain and limited shelter pose additional hazards.

Equipment

It is vital to have full training and equipment for mountain climbing and ice climbing, as you cannot afford to take risks. If you experience an accident in a mountainous region, your priority is to get down to a lower level as soon as possible in order to get out of the extreme weather conditions and to find food and shelter.

When moving in mountains, make sure that you can see where you are going. Do not attempt to negotiate mountainous terrain at night. You can easily slip and fall over a steep edge.

Glaciers

Glaciers pose dangers, so try to cross them in the early morning, while it is still cold and before the ice has turned to meltwater. Make sure you and any companions are roped together, whatever the conditions. Crevasses may be hidden by fresh snow, so be ready. Allow enough rope between walkers so that no two people fall in the same crevasse. This varies, but a distance of about 30 feet (9 m) should be maintained between walkers at all times. Make sure that the rope is taut. If somebody falls into a crevasse, the rest of the team should immediately move backward and fall back on their haunches to take the strain.

LANDSLIDES, AVALANCHES, AND CAVING   151

Descent

When descending down a steep gradient on a mountainside, make steps in the snow with the heel of your boot, keeping your leg slightly bent. Use the ice axe for support, with the pick pointing backward.

If you slip, drive the shaft of the ice axe into the snow, and hold onto it at the base. Try to kick both toes into the snow to form a foothold. If the snow is hard, use the sharp pick of the axe to dig into the snow.

Braking position

If you begin to slide down a slope, keep your head upward, and place one hand on the head of your ice axe and the other on the shaft. With the hand on the axe head, place the spike into the ice. Keep the other hand on the shaft. Then lean into it, pushing down so that the ice pick is forced into the slope. Put as much pressure as possible on the axe and on your knees, keeping your feet off the ground.

If you are without an ice axe, roll onto your front, and then push up from the slope with your arms, so as to maximize and focus the pressure on your toes, forcing them into the slope. The idea is to create a wedge effect, which will bring you to a halt. Alternatively, spread your legs and arms to create maximum drag.

When descending, keep an eye out for worn paths or for any other indication that the route has been used before. If scrambling down a hillside, face inward toward the rock. Make sure to avoid gullies due to the risk of falling stone.

152 LANDSLIDES, AVALANCHES, AND CAVING

Climbing cam

Spring-loaded climbing cams can be inserted into cracks in rocks. Once downward pressure is applied to the cam, from attached ropes, the cams are forced outwards to grip the rock, and provide a stable anchor.

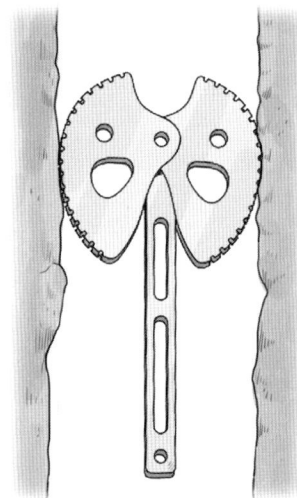

Descending without rope

The method of descending a gradient depends on how steep it is. If you are on a steep gradient, keep facing into the rock as you descend. Keep weight balanced on your legs, and keep legs bent. Your arms should be straight.

If the gradient is reasonably moderate, you can move downward in a sideways stance, but make sure to maintain three points of contact with the ground. This could be either two hands and one foot or one hand and two feet.

On a shallow gradient where you feel reasonably confident, you can descend with back to the hill and face out. This will make it easier to look for footholds where you can jam the heel of a boot to prevent sliding. If the ground is soft enough, you can kick the footholds.

Descending with rope

A rope can assist in descending a gradient that is not vertical or not very steep. Fix the rope to a secure anchor, with a backup if necessary, and make sure that the end of the rope is long enough to reach to a secure area targeted below. Position your side toward the anchor with the rope behind your back. Keep a firm grip at all times.

Begin to walk down the slope sideways (A), allowing the rope to pass slowly through your hands (B). To slow or stop, bring the hand controlling the lower end of the rope, sometimes called the brake hand, in front of the body, and turn to face the anchor (C). This will help lock the rope.

A

B

C

Mountain shelters

To avoid moving on a mountain at night, you can make a temporary shelter near the protection of a boulder or in a natural cave. If there is snow, you can build a snow cave by cutting into a drift or by piling snow. Each wall base should be thicker than the ceiling. The walls can be curved to prevent water from dripping. You can seal the top of the entrance with tightly packed snowballs. Then you can use a backpack or a bag of snow to seal the entrance. Just make sure there is at least one ventilation hole at a 45-degree angle from the door.

Snow tree shelter

A snow tree shelter takes advantage of the fact that the branches of a pine tree provide a natural and dense form of overhead shelter. Dig out the snow from around the base of the tree and line the floor with thick layers of foliage. With you hunkered down beneath, the low-hanging branches above you will provide some degree of waterproof and windproof protection.

CAVING

Caves are formed in different ways. Some are created by a chemical reaction between water and bedrock; some, by after-effects of volcanic eruptions; some, by glacier movement; and some are created by the action of wind and water such as coastal erosion.

Caves present numerous safety hazards. Underground chambers can be very deep and extend long distances through complex tunnels, in which there is real danger of getting lost. Steep or sheer drops can occur. Caves are also susceptible to surface waters running inside and creating drowning hazards. Underground areas have little or no natural light, making cavers totally dependent on reliable portable light sources. Far from the rays of the sun, caves are often very cold, presenting a danger of hypothermia.

This caver is wearing the appropriate clothing and safety equipment, including a thermal suit, climbing harness, rope, and protective helmet with mounting lights.

Clothing

When dressing for caving, follow the same principles of layering as you would for cold or wet weather aboveground. Do not wear cotton clothing, as it absorbs water and perspiration and will not dry underground. Wear tough outer garments to withstand scrapes and mud.

FOLLOW PLOW

P: Previous weather and water conditions. Has it been raining, and is the ground wet, dry, or frozen?

L: Local knowledge of both the cave and the catchment area. Find out how the cave floods and the usual time delay. Do you know the route? Do you have a guidebook or a local guide familiar with the area?

O: Observation. What is happening now? Is it raining, or are there obvious signs of rain to come? What do local cavers think? Are other cavers coming out when you are planning to go in? If so, why?

W: Weather forecast. Get two independent weather forecasts for the immediate area. Have a wet-weather-alternative plan.

Team check

Is each member of the team competent, fit, and healthy? Do you have the appropriate personal and technical kit, and the knowledge and ability to use them correctly? Do you have an emergency kit, such as a spare light, a whistle, first aid, dried food and clothing, survival bag or group shelters, spare rope, knife, and so on?

- Do you have details in case of an emergency?
- Participants' details, including contacts with cell numbers
- Cave name, grid reference, location, and intended route
- Parking place and car registration
- Time of entry and callout time if no contact has been made
- Whom to call in case of an emergency
- Emergency rescue services in the country and the local area

Dried food, ready meals, and candy provide instant energy when cut off from normal food sources. The U.S. military issues its personnel with Meal, Ready-to-Eat (MRE) rations for combat deployments.

CAVER EQUIPMENT

Cavers should consider wearing or carrying the following equipment:
- Thermal underwear
- Sturdy long trousers
- Shirt with long sleeves
- Mid-layer fleece for warmth
- Protective jacket
- Gloves
- Boots
- Socks
- Helmet with light
- Spare set of clothing and shoes
- Kneepads and elbow pads
- Backpack
- Spare lights
- Spare bulbs
- Spare batteries
- Whistle
- Duct tape
- Food
- First aid kit and medications
- Space blanket
- Markers to find a route out

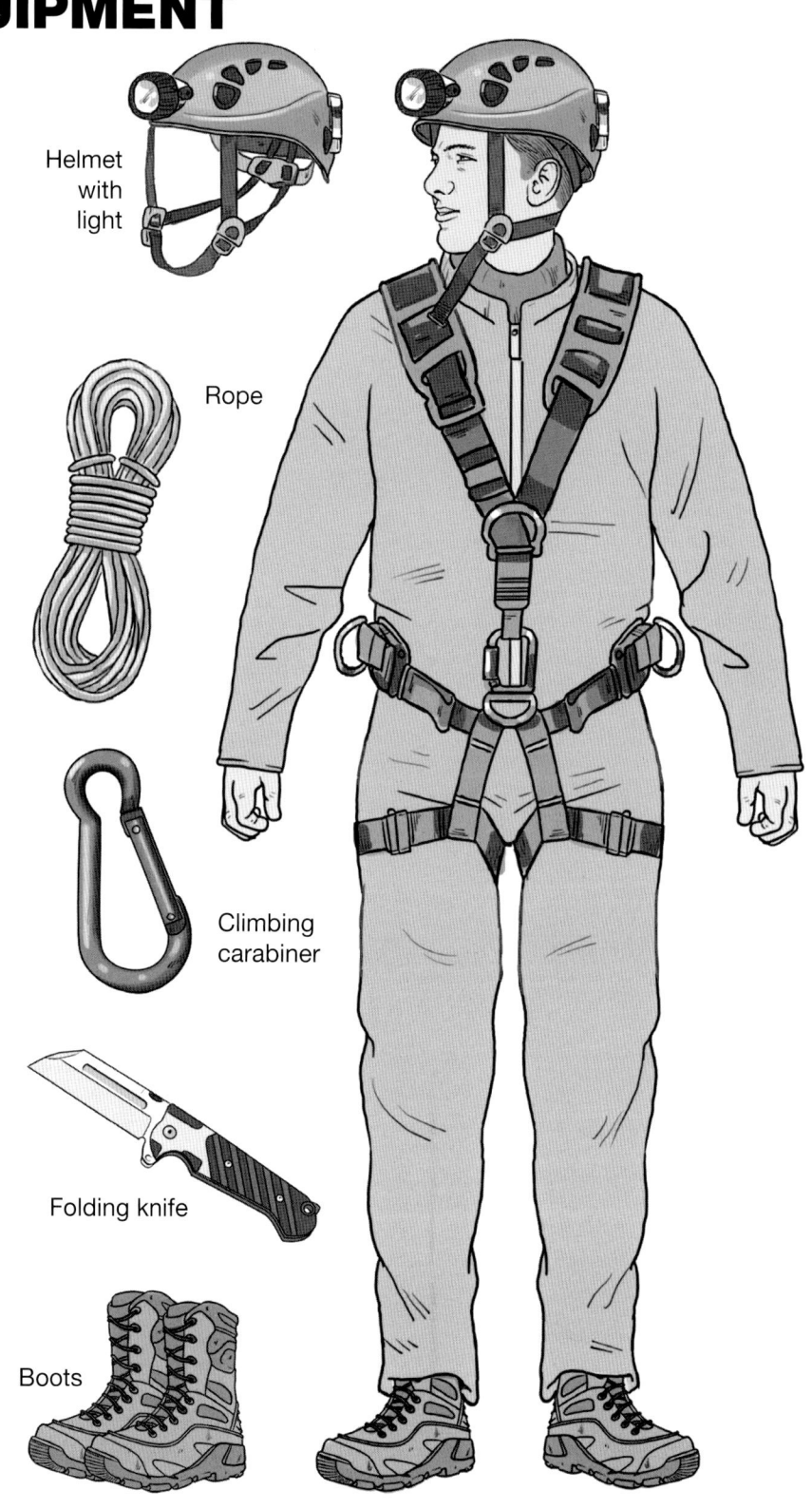

Helmet with light

Rope

Climbing carabiner

Folding knife

Boots

LANDSLIDES, AVALANCHES, AND CAVING 157

Reducing the likelihood of caving accidents

Some of the main causes of caving accidents are falls, getting hit by falling objects, or hypothermia.

Falling:
Avoid jumping, and do not slide down slopes. Make sure you have proper footwear. Check all climbing equipment to make sure it is not faulty. When moving through difficult areas, you should have three points of the body supported by stable objects always, such as handholds and footholds.

Falling objects:
Always wear a helmet to protect from being injured by falling objects. If possible, clear the bases of drops or climbs. Make sure that all personal equipment is secured, so it does not fall and hit another caver. Know your group warning for falling objects.

Hypothermia:
Extended exposure to cold temperatures can lead to hypothermia. Make sure that you have enough warm clothing, especially when you stop for rest or for food.

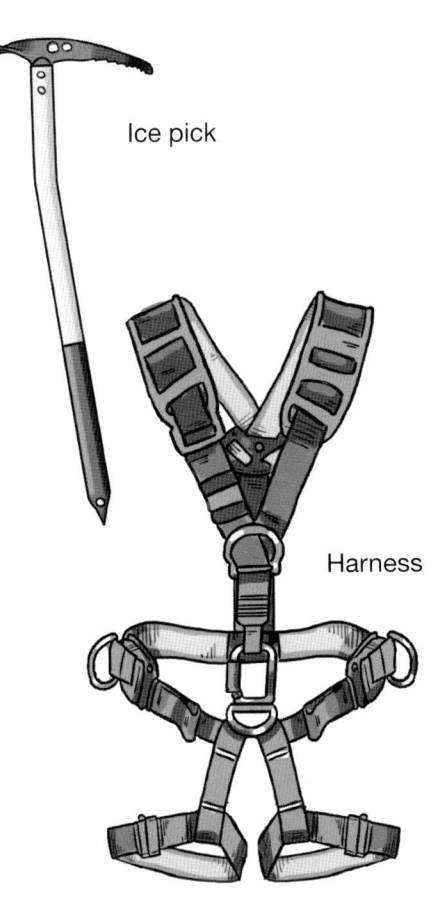

Ice pick

Harness

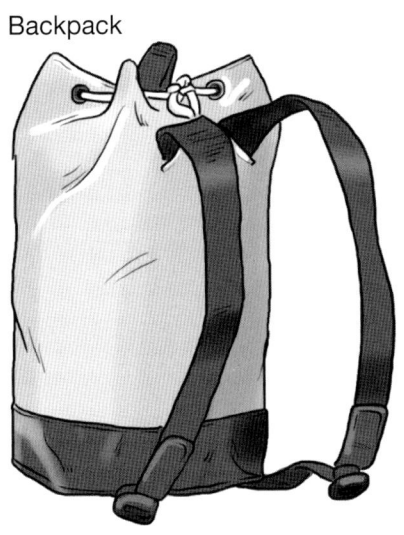

Backpack

ACTION IN A CAVE ACCIDENT

Make sure it is safe before attending to a patient. If necessary, move the patient to a safe area, checking first for any signs of back or neck injuries.

Immobilize any fractures if you can. Make sure the patient is kept warm until help comes. If there is a neck or spinal injury, wait for a professional rescue team. If the patient can walk or crawl, assist with movement out of the cave. If medical equipment or a stretcher is needed, let the team at the surface answer those needs.

THAILAND CAVE RESCUE

On June 23, 2018, a soccer team consisting of 12 boys, along with one of their coaches, entered Tham Luang cave in Chiang Rai Province, Thailand. Soon afterward, there was heavy rain, which filled parts of the cave with water. The group moved deep into the cave system as passageways flooded. Attempts to locate the group were hampered by flooding. Initial diving probes revealed little due to heavy silting of the water. Attempts to access the cave from above, using sniffer dogs and probes,

came to no avail. International rescue teams began arriving to supplement the contingent of Royal Thai Navy SEALs working on the rescue. The rescuers included the British Cave Rescue Council, the U.S. Air Force Pararescue, and the Australian Federal Police Specialist Response Group, as well as Chinese divers.

On July 2, two divers managed to reach the boys while laying guidelines. Although there was huge relief that the boys had been found and were apparently well, the challenge remained as to how to get them out. None of the boys could swim.

Rescuers made their way to the boys' location to provide high-energy food and medical assistance. Meanwhile, expert divers placed backup oxygen cylinders along the route. Major pumping operations were set up to manage the water levels, as a threat of rain was present. During these operations, former Thai Navy SEAL Saman Gunan lost his life.

It took experienced divers six hours to reach the boys' location, traveling against the current. The return journey was about five hours long. The boys could not manage on their own, so a method had to be devised to provide them with oxygen while guiding them. Divers practiced with local Thai boys in a swimming pool to figure out the best way to do this.

Members of the rescue team attached each boy to a safety line. Each boy was given a full facemask and an oxygen cylinder strapped to the chest. A handle was attached to his back, so a diver could guide him. The boys were sedated to reduce the danger of panic.

In the flooded passageways, some sections were so narrow that rescuers had to remove the oxygen tanks and push them through narrow gaps. The boys had to be eased through the tight areas carefully, so their facemasks would remain functional. After surviving their trip through the flooded areas, the boys were placed on stretchers on a pulley system to get them over a steep part of the cave system. In other areas, they were passed from one rescuer to the next until at last each boy reached the mouth of the cave and safety. The coach and the boys were feted as heroes in Thailand following their dramatic rescue.

The episode was a reminder of the dangers of caving in rainy conditions. It also highlighted the need for specialist skills for cave rescue. After the operation, the Thai Navy SEALs, normally trained for open-water diving, also began to receive training for cave diving.

Opposite: Members of the Royal Thai Navy are supported by volunteers from other parts of the world in launching a rescue of the schoolboys trapped in the Tham Luang cave in Chiang Rai province. Here they are carrying oxygen cylinders for divers.

TERRORISM

After numerous terrorist attacks in the United States, Europe, and elsewhere around the world, it has become clear that terrorists can strike anywhere at any time. No longer is terrorism the preserve of nations with significant internal or external conflicts. Civilians in otherwise peaceful nations need to be aware of the possible dangers. Whether at home or abroad, terrorists may strike at high-profile events or in public places, including pop concerts, airports, hotels, clubs, restaurants, and religious venues.

Rescue workers search through the rubble of the World Trade Center, New York City, following the terrorist attack of September 2001.

PREVENTION AND AWARENESS

In public venues, be aware of suspicious-looking individuals, and report them to police. Suspicious people are best identified not by physical appearance and dress but by behavior. Are they loitering? Do they appear to be observing buildings?

In airports, minimize the time you spend in open areas, particularly in the arrival area, and move through the security checks into secure areas as soon as possible. Report any suspicious abandoned bags. Do not leave your own baggage or packages lying around. Keep a low profile, and do not advertise your nationality with clothing, flags, or other identifying marks.

Formulate a plan of action if a terrorist incident should take place. This should include identifying police stations, hospitals, or other safe areas. Remember these three reactions: Run, hide, or fight. If possible, run; if necessary, hide; and fight off assailants only if in immediate danger without other options.

Airport security is designed to detect weapons and dangerous devices and materials from being carried onboard an aircraft.

Vehicles

If using a taxi, ensure that it has the correct license details displayed. If renting a car, check it over for signs of suspicious attachments. Keep car windows closed in urban areas, and check that doors are locked. Ensure that you have plenty of spare fuel.

Hotels

When traveling abroad, do not follow a regular routine. Vary the time and route of travel. Be aware of each hotel's evacuation plans and routes. Check the identity of visitors to your room, and do not accept unidentified packages. Report anything suspicious to the main desk, including unidentified objects.

Spotting suspicious behavior

In a multicultural society, terrorists may not be easily identified visually. However, if you are aware, you may be able to spot someone who is behaving suspiciously or carrying something suspicious. Has something been delivered that no one remembers ordering? Double-check rather than assume it is okay.

QUESTION WHAT YOU SEE

Notice if someone is hanging around an area or a building with no apparent purpose. Is that person particularly interested in entrances or exits? Is that person searching for security cameras or personnel?

Question what you see and hear. Is someone asking unusual questions? Has a vehicle been left in an unusual place? Have you noticed a vehicle that's being driven with no apparent sense of destination?

Next steps

If you think someone is acting suspiciously, you can opt to challenge him or her assertively but politely, and then make a judgment whether the answer is credible or if it increases your suspicions. Ask open-ended questions that require explanations. If the answers do not allay suspicions, report the event with accurate details, including a description of the person, his or her clothing and appearance, what aroused suspicion, the location, and the time.

Noticing the unusual involves an awareness of what might be expected in your particular environment. Terrorists sometimes organize attacks during religious festivals or times of unrest, so be especially alert during these times.

U.S. DEPARTMENT OF HOMELAND SECURITY ADVICE ON SUSPICIOUS BEHAVIOR AND PATHWAYS TO VIOLENCE

Potential warning signs include the following:

- **Increasingly erratic, unsafe, or aggressive behaviors**
- **Hostile feelings of injustice or perceived wrongdoing**
- **Drug and alcohol abuse**
- **Marginalization or distancing from friends and colleagues**
- **Changes in performance at work**
- **Sudden and dramatic changes in home life or in personality**
- **Financial difficulties**
- **Pending civil or criminal litigation**
- **Observable grievances with threats and plans of retribution**

At work, help ensure everyone's safety by doing the following:

- **Be aware of drastic changes in a colleague's attitude toward others.**
- **Take note of any escalations in behavior.**
- **Concerned? Contact a supervisor or the human resources department.** Provide information that may facilitate intervention and mitigate potential or emerging risks.

SUSPICIOUS ITEMS

If you see an item that arouses suspicion, think about how it looks or why it might have been left where it is. Follow the HOT mnemonic:

H — Hidden

O — Obvious

T — Typical

Has there been an attempt to conceal the item? People lose things but do not normally hide items on purpose. Is there something suspicious about the object, such as wiring, batteries, or liquids? Does the object fit in with items expected in a particular place? Does the item have identifying tags or labels?

If you have suspicions, confirm them by asking questions of people nearby. Are they aware of the object or know whom it might belong to? If you remain suspicious, ask people to move a safe distance from the item. Do not touch the item. Make sure that you are a minimum of 50 feet (15 m) away before using your phone to contact authorities, as the phone may trigger a device. Anyone in the area should move at least 325 feet (99 m) away and out of the line of sight. Make sure people stay away from glass windows or similar structures.

WEAPONS ATTACKS

If gunfire is heard, think of the safest options. The priority is to run to safety, but take time to think about the best escape route. Make sure that everyone with you acts fast and leaves belongings behind. Find alternative routes if necessary, and avoid dead-ends.

If there are no safe escape routes, hide. Choose a hiding place with solid physical protection. If possible, move to a room where the door locks. Barricade it if possible. Keep away from the door.

Put cell phones on silent, and switch off vibrate. Communicate as silently as possible. Do not move about or make any sound.

Calling police

If you have managed to escape to a safe area, call the police. Tell them:

- where the attack is
- where you are, and
- how many attackers were seen.

Provide descriptions of the attackers, including their clothing and weapons as well as where they were heading.

BOMBING

If there has been a bomb incident and there are casualties, use triage to assess the casualties. Consider degrees of urgency.

1. Who is bleeding severely?

2. Who is walking?

3. Who is talking?

Call an emergency hotline to provide as much information as possible. Move the walking wounded to a safe area, pending the arrival of emergency services. When assessing a patient, check for the following:

- Breathing
- Severe bleeding
- Lack of response
- Broken bones
- Burns

In July 2011 a car bomb was detonated in central Oslo, Norway, killing eight people and injuring more than 200.

Police SWAT Team

When police arrive

Police will deal with the immediate threat and neutralize it if possible. Police will not immediately be able to distinguish between innocent bystanders and potential assailants, so do exactly what they say. Do not make sudden movements or gestures or reach into pockets. Stay calm. Keep hands visible, so it is obvious that you are not holding a weapon.

If assailants are close

If the assailants are close or you are under immediate threat of attack, use whatever is available in defense. This may include sharp or pointed objects, such as pens, keys, umbrellas, hairbrushes, or high-heeled shoes. Aim for the face to confuse or delay an assailant so that you can make an escape.

If you are being followed or chased by an assailant, pull objects into his or her path, such as chairs, bins, crates, or tables. Bang on cars to set off car alarms to attract the attention of any police nearby.

TERRORISM

Active shooter

In countries such as the United States, where civilians are permitted to own and carry firearms, the threat may be a disturbed individual with a desire to take revenge on society. Usually innocent people of all ages are in the firing line. As an active shooter does not usually seek to take on security forces directly, there will usually be a time delay before security forces can intervene. In these cases, civilians need to know how to cope to the best of their ability with an unexpected attack.

The principle of training and practice remains the same: you stand a better chance if you have practiced and trained beforehand so you can act quickly and automatically if an incident should arise. Make sure to take part in any training exercises in schools or workplaces.

FEMA ADVICE REGARDING ACTIVE SHOOTERS

Quickly determine the most reasonable way to protect life. Remember that customers and clients are likely to follow the lead of employees and managers during an active shooter situation.

1. RUN

If there is an escape path, attempt to evacuate the premises. Do the following:

- Have an escape route and plan in mind.
- Evacuate regardless of whether others agree to follow.
- Leave belongings behind.
- Help others escape, if possible.
- Prevent individuals from entering an area where the active shooter may be.
- Keep your hands visible.
- Follow the instructions of any police officers.
- Do not attempt to move wounded people.
- Call 911 when you are safe.

2. HIDE

If evacuation is not possible, find a place to hide where the active shooter is less likely to find you. The hiding place should have these features:

- Be out of the active shooter's view.
- Have protection if shots are fired in your direction. For example, choose an office with a closed and lockable door.
- The spot should not trap you or restrict your options for movement.

To prevent an active shooter from entering your hiding place, lock the door. Blockade the door with heavy furniture.

3. HOW TO BEHAVE WHEN AN ACTIVE SHOOTER IS NEAR

- Lock the door.
- Silence your cell phone, including vibration.
- Turn off any source of noise such as televisions.
- Hide behind large items such as cabinets.
- Remain quiet.

If evacuation and hiding out are not possible:

- Remain calm.
- Dial 911, if possible, to alert police to the active shooter's location.
- If you cannot speak, leave the line open, and allow the dispatcher to listen.

4. FIGHT

As a last resort, and only when your life is in imminent danger, attempt to disrupt or incapacitate the active shooter. Consider the following:

- Act as aggressively as possible against the shooter.
- Throw items, and improvise weapons.
- Yell.
- Commit to your actions.

WORLD TRADE CENTER, NYC

On September 11, 2001, both of the twin towers of the World Trade Center were attacked with hijacked airliners, leading eventually to their collapse. That day, Michael Wright was on the eighty-first floor of the north tower, kicking off a routine Tuesday with a cup of coffee and a muffin. At about 8:45 a.m., he and his colleagues felt the shock of what seemed like an earthquake, causing those who were standing to lose their balance. Huge cracks appeared in the floor, and the elevator doors were blown out, leaving a dark void that no one wanted to approach. Smoke was billowing.

Michael and his colleagues went to a stairwell and began to descend with others in two lines, according to their fire drills. By the time they reached the fortieth floor, they met firefighters coming up. As the workers continued to descend, injured people from other offices joined them. When they reached the mall at the base of the tower, any sense of relief that Michael might have felt was dispelled when he saw bodies lying on the ground.

Shocked, he and others headed for the mall's escalator to get to the street level. As rescue workers signaled to them, Michael saw in the reflection of windows that the second tower was collapsing. He ran back into the building to be protected from falling debris, but the building above him started to collapse, too.

Michael was choking dust, but he had been buried with a firefighter who had a flashlight and a tool to break doors. The firefighter smashed a door leading into a bookshop. Then they and others ran through the dark and dust to emerge outside. As Michael ran into the streets, he heard a loud, unforgettable sound. It was his tower, his office, crashing down.

A New York City firefighter signals for more rescue workers in the ruins of the Twin Towers, four days after the terrorist attacks of September 11, 2001.

BATACLAN, PARIS

On November 13, 2015, at 9:20 p.m., a suicide bomber blew himself up outside the Stade de France, where the French president and a large crowd were watching a friendly football match between France and Germany. This was the first of a series of attacks that would take place that evening in Paris, including attacks with automatic weapons on cafes and restaurants. Three terrorist teams struck six separate venues within minutes. The most devastating attack took place at the Bataclan theater, which was packed with people listening to an American rock band. Gunmen opened fire on the crowd with military-style automatic assault weapons.

Some of the concertgoers managed to escape through emergency exits, some climbed onto the roof, and others hung outside the windows, risking a dangerous fall. A police officer arrived 15 minutes later. He had only a pistol, but he managed to shoot one terrorist. The intruder was wearing a suicide belt, which blew up. This caused the other terrorists to retreat from the main hall, along with some hostages. It would take half an hour for a special police force to arrive.

During the chaos, Isobel Bowdery flung herself to the floor. People were being shot around her, and she expected any moment that the bullets would reach her as well. People were dead or dying, and she was covered with blood. Isobel played dead, hoping not to be noticed. After an hour or so, a man near her stood up and put his hands on his head. Isobel did not know whether the gunmen were taking hostages. Then she heard instructions from police officers. So she got up, and the police told her to get out of the building fast.

Across the city, 130 people died from the attacks, and 89 of them were killed in the theater.

Crowds gather to light candles for the victims near the site of the Bataclan nightclub attack in Paris, France, November 2015.

VEHICLE RAMMING

The problem for the public and for security services is that it is very easy for potential assailants to rent a truck, a van, or another vehicle, and it is also easy to identify public events at which to carry out an attack.

Between 2014 and 2017, there were about 20 serious events where vehicles were used in terrorist attacks against citizens. This marks a tendency toward the encouragement of do-it-yourself violence, fomented originally by the terrorist group Al Qaeda and then by the so-called Islamic State. Whereas organized terrorist attacks can be largely thwarted by national and international intelligence and security services, it is very difficult to counter the acts of "loners," individuals who commit atrocities for a "cause," although they may have no connection with the cause's organizational center.

Israeli security forces and forensic teams inspect a destroyed vehicle that was used by a Palestinian assailant in a car-ramming attack targeting a group of Israeli soldiers in the West Bank, March 2018.

ACTION DURING A VEHICULAR ATTACK

- Run to get out of the way.
- Take cover behind something solid, such as a barrier or wall.
- Keep moving away from the area, in case there is a secondary attack after the vehicular attack.
- Notify police as soon as possible. Law enforcement officers will deploy quickly and have the ability to stop the threat.

Preventing vehicular attacks

It is easier to prevent an attack through observable indicators than it is to protect each and every potential venue. Friends, family, and employers are in the best place to notice unusual behaviors in individuals that may indicate upcoming violence.

Organizations involved in the rental of trucks, vans, and other vehicles need to be aware of any indicators that a rental may not be benign. This may include a range of suspicious behaviors, including asking for unusual modifications, renting at odd times, or heading toward suspicious destinations.

Barriers

Intelligent placement of either permanent or temporary barriers such as planters in areas where civilians gather is a good way of deterring attacks. When visiting a public place, look around to check what protection, if any, is in place. If there is no protection, think about what you could use as a barrier and safe place if threatened by a rogue vehicle attack. At some venues where there is little physical protection in place, large vehicles such as buses may be used to "circle the wagons" against a potential attack by an assailant.

NUCLEAR EXPLOSION

A nuclear weapon employs a nuclear reaction to cause an explosion. These weapons are built to cause devastating immediate destruction, followed by highly dangerous fallout in the first few hours after the explosion.

The time between the initial explosion and the arrival of fallout may be as short as 15 minutes. If such an explosion occurs, get into the safest place possible to minimize or prevent exposure to radiation.

Take refuge in the nearest building. Ideally this should be a brick or concrete building. Keep away from windows, and get into the most central room or a basement or cellar. Keep in touch with broadcasts by authorities, and do not come out before 24 hours have passed unless advised to do so by the authorities. Battery-operated radios may work, but other services may be disrupted.

If there is a warning of a nuclear explosion, have an emergency supply kit prepared.

Decontamination

If you think you have been exposed to nuclear fallout, remove outer clothing. If possible, take a shower, and wash all parts of your body that may have been exposed. Use soap and water. Consume only food and drink that has been inside the building during the explosion and fallout period.

FEMA ADVICE ON WHAT TO DO DURING A NUCLEAR EXPLOSION

- If warned of an imminent attack, immediately get inside the nearest building, and move away from windows. This will help provide protection from the blast, heat, and radiation of the detonation.

- If outdoors when a detonation occurs, take cover from the blast behind anything that might offer protection. Lie face down to protect exposed skin from the heat and flying debris. If in a vehicle, stop safely, and duck down within the vehicle.

- After the shock wave passes, get inside the nearest, best shelter for protection from potential fallout. You will have 10 minutes or more to find an adequate shelter. Be inside before the fallout arrives. The highest outdoor radiation levels from fallout occur immediately after fallout arrives and then decrease with time.

- Stay tuned for updated instructions from emergency-response officials. If advised to evacuate, listen for information about routes, shelters, and procedures.

Finding shelter in gullies, ravines, ditches, natural depressions, beneath fallen trees, and inside caves can reduce your exposure to nuclear fallout. Also a car parked over a ditch or hole can provide cover.

STAGES OF A NUCLEAR EXPLOSION

1. **BRIGHT FLASH:**
   This can cause temporary blindness for up to a minute.

2. **BLAST WAVE:**
   Depending on the size of the device, the blast can cause massive structural damage around the center of the explosion, as well as death or serious injury to humans.

3. **RADIATION:**
   This can cause damage to cells of the human body and in large enough doses can cause radiation sickness. The less time exposed to radiation and the greater your distance from the radiation source, the less radiation will affect you.

4. **FIRE AND HEAT:**
   This can also cause death, serious injury, and damage to buildings and nature for miles (kilometers) around the center of the explosion.

5. **ELECTROMAGNETIC PULSE (EMP):**
   This can cause damage and disruption to electronics in a wide area, making communications difficult.

6. **FALLOUT:**
   This arrives in the form of debris raining down from the sky. It is radioactive and should be avoided at all costs. Get inside as soon as possible, and stay inside until authorities say it is safe.

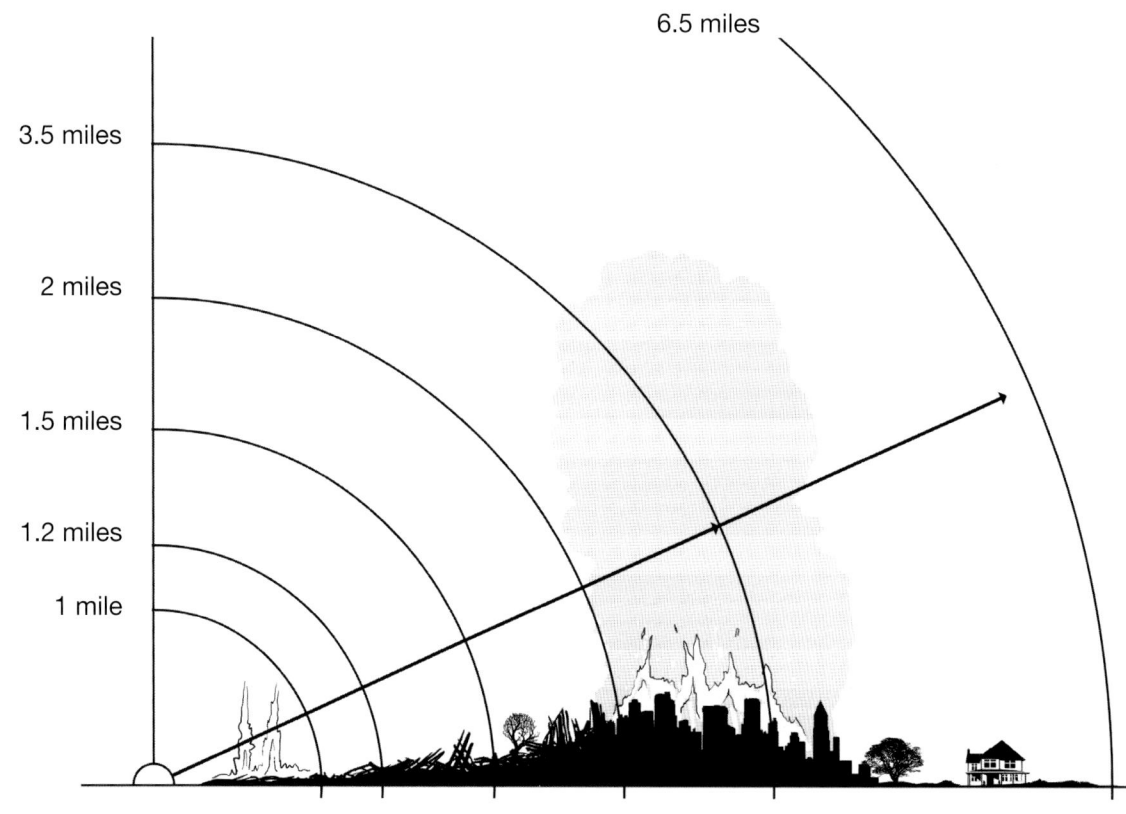

Variations of blast effects associated with positive and negative phase pressures over time:

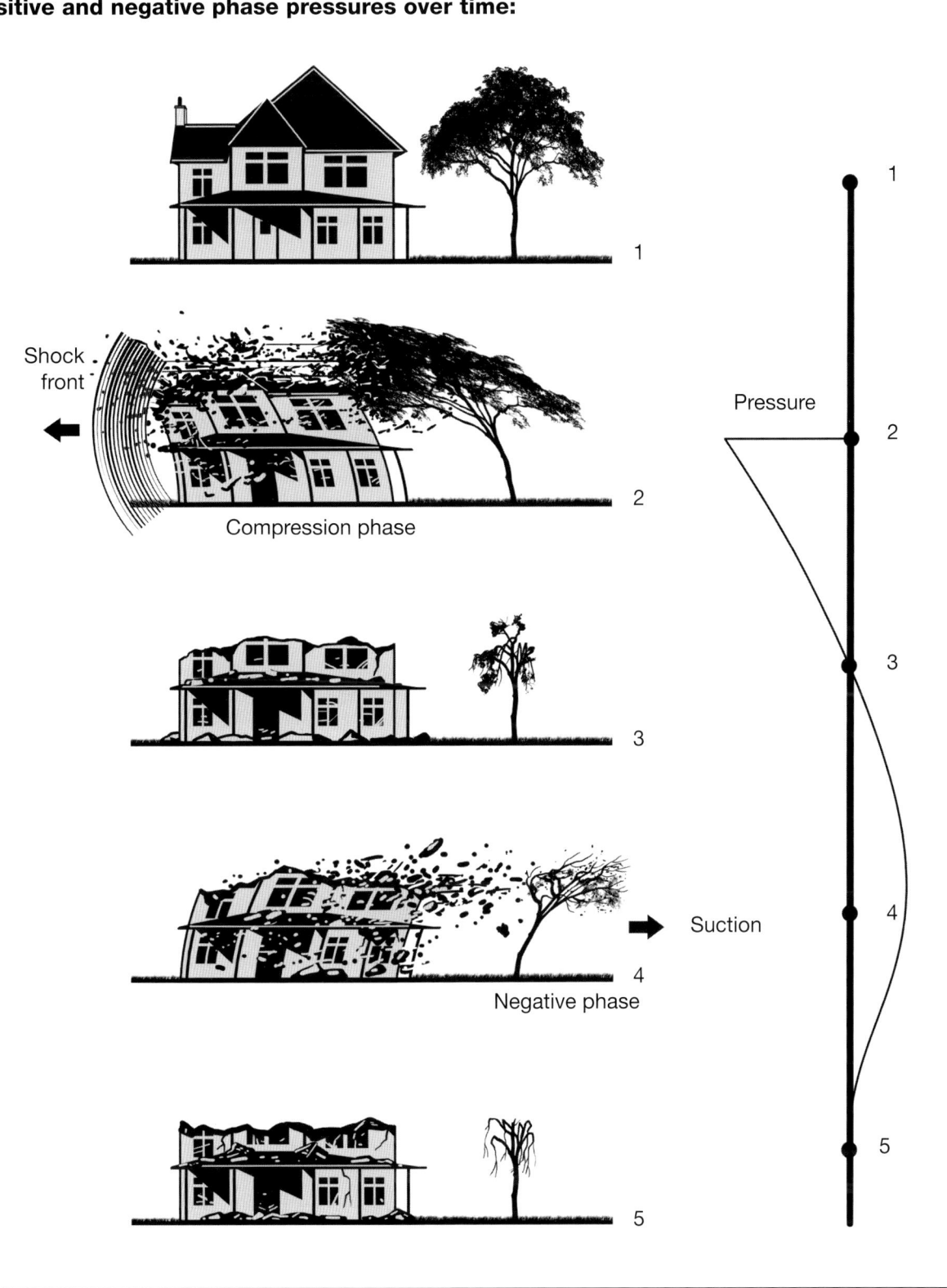

BIOLOGICAL ATTACKS

Biological weapons have potentially lethal and longstanding implications, as by their nature they can be very difficult to control. Weapons can include a variety of agents, including bacteria, viruses, or toxins.

An example of a toxin attack is the use of sarin in the Japanese subway system in 1995 by the Japanese sect Aum Shinrikyo. In September of 2001, there were anthrax attacks in the United States.

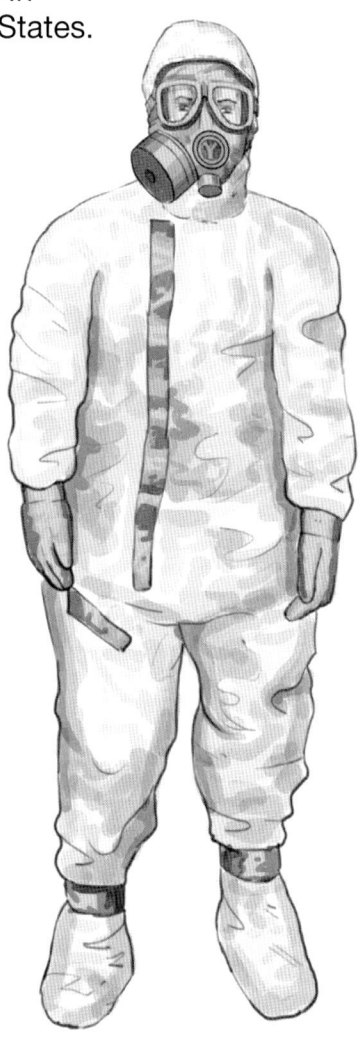

Delivery and protection

Biological agents are normally delivered in aerosol form. The best protection against such attacks is a protective mask along with protective clothing. In the military, a CBRN uniform and gas mask would normally be put on if there is warning of a CBRN attack. Decontamination would also be deployed according to regular training regimes. Whereas military personnel are regularly trained in CBRN methods and routinely carry CBRN suits and gas masks, it is more complex to provide adequate defense for a civilian community.

CIVIL DEFENSE

Although countries such as the United States have large supplies of vaccines for biological agents, such as anthrax and smallpox, there are smaller supplies for agents such as cholera. Apart from the availability of inoculations, a biological attack also requires high levels of training and coordination among responders. Each U.S. state now has a planning system for emergency response to a biological attack, and there are emergency stockpiles of vaccines positioned around the country. The National Guard is trained to support police, fire, and medical responders.

FEMA ADVICE ON ACTION DURING A BIOLOGICAL ATTACK

The first evidence of an attack may be symptoms of a disease caused by exposure to an agent. In the event of a biological attack, public health officials may not immediately be able to provide information. It may take time to determine the exact illness, its treatment, and those in danger. Follow these guidelines during a biological threat:

- Watch television, listen to the radio, or check the Internet for official news and information, including signs and symptoms of the disease, areas in danger, whether medications or vaccinations are being distributed, and where to seek medical attention if illness occurs.
- If you are aware of an unusual, suspicious substance, quickly get away.
- Cover your mouth and nose with layers of fabric that can filter the air but still allow breathing. Examples include two to three layers of cotton, such as a T-shirt, handkerchief, or towel.
- Depending on the situation, wear a face mask to reduce the chance of inhaling or spreading germs.
- If you have been exposed to a biological agent, remove and bag your clothes and personal items. Follow official instructions for disposal of contaminated items.
- Wash with soap and water, and put on clean clothes.
- Contact authorities, and seek medical assistance. You may be advised to stay away from others, or you may be forced into quarantine.
- If your symptoms match those described and you are in the group considered at risk, immediately seek emergency medical attention.
- Follow instructions of doctors and other public health officials.
- If the disease is contagious or not, expect to receive medical evaluation and treatment.
- In a declared biological emergency or developing epidemic, avoid crowds.
- Wash your hands with soap and water frequently.
- Do not share food or utensils.

U.S. ANTHRAX ATTACKS

A week after the devastating terrorist attack on the World Trade Center, several letters containing anthrax spores were mailed to two Democratic senators and to news media outlets, including ABC News, CBS News, the *New York Post* and the *National Enquirer*. Five people were killed in the attack, and 17 were infected.

The senators did not open the letters personally. One letter was opened by an aide, after which the U.S. government mail service was shut down, and the other was opened by a postal worker, who inhaled the anthrax spores and became infected.

The FBI mission to trace the perpetrators was complex, involving hundreds of agents and interviews of more than 9,000 people. The investigation concluded that the attack was not related to the 9/11 attacks, although there was considerable political pressure at the time to make that link. Later, the FBI concluded that a government specialist, Bruce Ivins, was the perpetrator.

The attacks not only killed or infected several people, but they also led to the contamination of several buildings, which required extensive decontamination procedures.

CHEMICAL ATTACKS

The threat of a chemical weapons attack has been growing in recent years. For example, in 2016, the Islamic State (ISIL) released toxic hydrogen sulfide gas in Iraq, and chemical weapons have been used regularly in the war in Syria in the form of chlorine and sarin gas.

Chemical weapons were used in Ghouta in August of 2013, causing more than 1,300 deaths, and chemicals were also used in Aleppo in December of 2016. These activities run against the Geneva Protocol signed in 1925 in an effort to prevent the repetition of the shocking use of chemicals in the First World War.

In February of 2017, the chemical nerve agent VX was used in the assassination of Kim Jong-nam, the half-brother of the North Korean dictator, Kim Jong-un. VX is several times more toxic than sarin.

On March 4, 2018, the nerve agent Novichok was used in an alleged assassination attempt on Sergei Skripal

A New Jersey bomb squad officer checks a simulated suspect vehicle during a terrorism response exercise coordinated by the U.S. Department of Homeland Security in 2005.

and his daughter, Yulia, in the English city of Salisbury. Novichok is about a thousand times more toxic than sarin. Even the smallest doses can be lethal. The Skripals were fortunate that two doctors on duty at a local hospital had recently returned from a course at the nearby British chemical weapons facility. They were therefore well equipped to recognize the symptoms of nerve agent poisoning.

Such is the potency of Novichok that a British police officer who had gone to help the Skripals was also hospitalized, and later a woman who had apparently handled an object that had been contaminated by the agent died, and her partner was hospitalized. The attack in Salisbury led to the deployment of hundreds of military personnel as well as police to sanitize the area and trace the culprits.

In September of 2018, British police publicly identified two Russian military intelligence officers as the most likely assailants.

FEMA ADVICE ON WHAT TO DO DURING A CHEMICAL ATTACK

- Quickly define the impacted area or where the chemical is coming from, if possible.
- Take immediate action to get away.
- If the chemical is inside your building, get out without passing through the contaminated area, if possible.
- If unable to get out or find clean air without passing through an affected area, move as far away as possible, and shelter in place.

If instructed to remain in your home or office building, you should:

- Close doors and windows, and turn off all ventilation, including furnaces, air conditioners, vents, and fans.
- Seek shelter in an internal room with a disaster supplies kit.
- Seal the room with duct tape and plastic sheeting.
- Listen to the radio or television for instructions from authorities.

If you are caught in or near a contaminated area outdoors:

- Quickly decide the fastest way to find clean air. Either move away immediately, upwind of the source of contamination, or find the closest building to shelter in place.

JAPAN'S SARIN INCIDENT

On March 20, 1995, the doomsday cult Aum Shinrikyo carried out a chemical attack on the Tokyo underground system. The group released sarin gas in five subway cars located throughout the underground network, killing 13 people and sickening thousands.

The cult's leader, Shoko Asahara, had taught followers that the world would have to be destroyed to become pure again. To this end, the cult had been stockpiling biological weapons, in addition to committing other crimes. To test the use of sarin, members had used a refrigerator truck outfitted with sarin spray in June of 1994. There were eight fatalities. Upon hearing that police were preparing to raid the group's stockpiles, the cult leader organized the metro attacks. He hoped the confusion would start World War III and bring about an apocalypse.

The attack, launched in one of the busiest subway systems in the world, occurred at peak morning rush hour. This time the sarin was in liquid form, held in plastic bags covered by newspaper. Five terrorists carried two bags each along with umbrellas with sharp tips to pierce the bags. When the trains reached selected stations, the terrorists dropped their packages and pierced them. Then they headed for exits where getaway cars were waiting.

As sarin evaporates quickly, those passengers who either had contact with the liquid or with the vapor were the ones most seriously affected.

Medical staff help the injured during the sarin attack on the Tokyo subway in 1995.

TRANSPORT SAFETY

A car can feel like a safe place, especially when outfitted with the latest advances in vehicle safety, soundproofing, and comfort. The technology involved in the automatic braking system (ABS), for example, made brakes more efficient. ABS sensors help to reduce a car's speed before it hits something. Car protection systems, including air bags, increase the likelihood of passengers surviving a crash. Despite improvements, however, vehicles move at high speeds, and any impact can be potentially disastrous.

A convoy of evacuees drives south as flames and smoke rises along the highway near Fort McMurray, Alberta, May 2016.

TRANSPORT SAFETY

DRIVING SAFETY

The greatest contribution to driving safety is an alert and prudent driver. There is no such thing as a routine journey. Anything can happen and every journey involves potential hazards. A well-maintained vehicle is another essential factor in safe driving.

Speed limits are imposed for a reason. They are calculated as the safest maximum speed that a particular road can be traveled, taking into account stopping distances, visibility, intersections, the location of buildings, and so on. The speed limit is not a target. In addition, drivers may need to travel at lower speeds under certain conditions, such as snow or rain, in order to remain safe.

Driving in fog can be challenging for even the most experienced drivers.

Driving in fog

Even the most experienced drivers should fear driving in fog. Driving through fog is much the same as flying through a cloud. However, pilots are unlikely to run into a stationary plane in front of them—but car drivers might crash into another car.

Fog can cause visibility to fall, giving the driver very little thinking time and braking distance. In these conditions, keep the headlights on a low beam, as full beams will reflect off the fog. It is difficult to judge speed in fog, as there is little or nothing visible to measure movement against. Therefore, keep a close eye on the speedometer. In addition, take more time to rest in foggy conditions, due to the high levels of concentration required.

Use brake lights well in advance of a stop to warn other drivers that you are slowing down. Make sure that brake lights are operational, as well as rear fog lights should you have them, so they work if needed. However, do not drive with rear fog lights on. Fog lights should only be used when visibility is below 328 feet (100 m). Other drivers may confuse the lights with brake lights.

VEHICLE EMERGENCY KIT

A good vehicle emergency kit should include high-visibility gear, jump leads, blanket, warning cone, tire inflation systems (electrical and canister), flashlight and batteries, basic tools for performing maintenance, and a shovel (folding types pack away easily in the trunk).

Driving shoes

Shoes make a big difference when driving, as they affect contact with and grip on the pedals. Flat shoes or athletic shoes are ideal, as they provide even contact and some traction. Do not wear high heels or platform shoes when driving, as they affect the efficiency of pedal movement. Do not wear flip-flops or light sandals, as they can slip on the pedals or get stuck under them.

BASIC VEHICLE CHECKS

- Check that the windshield and rear and side windows are clean.
- Check that mirrors are clean.
- Check that the lights, front and back, are working.
- Check indicators and hazard flashers.
- Check that the brakes work.
- Check tire pressure, and inflate if necessary.
- Check that the tire tread is within the legal limit, bearing in mind that this is a minimum. You may want to change tires before treads reach the limit. The tread needs to be even across the tire for maximum safety.
- Check that the tires do not have cuts, bulges, or abrasions.

Driving and tiredness

Falling asleep while driving can be fatal, not only for you, but for others on the road. Sleep-related accidents are three times more likely to cause death or serious injury, due to the fact that the driver completely loses control of the vehicle. Microsleep is a fleeting sleep episode that can occur when driving. It can last up to 10 seconds, during which time a vehicle can cross lanes or run into stopped traffic.

The body's circadian rhythm cannot easily be overridden, so avoid driving if possible between midnight and 6 a.m. There is a secondary circadian rhythm dip between 2 p.m. and 4 p.m. If driving during these hours, plan ahead to stop for breaks. If you feel drowsy when driving, pull over whenever it is safe to get rest, to walk, and to breathe deeply, or to take a short nap. Drink coffee, tea, or some other caffeinated drink. However, keep in mind that although caffeinated and energy drinks provide temporary relief from tiredness, they are no substitute for proper sleep.

Dehydration when driving

Do not drive under the influence of alcohol, but do make sure that you are well hydrated with water, juices, or other drinks, such as tea or coffee. Lack of water can cause drowsiness, delayed reactions, or poor decisions, which can be as dangerous as the effects of drinking alcohol. Health authorities commonly encourage people to drink 1 gallon (2 l) of water per day for health.

Steering position

When driving a car, try to be in maximum control. A driver's seat is not an armchair. To check the correct distance between the steering wheel and the back of the seat, place your shoulders comfortably in the seat back, and place your wrists on top of the steering wheel.

Adjust the seat forward or backward so that your wrists lie comfortably on the top of the steering wheel. Then grip the steering wheel in either the ten-to-two or nine-and-three position, whichever is more comfortable and suits the layout of the vehicle. Some steering wheels will have hints in their design as to which is the optimum place to grip.

STOPPING DISTANCES

Try not to brake suddenly unless you have to in order to avoid an accident. Brake lightly to slow down, and increase the pressure gradually on the pedal while coming to a halt. If the car does not have ABS, which is designed to avoid wheel lock and skidding, brake as firmly as possible without locking the wheels.

TYPICAL THINKING, BRAKING, AND STOPPING DISTANCES

At 30 mph (48 kph): Thinking 30 feet (9 m); braking 45 feet (14 m)
TOTAL distance: 75 feet (23 m)

At 50 mph (80 kph): Thinking 50 feet (15 m); braking 125 feet (38 m)
TOTAL distance: 175 feet (53 m)

At 70 mph (113 kph): Thinking 70 feet (21 m); braking 245 feet (75 m)
TOTAL distance: 315 feet (96 m)

In order to reduce the danger of a crash with any car in front, maintain a safe stopping distance. Allow a minimum of two seconds between your vehicle and the vehicle in front. Measure this against a marker on the side of the road, such as a road sign or lamppost. Double the distance when on a wet road, and increase it even more if on icy roads.

Traffic in the LA area fills a five-lane highway. In built-up urban areas people rarely leave enough braking distance with the vehicle in front.

Driving out of a skid

A skid can be caused by traveling with too much speed on wet, icy, or slippery roads. For example, roads may be oily and slippery after a heat wave. Skids can also be caused by cornering too fast, by accelerating too fast, or by sudden braking. If your car enters a skid, take your foot off the accelerator or the brake, and turn the steering wheel in the direction of the skid.

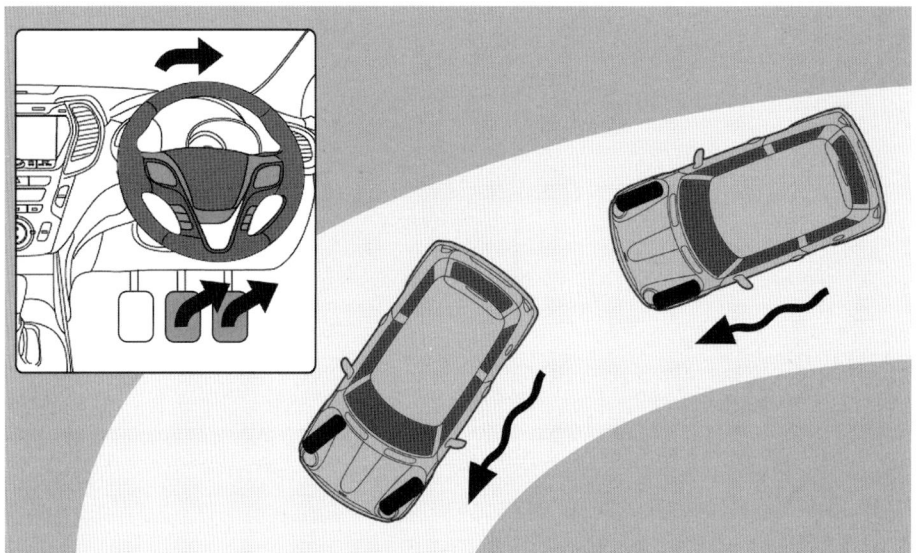

CASUALTIES

If people are injured in an accident, try to assess their condition, and inform emergency services if able to do so.

LIKELY INJURIES

REAR IMPACT:
Whiplash injury, affecting the spine and neck, as well as facial injuries

FRONTAL IMPACT:
Fractures, lacerations, head and spinal injuries, and an impacted pelvis

SIDE IMPACT:
Fractures to the leg and arm on the side of the impact, as well as shoulder and upper-arm injuries, and head injuries

If the accident involves a motorcycle, there may be leg and arm fractures, head injuries, and severe wounds. If the accident involves a pedestrian, injuries may include multiple fractures, head and spinal injuries, and multiple other traumatic injuries for the walker.

Vehicle accidents

If involved in an accident, such as a pileup on a highway, phone for rescue services, or get someone else in the vehicle to do so. Assess the area for immediate danger, such as oil spills or scattered metal, and get away from the area if necessary.

Check for any other vehicles approaching the scene, especially in fog. Do not venture across the lanes of the street or highway unless you are sure it is safe. Turn on the hazard warning lights, and get other drivers to do the same.

If it is safe to walk down the road, put out early warning reflective triangles about 82 feet (25 m) behind the scene of the accident. Wear a high-visibility reflective safety jacket if you have one. These garments are a legal requirement in some countries.

Vehicles are potential death traps when involved in an accident.

Vehicle fire

If your vehicle catches fire, which may first be detected by seeing smoke coming out of the hood, slow down, and bring the car to a halt whenever it is safe. Put on the hazard warning lights, and get out of the car. Tell any passengers to get out. Have them move to a safe place; make sure they do not stand behind the car.

If you have a fire extinguisher, point the nozzle through the front grill, and then spray the fire. Do not open the hood, as this will give oxygen to the fire, which may flare up in your face.

Defensive driving

Bad drivers are those who are not driving with care and attention. Good drivers are those who concentrate on the business of driving once they get behind the wheel, rather than thinking about a host of other things.

Think ahead:
Thinking ahead and driving defensively will give you more time to react and to avoid accidents. When driving in towns and cities, the unexpected should always be expected. Drivers may make sudden decisions that require you to suddenly swerve or slam on the brakes. People may run across the road to try to get to a bus or taxi. Somebody may run out from behind a parked van.

Be careful with lights:
Do not flash your lights to indicate that someone should turn in front. Flashing of lights signals an emergency. Note that other drivers may not be paying attention and may have left turn signals on. Do not assume they are going to turn left or right until it becomes obvious by their actions.

Keep calm:
Perhaps most importantly, avoid road rage. Do not engage drivers who are driving erratically or making poor driving decisions. Report them to authorities instead.

Watch out:
If you are following a cyclist, watch out. He or she may suddenly swerve to avoid a curb or pothole. Do not signal to pedestrians that they have permission to cross the road in front if you have stopped and are waiting for the walkers to pass. An impatient driver, motorcyclist, or cyclist behind you may overtake you at the moment they are crossing. Keep an eye out for motorcycles on both sides of the car. In some places, cycles are allowed to drive on the centerline while other vehicles have slowed or stopped. Never open a car door when stopped without looking behind you.

MOTORCYCLISTS AND CYCLISTS

Motorcyclists and cyclists are far more exposed than drivers in enclosed vehicles. Both are especially at risk when turning corners and passing other vehicles. Speed and fatigue are also major factors in cycling and motorcycle accidents.

Motorcyclists are more likely not to be seen by other drivers, especially at intersections, due to their relatively narrow profile. Drivers often find it difficult to judge the speed of an approaching motorcycle.

Defensive riding

More than other kinds of drivers, motorcyclists need to be vigilant in case others do not see them on the road. This means taking nothing for granted. Motorcyclists need to anticipate hazards. Motorcycles are more agile than other types of vehicles, so motorcyclists sometimes maneuver into areas where motorists are not expecting them.

Motorcyclists often drive between lanes of traffic, making it difficult for other vehicle drivers to easily notice their movements.

Daytime running lights (DRLs)

Daytime running lights (DRLs) are designed to come on automatically when the engine is switched on and to turn off then headlights are turned on. DRLs on motorcycles have received mixed reactions from motorcyclists. From the perspective of other drivers, however, DRLs positioned at three points on a motorcycle often counteract the usual narrow profile of a motorcycle and make it much more visible.

TRANSPORT SAFETY

HEAD INJURIES

If you believe a cyclist or motorcyclist has hurt their head in an accident, keep their head and neck stable when removing their helmet.

Cycling safety

One of the major dangers to cyclists on the road is where the driver of a truck, a bus, or another large vehicle cannot see a cyclist passing on the inside when turning left or right.

If you are a cyclist and see a large vehicle indicating a left or right turn, keep far back, as the driver may not be able to see you. It is always a good idea to wear high-visibility clothing when cycling and to have lights on the front and back, even during daylight hours. If you are passing through an area with trees, for example, a driver may not immediately see you without a light.

Have flasher lights and a powerful front light to see with in dark areas or at night. Fix pedals with reflectors, and fix reflectors to the spokes on the front and back wheels. Reflective tape can be wound around the handlebars and frame. If you have saddlebags, place reflective triangles on them.

This cyclist is wearing a high-visibility jacket so car drivers will be aware of his movements.

TRAVELING BY TRAIN

Although traveling by train is relatively safe, you should always take precautions, especially if traveling alone at night. When waiting for a train at the platform, make sure you stand in a well-lit area. Keep a lookout for suspicious people, and remain in a group of regular passengers if possible.

Once on a train, do not sit alone in a train car, and avoid groups of people who may be rowdy or drunk. Move to another train car or contact security. To remain safe, find out where a security guard is located, and sit there. Choose a seat where you are close to a door or have a compartment barrier behind you, so that no one can approach you from behind unexpectedly. Try not to fall asleep on a train, as you will be vulnerable to pickpockets or attack, and you may also miss your stop.

Train accidents

Make sure you read the safety advice that is posted, and be aware of any emergency equipment. If the train is involved in an accident, indicated by heavy braking, a rocking motion, or a pitching sensation, lean forward with your head toward your knees, and put your arms over your head. If you have a coat, cover your head with it to be protected from flying objects and glass.

If the train has come to a halt, unless there is immediate danger, remain on the train, as there may be other hazards on the track, such as other trains, electric rails, or fallen cables.

If you do have to get out, use the doors if they will open, or use emergency equipment such as glass hammers to break through the windows. Do not cross the tracks unless you are specifically ordered to do so by an emergency official or unless you have correctly identified electric rails.

AIR TRAVEL

Under the stress of air travel, some passengers have exhibited air rage, or uncontrolled anger that poses a danger to others. Air rage includes a range of antisocial and abusive behaviors, including physical aggression.

Keep an eye out for anyone who appears to be drinking heavily before departure or on the flight, and warn the flight crew. If someone is drunk or aggressive on a flight, the priority is to contain the problem. Do not overtly react, due to the restricted space and danger to others. By stepping in personally, a passenger risks being identified as a troublemaker. If reported by the flight crew, this can lead to possible arrest on the ground. The aircraft crew are trained to deal with such incidents, so leave it to them.

Do not give an aggressive person the opportunity to vent frustration on you. Avoid eye contact, and do not stare at a loudmouth or troublemaker. Use minimum force if you have to defend yourself or another passenger. Maintain an assertive defense posture to avoid becoming part of the problem. Remember that it is a sign of strength to control your reactions, although it may not feel that way at the time. Be prepared, however, to lend a hand if requested by flight crew or if someone is being assaulted.

Air turbulence

Some of the worst turbulence is experienced when flying through cumulonimbus clouds, due to high levels of updraft. Turbulence is also caused by hot air rising from the ground, high-altitude jet streams, and wind.

It is not always possible for aircraft on particular flight paths to avoid areas of air turbulence. This can range from slight bumping to violent shaking of the aircraft. To avoid injury, it is best to remain in your seat with your seatbelt fastened securely. Make sure that any personal items are well secured. Because the aircraft is designed to withstand high levels of turbulence and because it is traveling very fast, turbulence normally lasts only a few minutes.

Hijackings

Although there was a spate of aircraft hijackings in the 1960s and 1970s, it is now a relatively rare occurrence, due to a massive increase in airport security. Aircraft crews are trained to know how to deal with hijackings, so do not get involved unless absolutely necessary.

Avoid eye contact with hijackers, and do nothing to provoke them. Blend into your surroundings as much as possible, but also be alert and aware. Make a mental note of the hijackers' movements and also of their appearance, in case you have to identify them to security forces later.

Once the plane is on the ground, remember that everyone's moves will be followed by the special forces on the scene. The security forces may have planned an assault on the plane. If so, their boarding may be preceded by stun grenades to cause confusion. Do not panic, but keep your head down. Do not move unless given direct orders by security personnel. Do not get in their line of sight. You remain a potential suspect until the plane has been cleared and all the terrorists have been apprehended.

PLANE CRASHES

Although the idea of a plane crash may seem too horrendous to think about, the reality is that most people survive plane crashes. Research shows that you can increase your chances of survival if you take certain precautions.

As in almost all survival scenarios, planning ahead and visualizing what you would do in an accident increases your chance of coming through. Part of that preparation should be to listen carefully to the safety advice given by the cabin crew. If the exit door is behind your seat, it is worth physically turning around to see how far it is, and it also helps to count the number of seats between your seat and the exit. You will then be able to feel your way to the right place if everything goes dark or is obscured by smoke.

Although it should be possible to remain relatively safe and to have a good chance of survival wherever you sit on a plane, some research has shown that the back of the plane is the optimum place to sit, due to reduced g-forces in that area on impact. However, aircraft manufacturers, who say that one seat in any part of the plane is as good as another, do not support this research. Much depends on how the plane impacts the ground or water.

Asiana Airlines Flight 214 crash-landed on its final approach to San Francisco International Airport in July 2013. Three passengers were killed and more than 180 injured.

SEAT BELTS

In traumatic events, we often act automatically. People are belted into car seats more often than seats on planes, so their instinct after a plane crash is to try to press a car-seat-style button on the belt. Yet aircraft belts are almost invariably of the buckle type. So make a mental note when you climb into an aircraft seat to remember that simple point. It could save your life. Also make sure that the seat belt is as tight as it can be while remaining comfortable. The less movement there is between you and the seat belt, the less your body will move in an impact.

Head down and hug knees

Alternative: Cradle head against seat in front

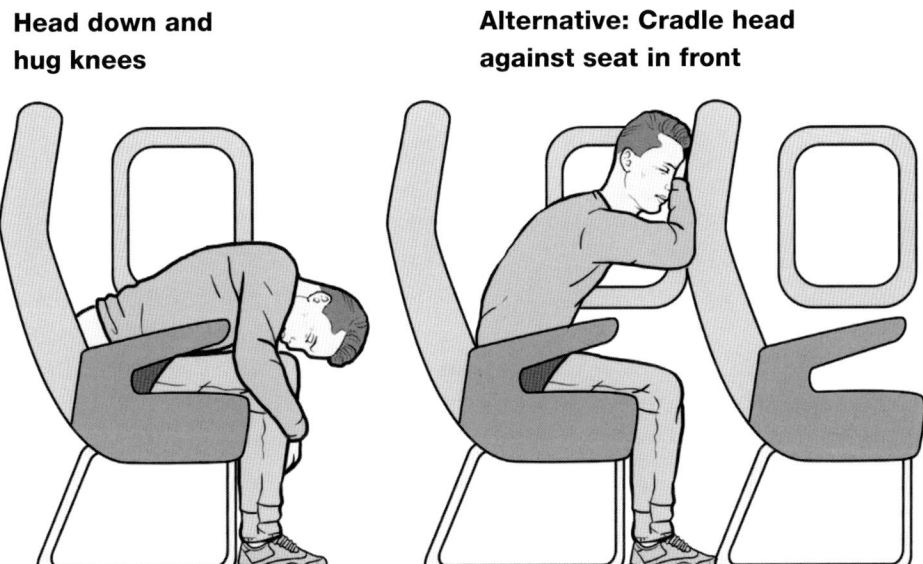

Brace, brace

Aircraft manufacturers and others say that the crucial difference for survival chances is between those who brace properly and those who do not. The brace position is designed to reduce the danger of lurching body movements, which can lead to broken backs, necks, and limbs. Placing feet firmly on the ground just behind the knees will also reduce the danger of the legs being flung forward under the seat in front. Baggage placed under the seat in front may also help to reduce this danger.

SURVIVING IN PERU

On December 24, 1971, Juliane Koepcke was in an aircraft flying over the Peruvian rain forest when the plane ran into a severe electrical storm. After entering a black cloud, the turbulence became extreme. Luggage started to fall out of the bins; objects were flying around the cabin. Then the lightning began. There was a bright flash from one of the engines, and the plane went into a nosedive.

Juliane was suddenly in freefall, still strapped to her seat. She blacked out.

Waking up the next day, she realized she had survived a disastrous air crash. She searched for her mother, who had been seated next to her, but realized she was alone.

Having lived in the area previously, Juliane was aware of the dangers of the jungle, including snakes, poisonous insects, piranhas, and alligators. She knew to follow water downstream, because small streams lead to larger ones, which are more likely to support people. Upon finding a hut and boat, she used gasoline found on the site to clear maggots from a wound in her upper arm. The next day, several men appeared and took her back to civilization.

Juliane survived the crash largely because she was strapped to her seat, although some luck was involved as well. It is unlikely that anyone survives when a plane breaks up in midair, as hers did. She survived in the jungle because her knowledge of the environment and her determination to find a way to safety helped her to find the hut and to get by.

Take action

After impact there may be a stunned silence followed by a bustle of activity. Do not wait too long for a flight attendant to appear and give instructions, as the attendants may be either hurt or stunned. It is up to you to get going and to help family or friends. Make sure you know where the nearest exit is located. Forget personal belongings, and focus on getting out of the plane as quickly as possible while remaining as calm as possible.

AIRCRAFT EVACUATION ROUTES

An evacuation slide is an inflatable device which facilitates the rapid evacuation of an aircraft. Most commercial aircraft include ample escape routes. Please follow the safety instructions issued by airline staff.

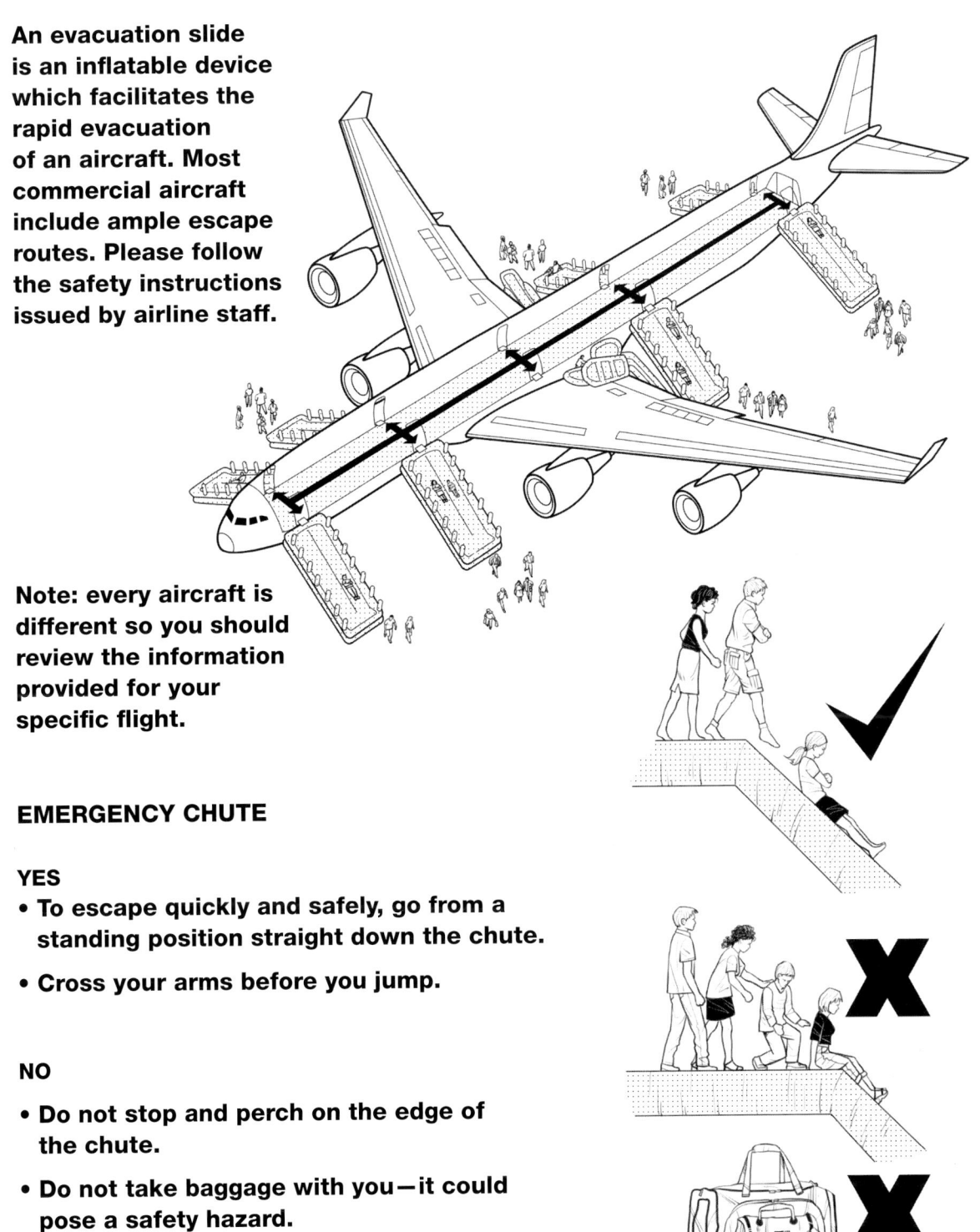

Note: every aircraft is different so you should review the information provided for your specific flight.

EMERGENCY CHUTE

YES
- To escape quickly and safely, go from a standing position straight down the chute.
- Cross your arms before you jump.

NO
- Do not stop and perch on the edge of the chute.
- Do not take baggage with you—it could pose a safety hazard.
- Do not wear high heels.

HUDSON RIVER CRASH

On January 15, 2009, U.S. Airways Flight 1549 took off from La Guardia Airport in New York City for a routine flight to Charlotte Douglas International Airport in North Carolina. Having reached an altitude of almost 3,000 feet (914 m), the aircraft ran into a flock of Canadian geese, some of which were sucked into the engines. The plane lost power, leaving the pilot with few options. The chances of reaching La Guardia by turning back were slim. There was almost no chance of reaching other airfields without power. The plane was flying over a densely populated area, so a crash would have catastrophic results.

The pilot made the best available choice, which was to ditch in the nearby Hudson River. The Coast Guard was warned, and vessels were put on standby to give aid when necessary. As the Airbus was passing over the George Washington Bridge at 900 feet (274 m), the captain warned the passengers to brace for impact.

Josh Peltz was sitting next to one of the emergency exits over the wings. As the plane started to descend, he read the safety instructions over and over again. He pulled his seat belt tight and braced himself. When the plane hit the water, other passengers sustained impact injuries as their heads hit the seats in front of them.

Josh knew that the priority was to get out of the plane before it sank. He pulled the handle of the emergency exit door and pushed it outward, having just been reminded by the safety leaflet that it opened outward. Guiding a fellow passenger, he stepped out onto the wing. They moved along the wing to give room to others who were climbing out. He saw other passengers coming out on the emergency slides that floated on the water.

Josh was immediately aware of the cold. The air temperature was 21°F (–6°C), and the water temperature was 38°F (3°C). The plane was sinking, and some people were already up to their waists in water. In conditions like these, it would not be long before hypothermia set in.

A ferry came to the rescue, and the passengers were taken on board. Later, when he had time to reflect, Josh credited his survival to taking things one step at a time. By working out his next steps, 10 seconds at a time, Josh held back panic and confusion, completed a successful escape, and helped other passengers survive as well.

River tugs take part in salvaging the wreckage of U.S. Airways Flight 1549 in the Hudson River.

RESCUE

Although you may be able to survive a disaster by getting to safety, sometimes your best hope is being rescued. When dealing with a disaster, it is essential to take time to assess the situation. First, get into a place where you can be as comfortable as possible, in order to think as clearly as you can. This can mean getting out of the hot sun in a desert environment or out of the cold in a mountainous or arctic environment.

Rescuers tend to one of the more than 500 people evacuated from the island of Lombok following the eruption of the Mount Rinjani volcano in July 2018.

CHECK YOUR SITUATION

Check for injuries, to anyone who may be with you as well as yourself. Check if anyone is suffering from shock. Give any first aid that can be administered. Assess whether your companions are too weak or injured to move.

Everyone involved needs to be mentally resilient and determined to reach safety if a long and potentially dangerous journey is ahead.

Food, water, and equipment

If in a vehicle or an aircraft accident in a remote area, check to see if there is food, water, or essential equipment that can be saved. Knowing the amount of food, water, and shelter available will help you to assess whether to stay or to travel to find help.

Assess whether you or others are confident enough in your or their navigational skills to get to a safe place where help is available. Getting more lost would likely lead to failure. You have to at least have an idea of which direction to travel.

BIG DECISIONS

1. **Whether to stay or move**

2. **Whether there is enough water and food, and how to ration it**

3. **How to contact rescuers**

How dangerous is the area? Crossing a desert requires a large amount of water. Clambering in mountains may be too dangerous, especially if someone in the party is injured. However, it may also be too dangerous to stay in place, especially if you are exposed to the elements.

SIGNALS FOR HELP

If you are involved in a plane crash or you suffer a vehicle breakdown in an isolated location, staying near the vehicle may provide the best chance of rescue, so long as there is no danger of burning fuel.

If flares are available, wait to signal to airborne rescuers until they are near enough to see the signals. Alternatively, build a fire, and have it ready to light as soon as an aircraft approaches (see page 210 for instructions).

A laser flare (illustrated here) offers a simple and effective way of indicating your position. At night, the light can be seen at a distance of up to 20 miles (32 km).

NUMBER SIX

Six is a number recognized internationally as a distress signal. This could be six blasts on a whistle or six flashes from a signalling device. When making noise or using flashes, wait a minute between each group of six.

Signals with mirrors

A mirror, a polished piece of tin, or a smooth piece of foil can be an effective way of sending signals to possible rescuers in the distance.

So that rescuers do not dismiss the signal as a random reflection, learn Morse Code for SOS, an international distress code. It is indicated by three dots followed by three dashes and three more dots:

... _ _ _ ...

- Frame the aircraft between the V of two fingers.

- Hold the mirror by your head and shine the reflected light through your fingers, toward the rescue aircraft.

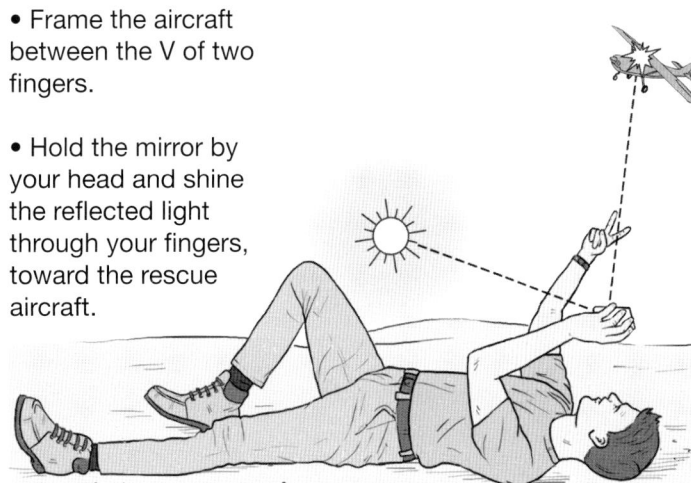

Ground signals

In addition to flares or smoke from a fire, you can create static ground signals that can be seen from the air, using rocks, sticks, and other materials that contrast in color with the ground. Follow International Ground-to-Air Codes to send specific messages to rescuers.

A capital "V" is a signal that assistance is needed. "X" indicates that someone needs medical help. "N" is for "no," and "Y" is for "yes." Arrows can be used to point the way.

1: Need doctor—serious injuries
2: Need medical supplies
3: Unable to proceed
4: Need food and water
5: Need firearms
6: Need map and compass
7: Need signal lamp/radio
8: Indicate direction to proceed
9: Am proceeding in this direction
10: Will attempt take-off
11: Aircraft seriously damaged
12: Probably safe to land here
13: Need fuel and oil
14: All well
15: No
16: Yes
17: Not understand
18: Need engineer

Signal fires

Signal fires are an international distress signal. Try to build three fires in a triangular shape if you have enough fuel and tinder. Do not light fires under trees, as you may cause a conflagration. If there is a single tree in a clearing, you may be able to set that on fire. You may be able to pile tinder around the lone tree so that when lit it becomes a burning torch.

If building signal fires, keep them covered, so the tinder is dry when it's time to light them. Prepare green wood and foliage to create thick white smoke that will stand out against a dark forest canopy. If in a desert or in a snowbound area, dark smoke will contrast better with the background. Burning rubber or oil can produce this.

If you have identified an area where an aircraft might land, make sure the fires are downwind of the landing area.

Three fires arranged in a triangular shape is a recognized international distress signal

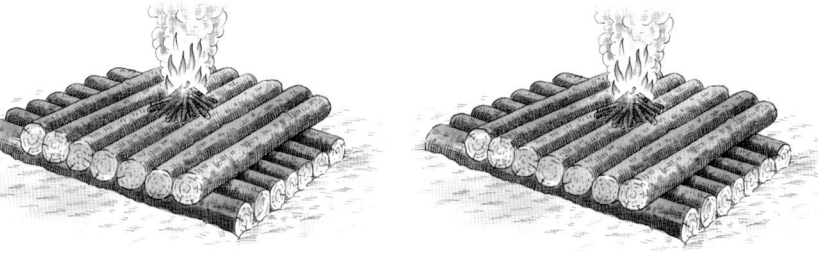

PERSONAL LOCATION BEACON

A personal location beacon (PLB) fitted with a global navigation satellite system (GNSS) receiver will help send signals to rescuers. The PLB should be used only in an emergency, as it sends distress signals via satellite to relevant rescue organizations.

Body signals

Body signals can communicate with rescuers in aircraft, giving information about your status and needs as well as whether the area is safe for a landing. If you are in a forested area, place brightly colored materials in the trees, so people in passing aircraft can see them. You can also try to find a clearing in a jungle to display a bright color.

Receiver is operating

Affirmative (yes)

Can proceed shortly, wait if possible

Need mechanical help or parts, long delay

Do not attempt to land here

Pick us up, aircraft abandoned

Use drop message

All okay, do not wait

Negative (No)

Land here (point in direction)

Need urgent medical help

RESCUE BY HELICOPTER

Find or clear an area, ideally on level ground, which is at least 165 feet (50 m) wide and long. Make sure there are no overhead obstacles such as wires. A helicopter will usually approach at about a 10-degree angle, rather than land vertically, and the pilot will need room to maneuver in high winds.

Remove large obstacles. Keep the area clear of loose material that may be blown around by the rotors. If in a snowbound area, try to stamp down the snow to minimize the danger of its billowing up in the updraft, which may obscure the pilot's vision. To indicate the landing zone, mark out an "H" with something such as colored stones. If using stones, make sure to dig them into the ground, so they are level with the surface.

Wait until the helicopter has landed before approaching it. Do not approach a helicopter from the rear. Beware of the main rotor, especially if the ground nearby is not level and your approach places you at the level of the spinning blades.

A mountain rescue member uses a signal flare to attract an approaching helicopter in northern England, following the rescue of a party of stranded climbers.

RESCUE

Winch rescue

In a winch rescue, either a member of the crew will descend from the aircraft or a rescue strop will be lowered. If a rescue strop is used, put it over your head and then under your arms and across your back. Tighten it if possible, so that it is secure. Cross your arms to keep the strap securely in place. When ready, give a thumbs-up to the winch operator so he or she can turn the crank to raise you.

HELICOPTER LANDING ZONE

A helicopter landing zone must be at least 115 feet (35 meters) wide for the aircraft's body and have at least 165 feet (50 meters) for the main rotor clearance. Also allow a landing strip approach of several hundred yards.

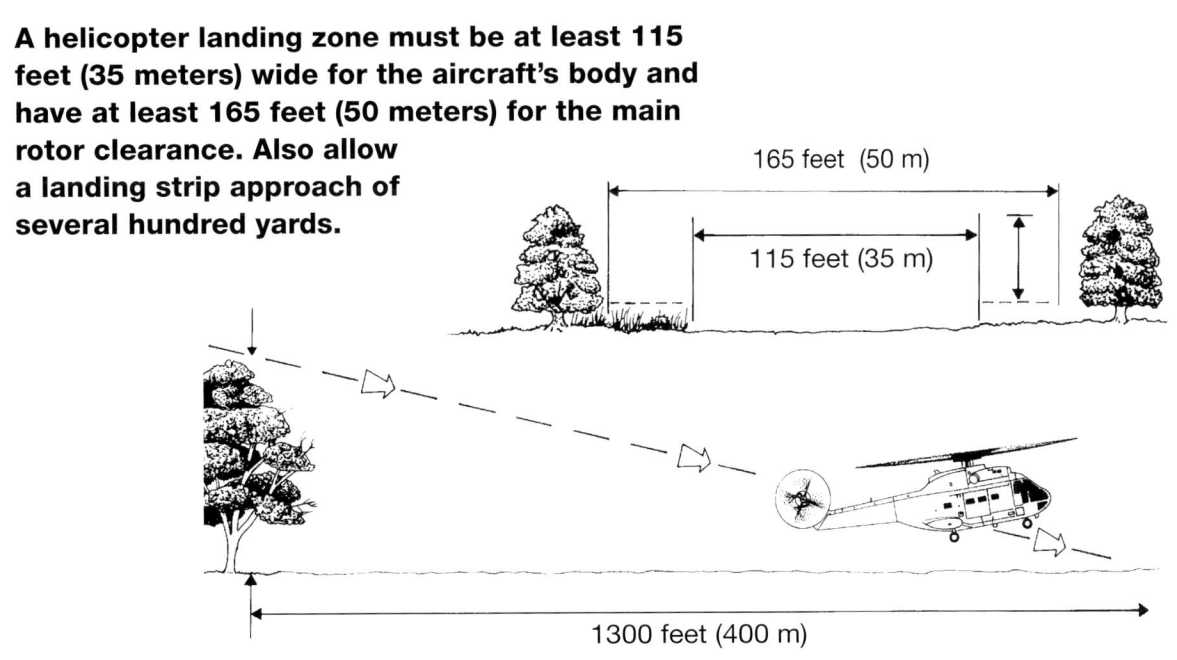

NAVIGATION

In a crisis or an accident, you may become separated from your maps, so it is important to have a reliable compass. Keep the compass with other personal equipment, or keep it around your neck with a lanyard.

Compasses can be set for different magnetic regions, depending on where you are in the world, so make sure you have the correct code for the region you are visiting: MN, NME, ME, SME, or MS.

Finding bearings

If using a Silva plastic compass and a map, place the compass on the map with the edge of the base plate connecting where you are with where you want to travel. Then turn the heading on the compass until the "N" marking north points toward magnetic north (MN) on the map.

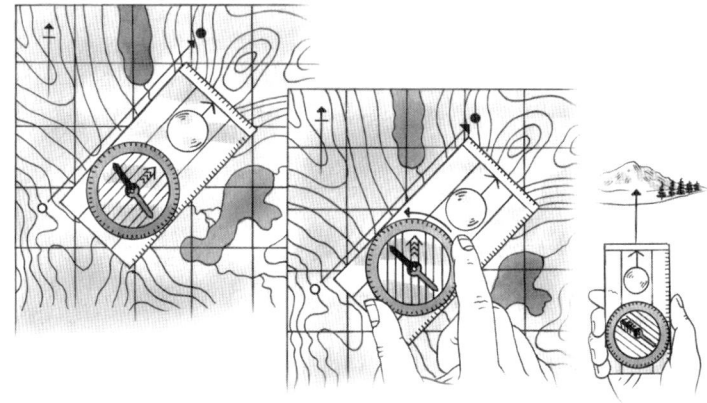

In order to follow the compass in the desired direction, take the compass off the map. Hold it level with the arrow that indicates direction of travel pointing straight ahead. Turn your body until that arrow lies over the arrow pointing to "N" on the dial. The compass is now pointing in the desired direction.

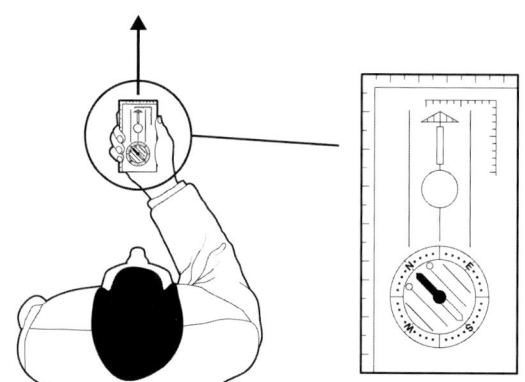

To stay on the route, focus on a landmark that is in line with the compass direction. Once the landmark has been reached, focus on a second one. Continue this way until reaching the destination. Take into account the possibility that you may lose sight of a landmark if you go downhill or enter a wood.

NAISMITH'S RULE

Designed by a Scottish navigator in the late 1800s, this rule is a way of estimating the time it will take to walk a route on hilly ground for an average walker. Allow 1 hour for every 3 miles (5 km) going forward. Add 30 minutes for every 1,000 feet (305 m) of ascent. When traveling with a group, figure the speed of the slowest in the group.

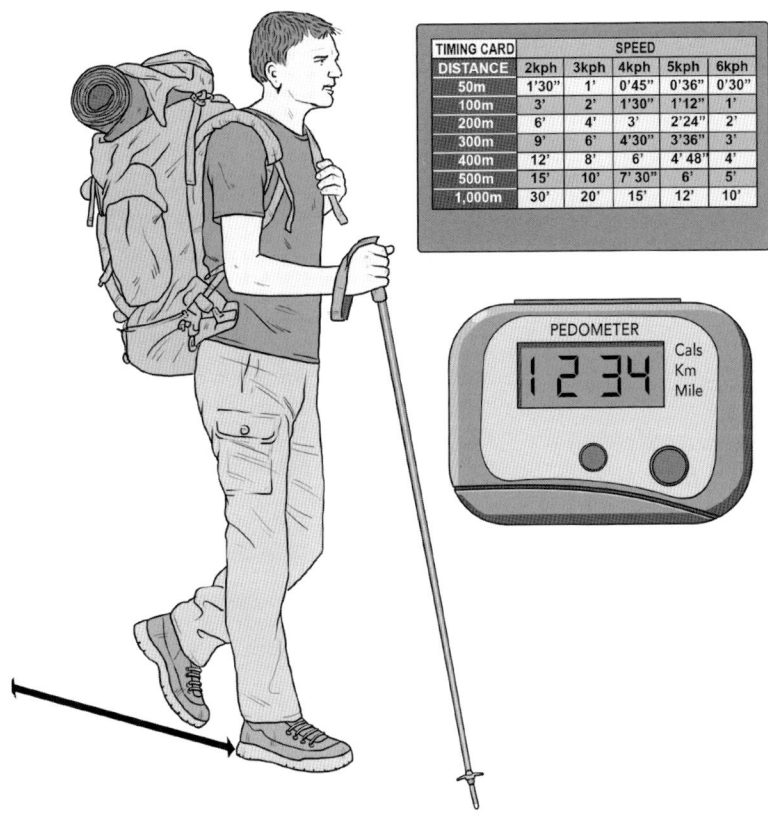

TIMING CARD	SPEED				
DISTANCE	2kph	3kph	4kph	5kph	6kph
50m	1'30"	1'	0'45"	0'36"	0'30"
100m	3'	2'	1'30"	1'12"	1'
200m	6'	4'	3'	2'24"	2'
300m	9'	6'	4'30"	3'36"	3'
400m	12'	8'	6'	4'48"	4'
500m	15'	10'	7'30"	6'	5'
1,000m	30'	20'	15'	12'	10'

Pacing

The best way to measure pacing is against a measured distance before you set out on an expedition. Measure a full pace each time your right heel hits the ground, and record how many paces occur in a measured distance while on a flat surface, while carrying a load, or while on hilly ground.

If you have a pedometer, make sure you know how to use it, and assure that it is adjusted to your individual pace. By using pacing, you can obtain a more accurate fix on your position as you progress toward a destination.

Keep a pacing and timing card on your person, such as in a wallet or pocket. Include details of the number of paces and the time it takes to cover particular distances in certain conditions. A tally counter can help track the information.

USEFUL OUTDOOR EQUIPMENT

High-tech outdoor watches may include features such as a global positioning system (GPS), an altimeter, a barometer, and a compass. Such watches often include special modes for different activities. You can preplan your route on the GPS and get weather alerts from the barometer.

However, high-tech gadgets such as this can have heavy battery use, so if you are in a remote area for a long time, it is good to have the backup of a rugged conventional analog watch.

You should also take a conventional compass and map as well as a waterproof notebook and grease pencil. In addition, an inclinometer, sometimes called a clinometer, or a slope angle card will help you to work out how steep slopes are.

Using an analog watch

After adjusting the time back an hour for Daylight Savings Time, should your watch currently be adjusted for that, hold the watch flat, and point the hour hand at the sun. Imagine a line that bisects the angle between the hour hand and 12 o'clock. This will give you the north–south line in the Northern Hemisphere. In the Southern Hemisphere, point the 12 o'clock mark at the sun. Draw an imaginary line bisecting the angle between the 12 o'clock mark and the hour hand to find the north–south line.

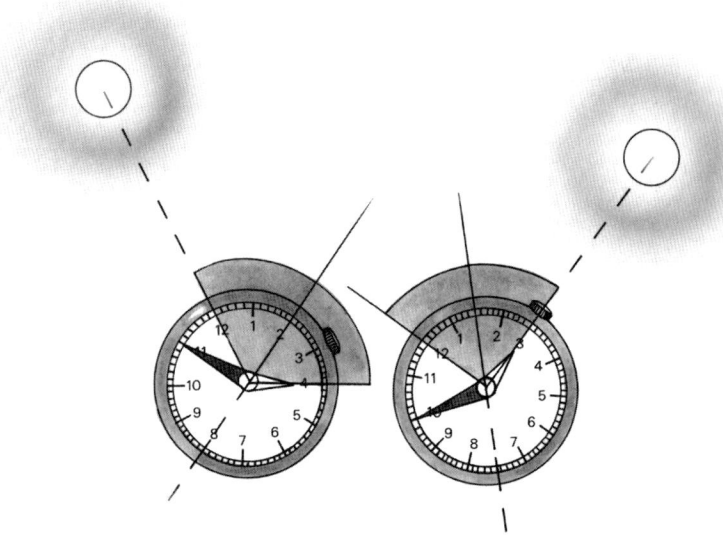

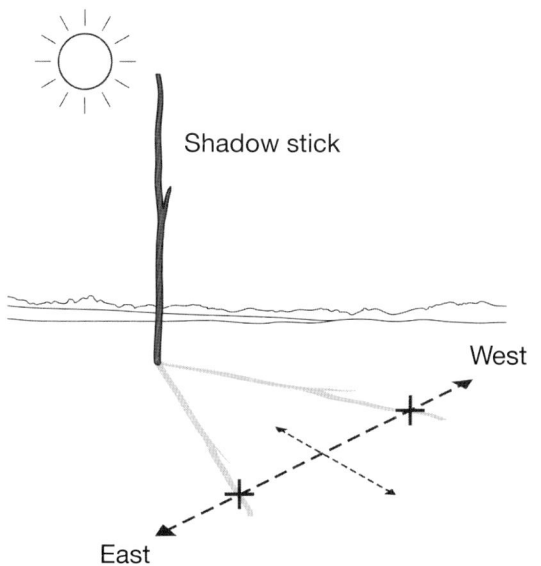
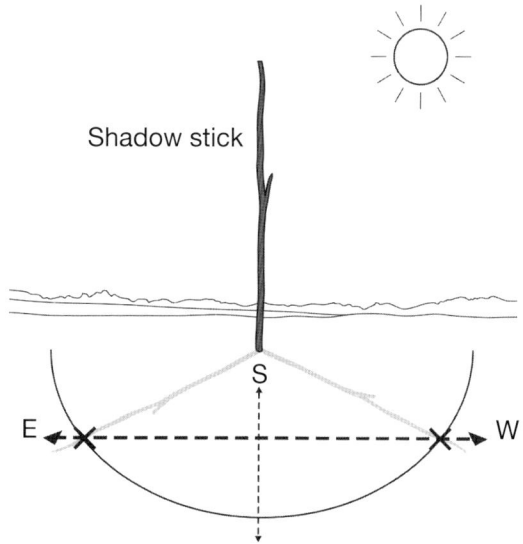

Navigating with the sun

If without a map or compass, the position of the sun will help with orientation. The sun rises in the east and sets in the west.

Place a straight stick in the ground, and mark the top of its shadow with a stone or similar object. Wait about 15 minutes. Ideally, place the stick 15 minutes before noon and make a second mark the same number of minutes after noon. With feet placed on each marker, you should be facing north.

If you draw a line between the two markers, this indicates an east–west line. If you draw a line at right angles to the first line, it indicates a north–south line.

STAR MOVEMENTS

Star movements can provide a general guide to direction.

IN THE NORTHERN HEMISPHERE:

A star rising is in the east; a star falling is in the west.

A star moving left is in the north; a star moving right is in the south.

IN THE SOUTHERN HEMISPHERE:

A star rising is in the west; a star falling is in the east.

A star moving left is in the south; a star moving right is in the north.

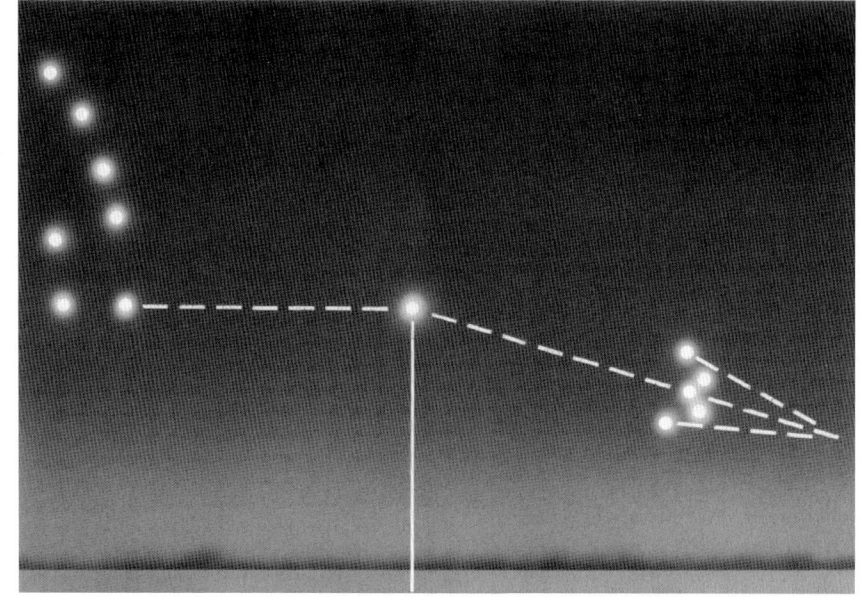

Big Dipper

Cassiopeia

North Star (Pole Star)

Stars

In the Northern Hemisphere, Polaris, also known as the North Star or the Pole Star, in the constellation Ursa Major, is the best indication of north. Polaris can be located using the constellations Ursa Major (Great Bear), Orion, and Cassiopeia. By calculating the vertical angle to Polaris, you can work out the latitude. As you move farther south, Polaris will appear lower in the sky.

In the Southern Hemisphere, to find south, use the Southern Cross constellation as well as the bright star in the Hydrus constellation, called B Hydrus. The Southern Cross can be found near a dark patch in the Milky Way known as the Coalsack. Draw an imaginary line between B Hydrus and the Southern Cross, and then extend the longer axis 4.5 times to mark a point which will be directly above geographic south.

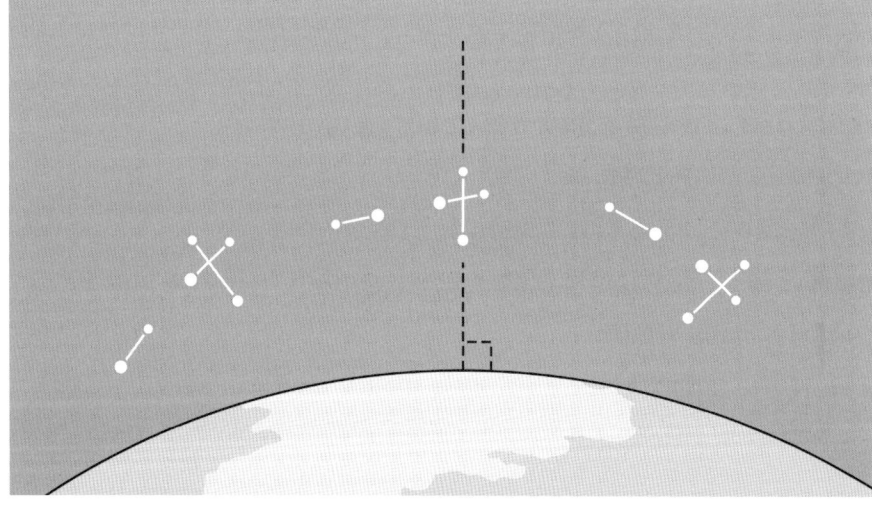

When the Southern Cross sits directly upright over the horizon as shown, the main axis of the group points at geographic south.

Moon navigation

As the moon turns in relation to the sun, the face of the moon alters. If the moon rises at dusk just after sunset, the illuminated face will be toward the west. After midnight, the illuminated face of the moon will be toward the east.

In the Northern Hemisphere, look at a quarter moon, and draw an imaginary line between the two horns of the moon down to the horizon. This point will be north. If you do the same in the Southern Hemisphere, the point on the horizon will be south.

Navigating nature

Knowing landmarks can help in finding the way forward. For example, if you know that certain ridges or rivers run in a certain direction, you can use those to navigate. The same applies to aircraft flight paths and to power lines. Overhead power lines often run in the same direction for long distances, so you can sometimes use them for navigation.

Look at trees, and see which side has more leaves. That will be the sunny side. If you are in the Northern Hemisphere, the sunny side will be south. At midday in the Northern Hemisphere, the shadow from any vertical object will be pointing north. It will be vice versa in the Southern Hemisphere.

Moss on trees will normally be thicker and bark will usually be darker on the north side. The roots of a tree will normally grow longer and thicker on the side opposite to the prevailing wind. If you know the direction of the prevailing wind, this should help with navigation. If you come across a tree stump, the rings should be more compact on the sunny side.

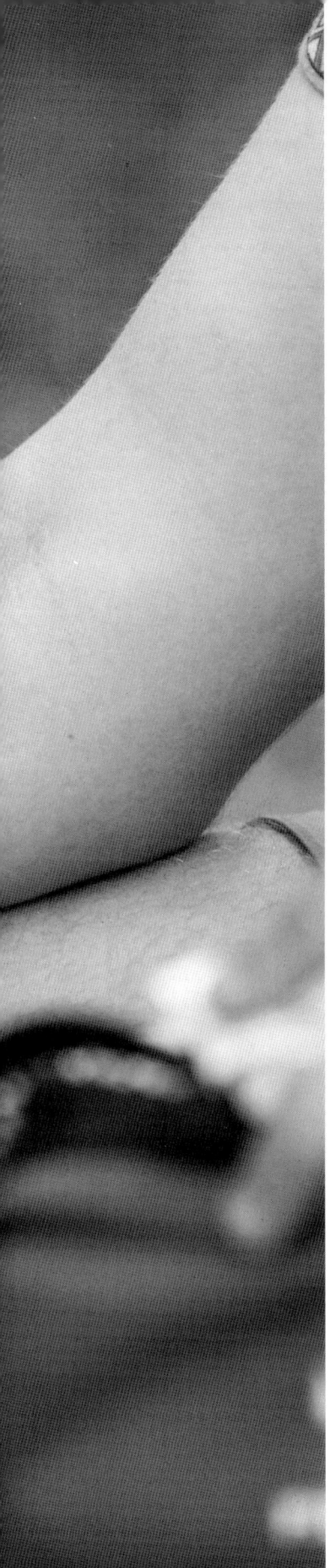

FIRST AID

First aid training can help you save lives. You may be ready and willing to help someone in an emergency, but without training, you may not know what to do, or you could inadvertently do something that causes more harm than good. Emergencies by their nature require quick responses. These are not good times for trying to work out what should be done, as taking time to plan could mean the difference between life and death for someone who is injured.

Knowing how to apply a bandage to a lesion or sprain could make all the difference in a crisis situation.

FIRST STEPS

If you have had first aid training and practiced some of its essential procedures, you will be better able to act automatically and swiftly in an emergency, and more likely to achieve a successful outcome.

There are basic questions to ask when faced with an accident or emergency.

Start by checking whether the area is safe. If you are on or near a road, is traffic a danger? Are there toxic liquids, are there downed power lines, or are you near an unstable area such as a rockfall?

Has anyone been hurt? Call the relevant emergency number for the country and area, or get someone nearby to call while administering first aid to a patient.

Helping a patient

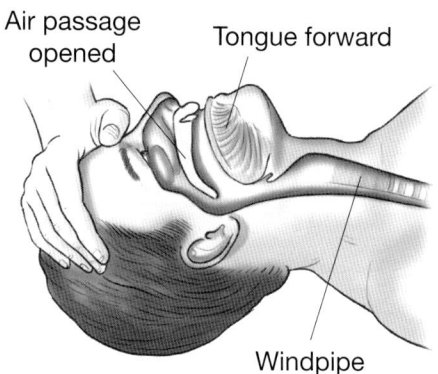

Airway:
Tilt the patient's head back, and lift his or her chin. Check for signs of airway blockage, and clear the mouth of obstructions, such as blood or vomit. Check that the tongue is not blocking the throat. Use an oropharyngeal airway, a special medical device, if necessary.

Breathing:
Put an ear near the nose and mouth of the patient to detect the sound of breath, or hold your hand near the nose and mouth to check whether you can feel breath. If there is no obvious sign of breathing, take immediate action.

Circulation:
Check for a pulse at the neck or on the underside of the wrist. If there is no pulse, administer cardiopulmonary resuscitation (CPR). Check the color of the patient's skin.

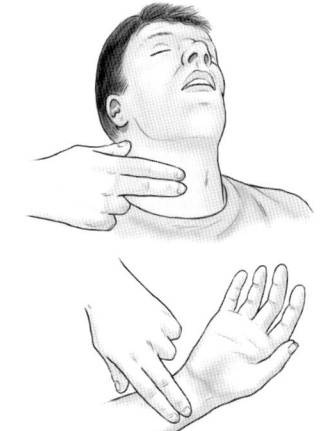

FIRST AID 223

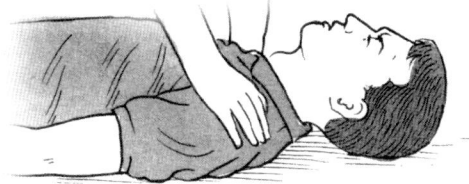
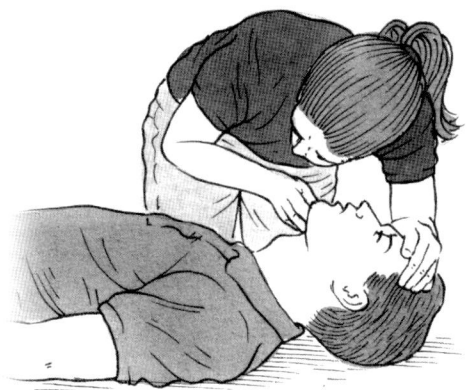

CPR in action

Deliver rescue breaths. Tilt the patient's head back slightly, and lift the chin. Then pinch the patient's nose shut, and place your mouth over the patient's mouth to make a complete seal. Blow into the patient's mouth until you see his or her chest rise. Give two rescue breaths, and then continue compressions.

If the patient's chest does not rise with the first rescue breath, tilt the head again before delivering the second breath. If the chest still does not rise with the second breath, the patient may be choking. Check for obstructions in the mouth and throat, and remove them if needed.

Continue with the CPR cycles of chest compressions and breathing until the patient shows signs of life, or until a trained medical responder arrives to take over.

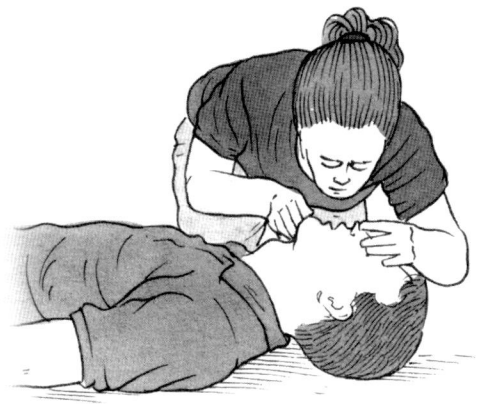
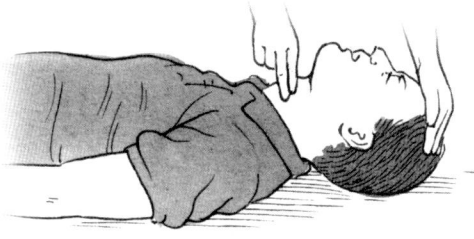
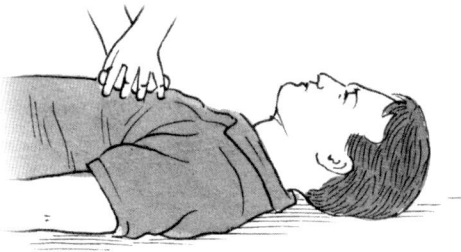

Recovery position

The recovery position can help a patient who is unconscious, but breathing. This works to prevent suffocation from vomiting. However, beware of a spinal injury, in which case the body should not be moved until the back can be fully supported.

- If the spine is not injured, kneel down next to the patient. Avoid pressure to the chest. Move one of the patient's arms at a right angle to the body, straight out and palm upward.
- Roll the body gently on its side toward the outstretched arm.
- Place the other arm across the chest, until it rests with the palm down on the outstretched arm.
- Lift and bend the knee from the upward side, and gently place the bent knee across the other leg. The knee of the bottom leg should bend slightly, too.
- In the end, the arms should be supporting the head, and the knee of the top leg should be resting on the ground.
- Tilt the patient's head back, and tilt the chin forward. Check that there are no obstructions and that the airway is open and clear.

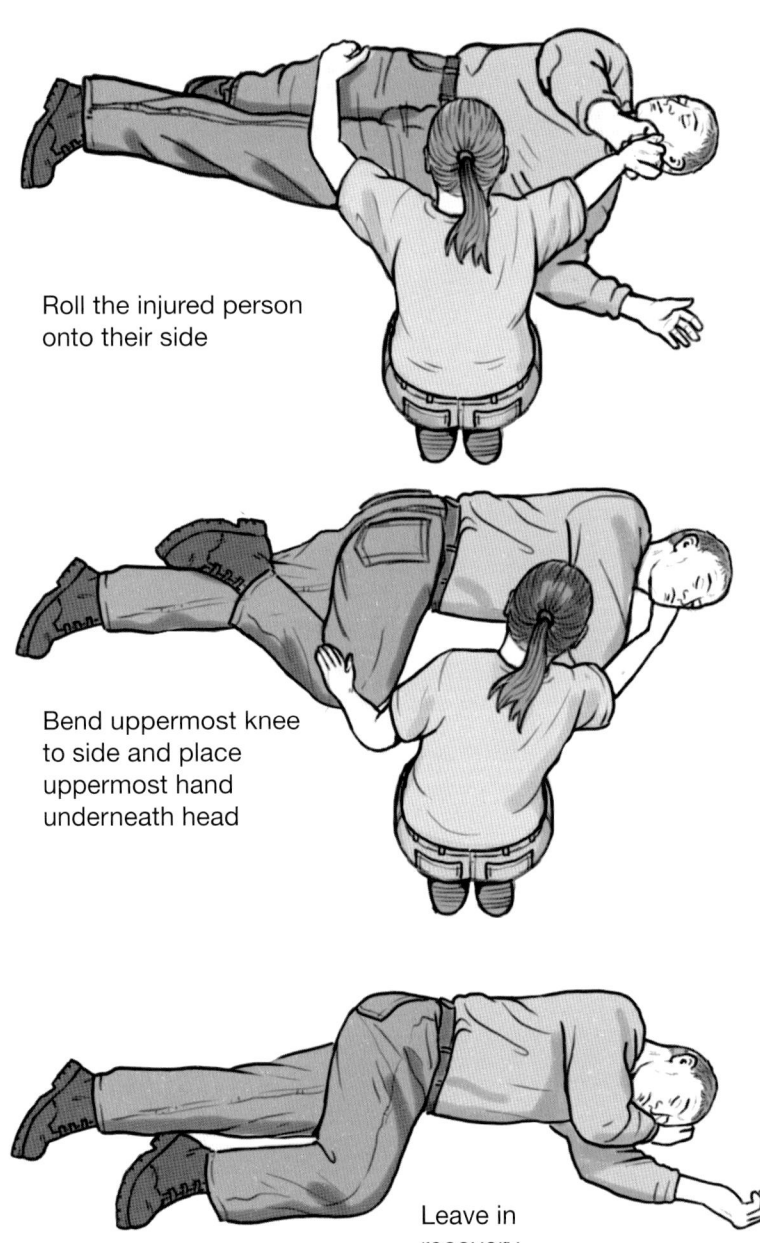

Roll the injured person onto their side

Bend uppermost knee to side and place uppermost hand underneath head

Leave in recovery position

EXAMINATION TECHNIQUE

When you come across someone who has suffered an accident, it may not be immediately obvious what is wrong. To check for breathing, follow the sequence called "Look, feel, listen." If checking a limb, follow the sequence known as "Look, feel, move." Areas to be checked include hands, pulse, blood pressure, head, neck, chest, abdomen, and limbs.

Treating shock

Shock occurs when vital organs are deprived of oxygen due to a failure of the circulatory system to provide enough oxygenated blood. Severe blood loss, severe burns, heart attack, vomiting, or an allergic reaction can cause shock. The signs of shock include pale, clammy skin; sweating; rapid, shallow breathing; dizziness; and a sick feeling.

Call an emergency number for help, but treat any injuries you can see, and raise the patient's legs. Cover the patient with a blanket or coat, and provide reassurance until help arrives.

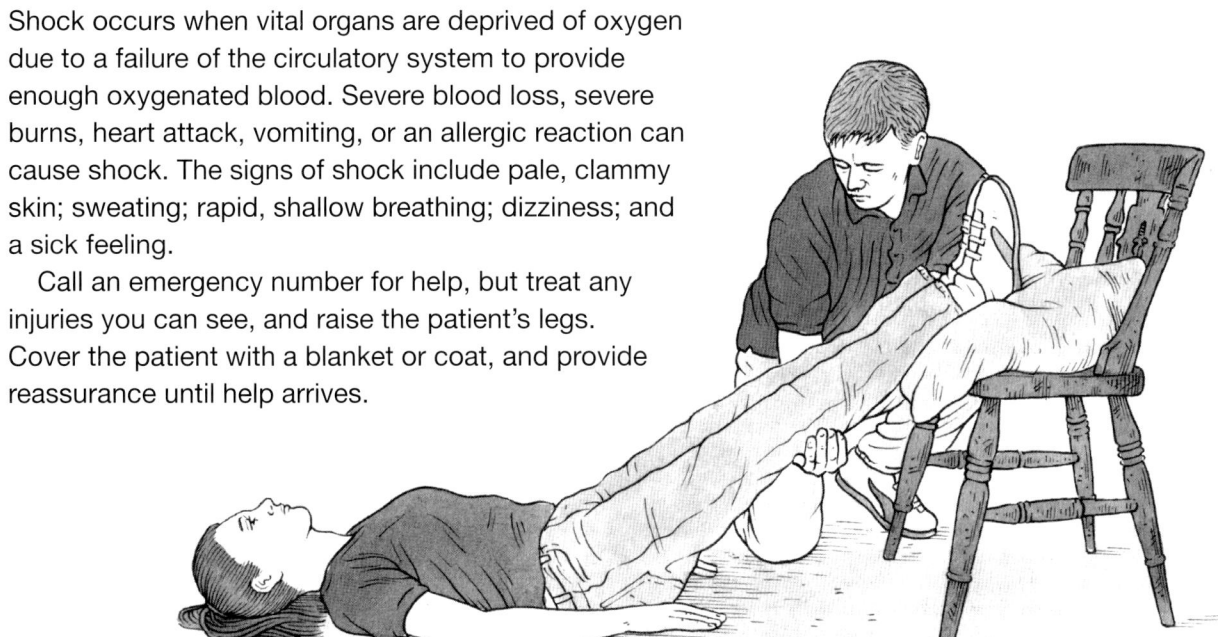

JAW THRUST TECHNIQUE

This technique may be used where a spinal injury is suspected and you do not wish to move the patient's body. It will ensure that the patient's airway is unobstructed.

Kneel behind the patient's head, and place your hands on both sides of his or her face. Lift the jaw gently with your fingertips, and avoid moving the neck. Remain with the patient, or take turns with another person, to support the head until emergency services arrive to provide professional assistance.

CHOKING

Severe choking can lead to unconsciousness because the patient cannot breathe properly. The patient will not be able to speak either.

Stand behind the patient and slightly to one side. Support his or her chest with one hand, and get the patient to lean forward so that the obstacle in the throat comes out of the mouth. If the object does not come out, give up to five sharp blows between the patient's shoulder blades with the heel of your hand. If the object still does not come out, you will need to give abdominal thrusts.

Treating an infant for choking

Lay the baby facedown along your forearm, with the baby's head low, and give five sharp slaps between the shoulders. If the obstruction remains, place the infant face up along your other arm, and place two fingers on the lower part of the breastbone. Give five sharp downward thrusts. Then look in the infant's mouth, holding the tongue down with one finger. Remove any visible obstruction. Carry on with above sequences until the blockage is cleared.

ABDOMINAL THRUSTS
- **Stand behind the patient.**
- **Place your arms around his or her waist, and make the patient bend forward.**
- **Place one fist in the area just above the belly button.**
- **Place your other hand on top of your first, and move it sharply upward.**
- **If the obstacle does not come out, repeat up to five times.**
- **If there is still no change, call emergency services, and keep attempting to move the obstacle in the same way.**

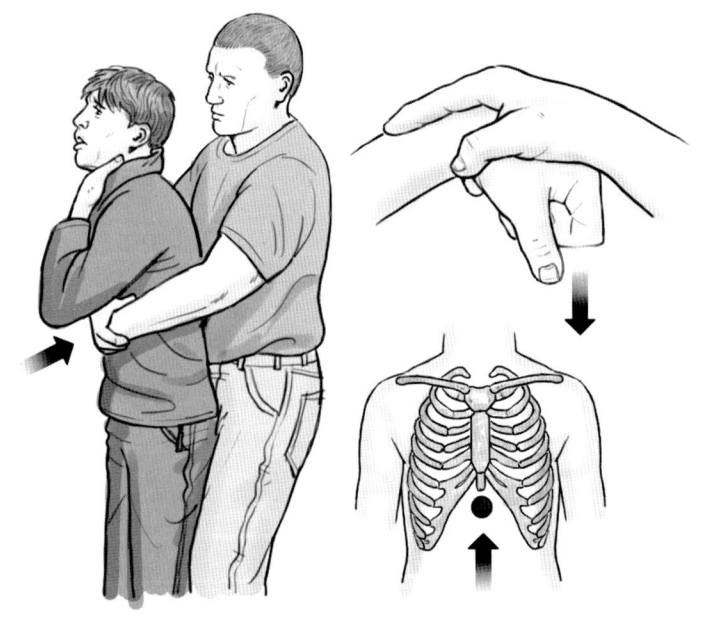

DROWNING

Do not jump into water to make a rescue unless you have a realistic chance of bringing the person back to safety. However, you should throw a lifebuoy or similar rescue tool if one is available, and you should call emergency services for help.

Once someone who has been immersed in the water is back on land, check for breathing. If there is no sign of breath, open the airway, and give five initial rescue breaths. Perform CPR for at least one minute before calling for help. Alternatively, ask someone else to call emergency services while administering CPR.

Symptoms of drowning include pale and cool skin, no sign of breathing, blue lips (cyanosis), a weak or absent pulse, and unconsciousness.

Keep the patient's head lower than the rest of the body to allow water to drain naturally from the lungs. If the patient is coughing or spluttering, keep him or her on one side. If the patient is unconscious, use the recovery position, and call for medical assistance. If providing artificial respiration, you may need to breathe more heavily to overcome the effects of water in the lungs. Required treatment for a near drowning may also include treatment for hypothermia and treatment for shock.

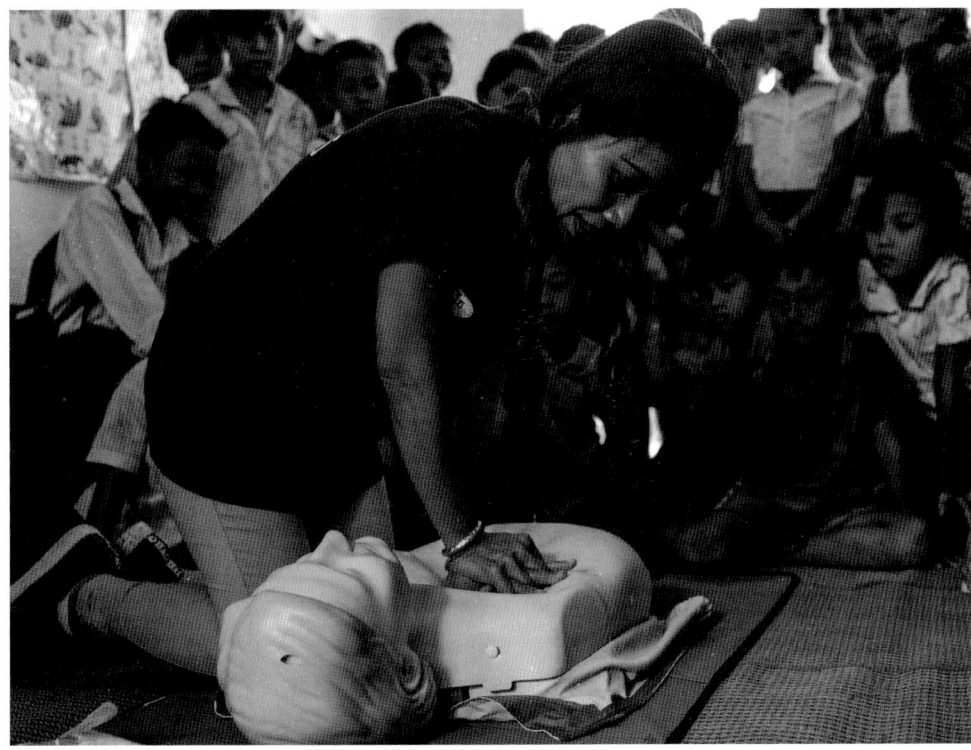

A medical professional demonstrates how to perform CPR on a mannequin during a water safety and drowning prevention class.

COLD AND HEAT

Extended periods of cold or heat can present a serious threat to a person's health and they require urgent treatment. Here are some methods of treating heat and cold injuries prior to medical assistance.

Hypothermia

A person may suffer hypothermia when body temperature falls below 95°F (35°C). This can be caused by long-term exposure to cold weather or immersion in cold water. The patient may appear drowsy or display shallow breathing and a low heart rate. He or she may lose consciousness.

The patient needs to be warmed urgently, but in an even and gradual way. Remove any wet clothing, and replace it with clean, dry clothing. Place the patient in a sleeping bag in a warm dry area. If necessary, someone else should share the sleeping bag to increase warmth. A warm bath is another solution if available. Provide artificial respiration if breathing stops, and seek medical assistance.

Chilblains

This is caused by lengthy exposure of the skin to low temperature, which constricts the small blood vessels just below the surface of the skin. If the skin is later exposed to heat, the blood vessels become wider, causing purple-red swellings on toes or fingers.

You should gently warm the affected part, but do not massage the skin or apply direct heat. Put hands in warm, dry gloves and feet in warm, dry socks.

Trench foot

This is caused by exposure of the feet to wet and damp conditions over a prolonged period. The symptoms include pale feet that then turn red. They become swollen and painful. If the feet are pale, warm them gently. If they are red and swollen, cool them gradually.

You should not massage feet or subject them to direct heat or cold. To reduce the risk of this condition, change socks daily, and make sure the socks are clean and dry.

Frostbite

British Royal Marines practice warm-up exercises to help prevent frostbite.

Frostbite is damage to skin tissue through long exposure to cold temperatures. The symptoms are white, cold skin, which then becomes red and swollen. Replace any wet clothing with warm and dry clothing, and keep the affected part of the body warm and dry. Seek medical help.

Heatstroke

This is caused by a failure of body cooling mechanisms after long exposure to heat and sun. The symptoms include red and dry skin; a rapid, weak pulse; headache; dizziness; and nausea. Treatment includes moving the patient to a cool, shaded area. Raise and support the legs. Give the patient water to drink if conscious. If you have enough water, use some to cool the patient. Massage extremities to improve blood flow. Monitor the patient, and seek medical assistance.

HEAT CRAMPS

This is caused by loss of body salts through excessive sweating, vomiting, or diarrhea. The symptoms include cramps in the arms, legs, or abdomen as well as heavy sweating and thirst. To treat heat cramps, move the patient to a cool, shady area, provide drinking water, and loosen clothing. Seek medical assistance if there are no signs of improvement.

Burns and scalds

If someone is burned or scalded, he or she needs to be separated from the heat source, and the burn area should be cooled immediately with cold water. Keep cooling the area for at least 20 minutes. Cover the burn area loosely with plastic wrap, or apply a clean, dry dressing. Refrain from using ointments and sprays.

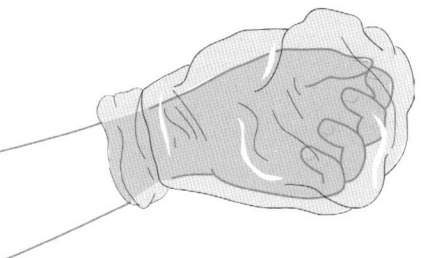

A burnt hand can be protected with a loose-fitting plastic wrap

First-degree burns involve the top layer of skin and often occur in sunburn. The skin first turns red and then peels. Treatment includes rehydrating cream for the skin and also treatment for headache or fever. Cool water should be taken at regular intervals.

Second-degree burns involve deeper damage to the skin, which can cause blisters on the skin as well as shock. Treatment includes antibacterial dressing. You may also leave the wound undressed but clean. Treat for shock as needed.

Third-degree burns involve damage to all layers of the skin. The patient will also be suffering from shock. This requires specialist treatment, and medical aid should be sought urgently.

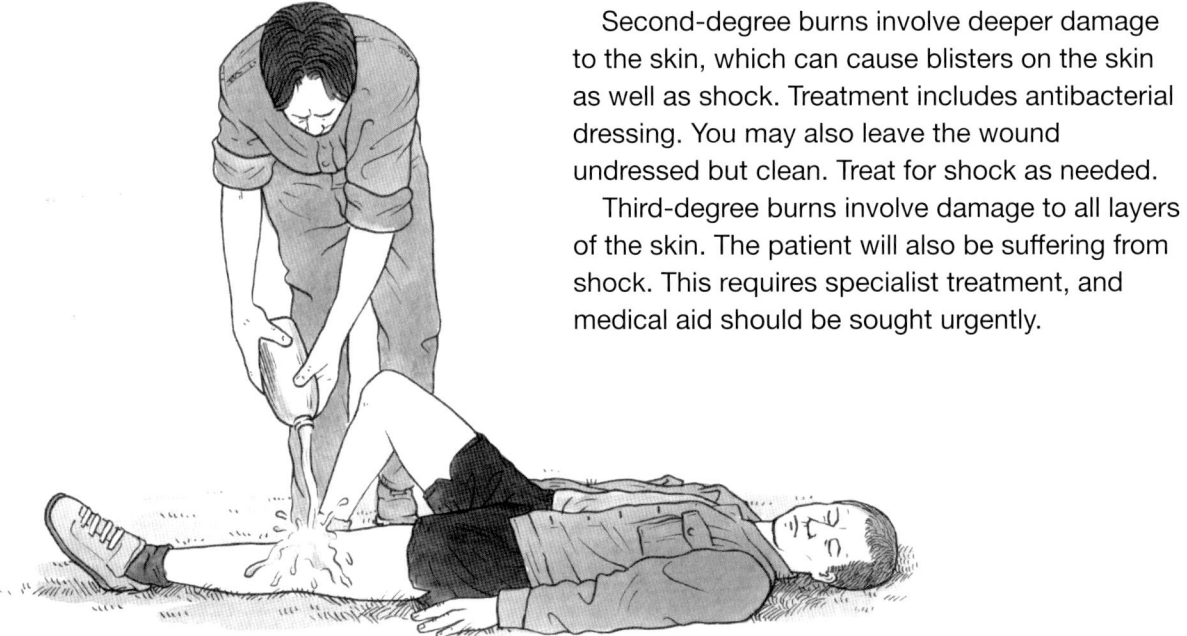

BLEEDING

Bleeding can be in different forms, depending on the seriousness of the wound. Arterial bleeding is characterized by its bright red color. Blood will spurt in time with the beating of the heart. Venous bleeding tends to be darker and is more easily controlled. Capillary bleeding results from minor cuts and grazes.

Press firmly on the wound to stop bleeding. If you have a dressing pad, this should be placed over the wound and either held or tied in place. If there is no dressing available, use another clean pad or a handkerchief. Keep pressure on the wound for up to 10 minutes.

Bandage the dressing in place but not so tightly that it will interfere with blood flow. If necessary, place another dressing on top of the first one, but do not remove the first.

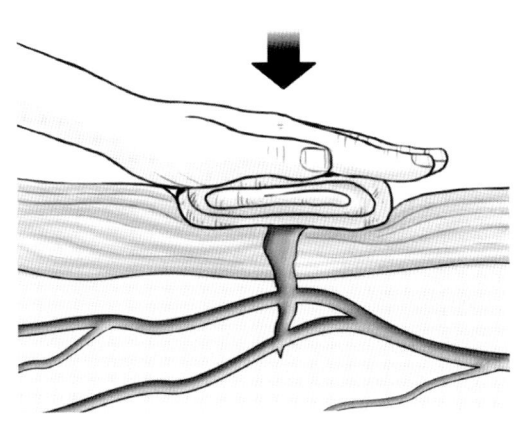

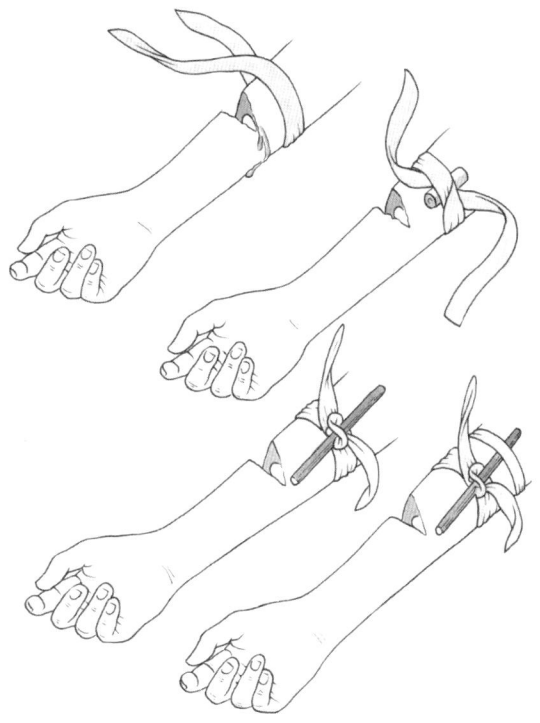

Applying a torniquet

Apply a tourniquet only if other methods of bleeding prevention have failed.

- Tie the tourniquet around the injured arm or leg, several inches above the injury.

- Place a stick on the knot and tie the loose ends of the tourniquet around it in another square knot.

- Twist the stick to increase the pressure until the bleeding stops.

- If possible, secure the stick to the upper arm to maintain pressure.

SUTURES

In the United States, law requires that medical personnel perform sutures or direct how they are done. In an emergency, if you have experience with suturing and have clean materials, you may be compelled to suture a deep wound.

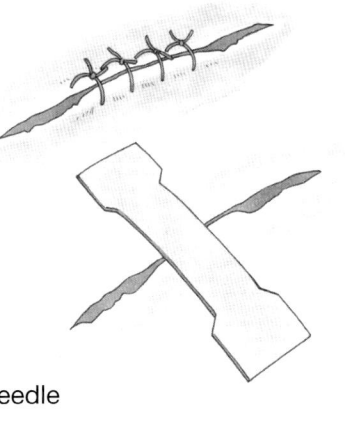

- Sterilize materials, and clean the wound.
- Pass the needle into one edge of the skin and out of the other edge.
- Take in equal amounts of skin on both sides to align the edges of the wound.
- Tie the sutures with a square knot.
- Loop over the needle holder, grasp the end through the loop, and pull tight.
- Loop around the needle holder in the other direction, grasp the end through the loop, and pull tight again.

Leave the sutures in place for about 10 days. When you take a stitch out, grasp the knot with forceps and tweezers, and then pull the stitch out with a firm pull.

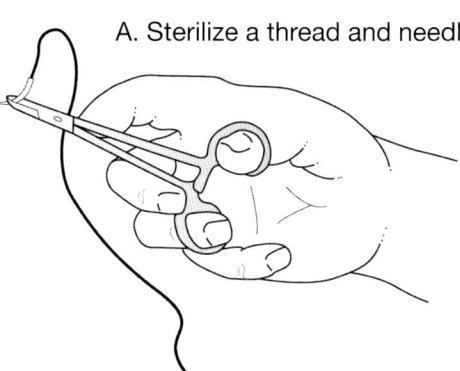

A. Sterilize a thread and needle

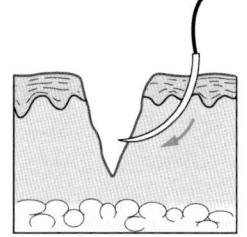

B. Make a stitch at the midpoint of the wound

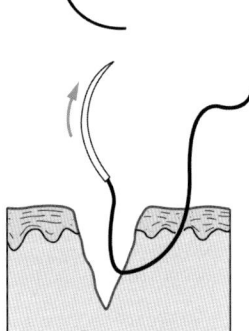

C. Pull needle through one side of the wound

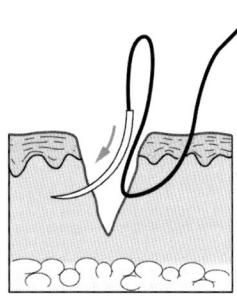

D. Then stitch through the other side

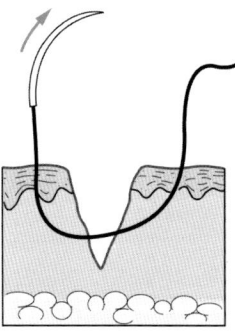

E. Draw the wound together

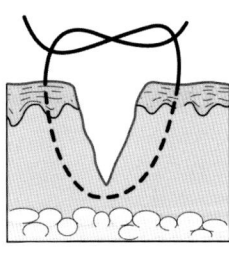

F. Tie stitch off

TO SECURE DRESSING

Follow these guidelines to make the most of a dressing:

- **Ensure the dressing pad extends beyond the edges of the wound.**
- **Place the dressing directly on the wound. Do not slide it around.**
- **If blood seeps through, do not replace it. Put another dressing over it.**
- **If there is only one sterile dressing, use this one directly on the wound, and use others to back it up.**

To secure dressings:

- **Wind a bandage around the limb and dressing to secure the pad.**
- **To secure the bandage, tie the ends in a square knot over the pad to exert firm pressure over the top of the wound.**
- **Check the circulation beyond the bandage. Loosen the bandage if necessary.**

If there is nothing else available, and the wound is gaping, you can use adhesive tape to close the wound, making sure it is sterile and clean first.

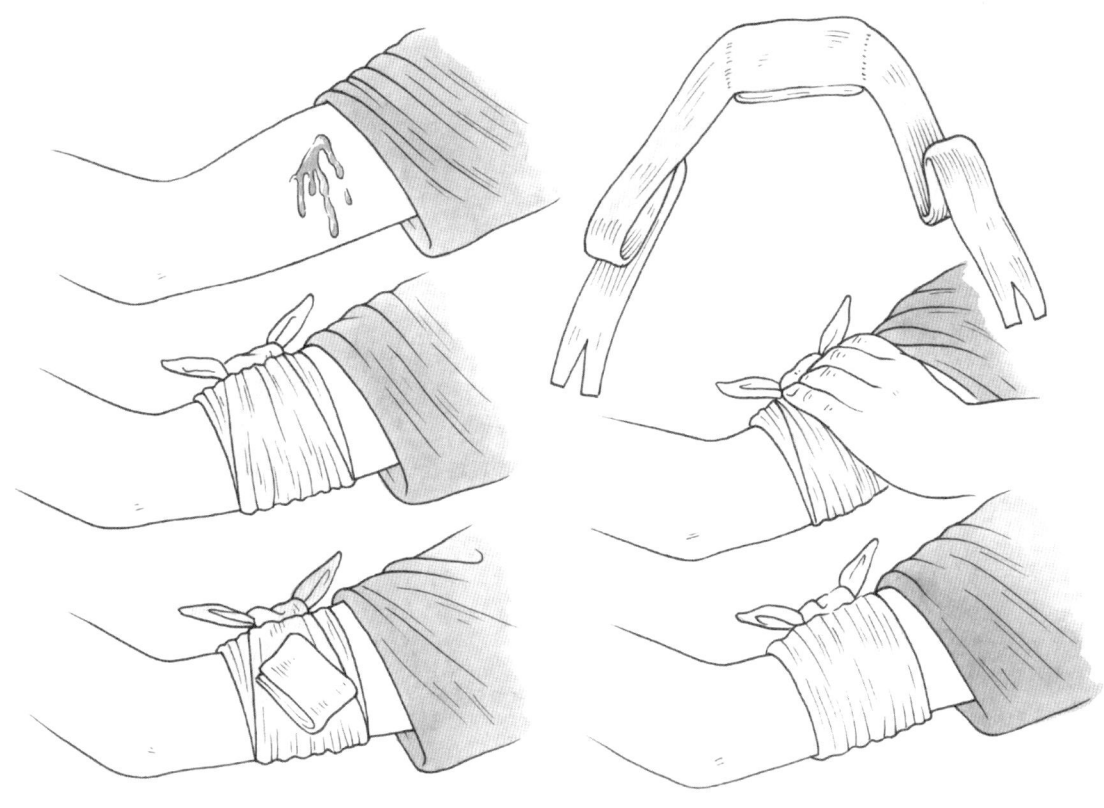

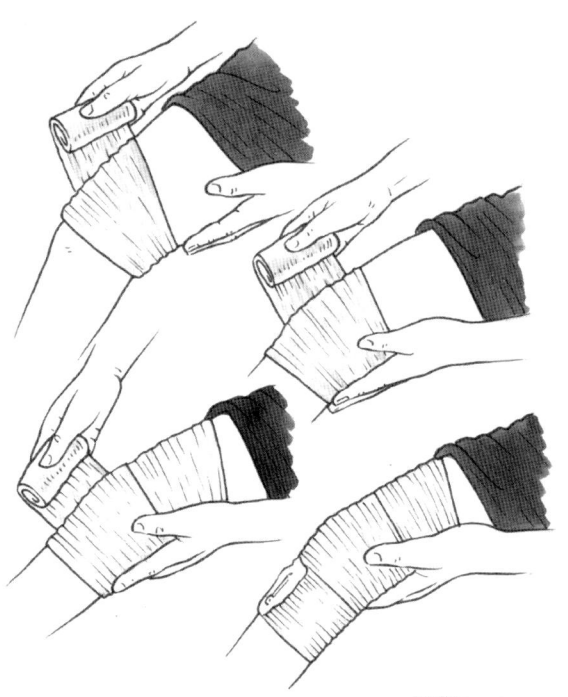

Large bandages

Leg bandage
- Place the center of a triangular bandage over the dressing that covers the wound.
- To begin a knot, take the left end over and under the right end on the other side of the leg. Then take the right end over and under the left end to finish the knot.
- Pull from both ends to make sure it lies flat.
- To apply a roller bandage instead, start on a diagonal below the dressing, and work upward, covering two-thirds of the bandage roll with each turn. Finish with a straight turn, which can be taped or pinned into place.

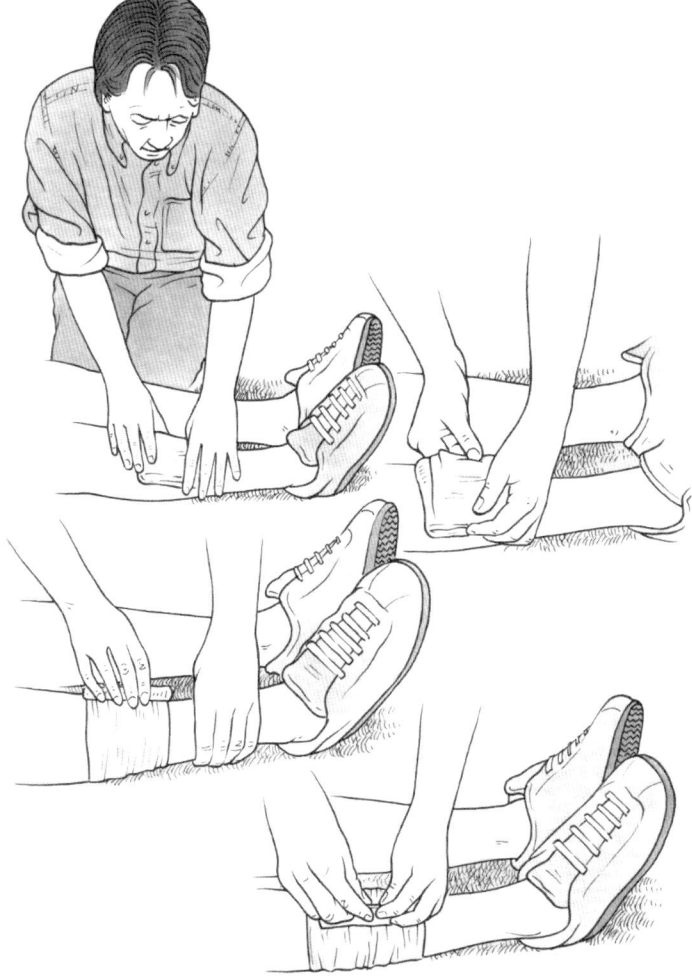

FIRST AID

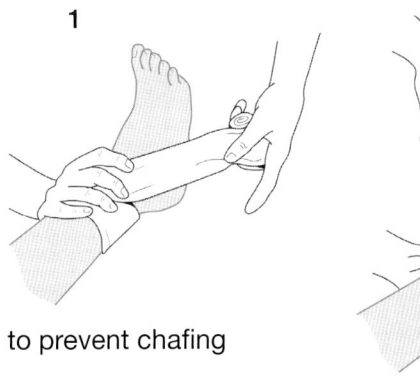
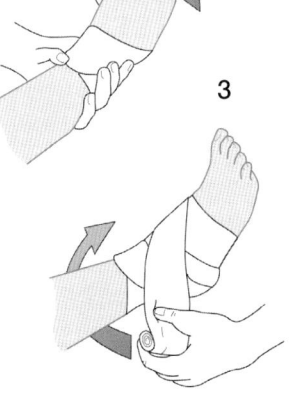
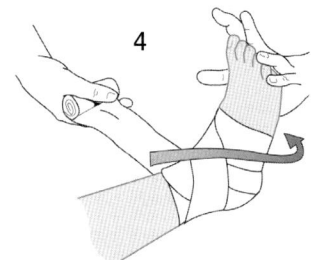

Foot bandage
- Place the foot in the middle of a triangular bandage with the heel well forward of the base.
- Separate the toes with absorbent material to prevent chafing and irritation.
- Place the forward point of the bandage over the top of the foot, and tuck any excess material into the pleats on each side of the foot.
- Cross the ends on top of the foot, pull the ends around the ankle, and tie them at the front of the ankle.
- To apply a roller bandage instead, cover the dressing, then pull the bandage around the ankle, and then pull it back over the back of the foot to the base of the little toe.
- Make a complete turn around the toes. Go back around the ankle again as well as back around the base of the toes, moving upward.
- Continue until the dressing is covered. Finish with a final turn around the ankle, and secure with tape or pin. The bandage should be wrapped from the ankle up to the middle of the foot, before looping back to the ankle.

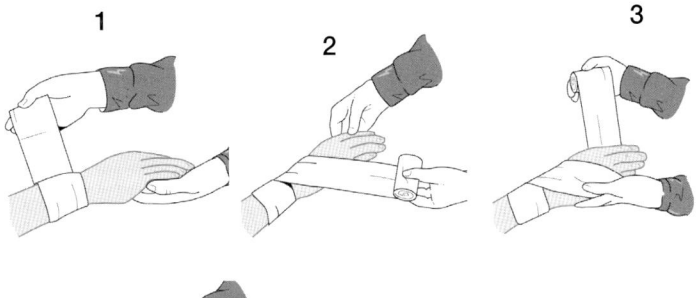

Hand bandage
- Place the hand on a triangular bandage with the wrist at the base.
- Separate fingers with soft material to prevent their chafing.
- Bring the apex of the bandage up and over the fingers.
- Bring the ends around to tie them at the wrist.
- Wrap the bandage around the wrist before crossing to the top of the little finger.
- Go under the hand, then return to the wrist across the back of the hand. Repeat and secure.
- To use a roller bandage instead, cover the dressing, and then pull the bandage around the wrist and over the back of the hand to the base of the little finger.

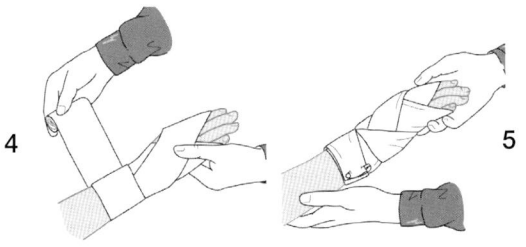

- Make a complete turn around the fingers. Go back around the wrist again as well as back around the base of the fingers. Continue until the dressing is covered. Finish with a final turn around the wrist, and secure with tape or pin.

FRACTURES

Fractures are not easy to identify. The patient may have a muscle or ligament injury instead of a broken bone. However, it is safer to treat related injuries as if they were fractures than to do nothing.

If the patient is bleeding or has difficulty breathing, this needs to be dealt with by stemming the blood flow.

Depending on the wound and availability of help, call an ambulance or attempt to get the patient to a hospital by car.

If you are far from any medical assistance, try to splint the wound to keep it in place. Do not try to reset bones.

Types of fracture

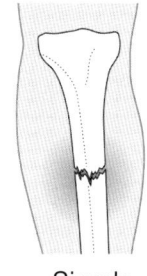
Simple

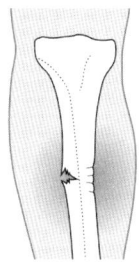
Greenstick

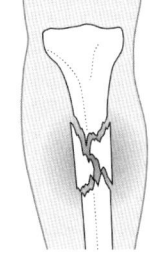
Comminuted

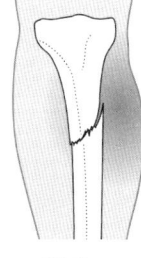
Oblique

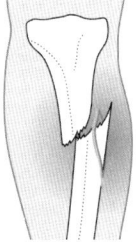
Compound

Splints

Splints can be made from whatever material is available, including sticks, tree branches, or even rolled newspaper. It is important that the splint is long enough to immobilize the limb above and below the wound.

Place padding between the splint and the limb. Tie the splint in place in two places above the fracture and in two places below. With a broken leg, you can use the other good leg as a splint by tying the two legs together.

Hip or upper leg
- Place splints on the inside of the leg with padding.
- Place a longer splint from the ankle to the armpit on the outside of the leg.
- If there are no splints, use the other leg as a splint with a blanket in between.

Lower leg
- Place splints on both sides of the leg, extending from the foot to above the knee.
- If no splints are available, use the other leg as a splint with padding in between.

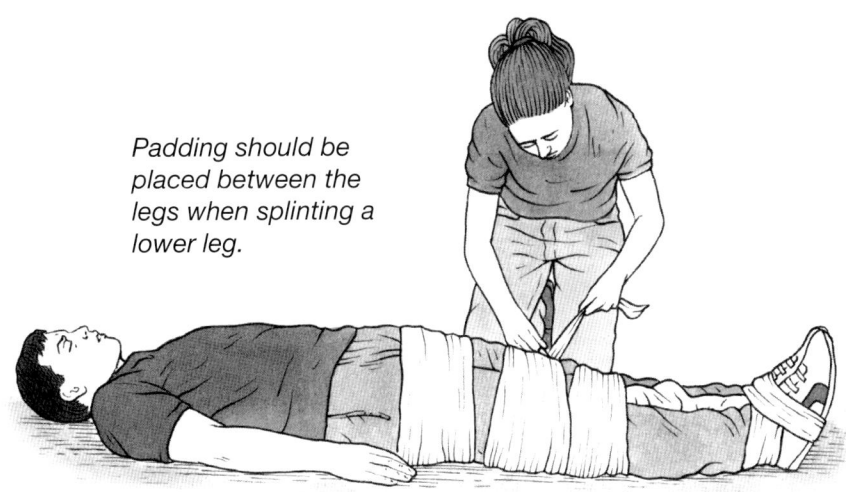

Padding should be placed between the legs when splinting a lower leg.

Ankle or foot
- Raise the leg, and support it.
- A boot will provide some support for the ankle or foot.
- Do not let the patient walk on the injured part.

Knee fracture
- Try to make the leg straight if possible, but do not force it.
- Place a splint below the leg, and provide support padding under the knee if it is slightly bent.
- If the leg is quite bent and cannot be straightened, strap legs together with padding below and above the knee.

A pelvis fracture should be stabilized with pads and splints.

Pelvis fracture
- Place a pad between the thighs, and tie at the knees and ankles.
- If the legs are bent, place padding beneath the knees.
- If possible, the patient can be strapped to a board or a door, with straps at the ankles, the waist, and the top part of the chest, under the arms.
- If there is no board available, strap the two legs together, with padding between and with bandaging at the feet, ankles, knees, and pelvis.

Neck fracture

Neck fractures are extremely dangerous. Only offer treatment if paramedics are not available.

- Immobilize the neck with a cervical collar. If one is not available, place a rolled towel under the neck to support it.
- Place two heavy objects on either side of the head to keep it stable. For example, a pair of boots can be used.

SKULL FRACTURE

Skull fractures are potentially very serious and require urgent medical attention.

Symptoms include the following:

- **Wound or bruise on the head**
- **A soft area on the scalp**
- **Semiconsciousness or slow responsiveness**
- **Clear fluid seeping from nose or ear**
- **Blood showing in the white of the eye**
- **Distortion of head or face**

**TO TREAT:
Place the patient in the recovery position. Get urgent medical assistance.**

Different types of brain injury

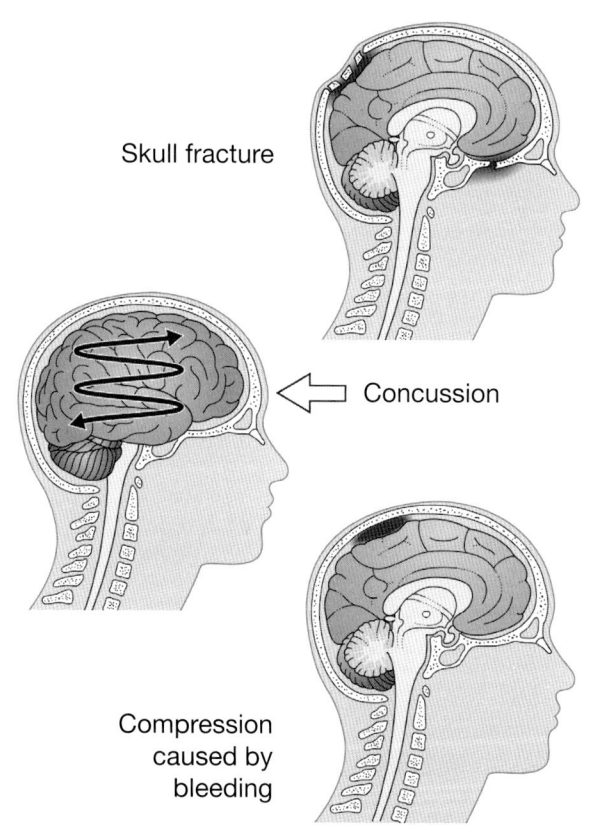

Skull fracture

Concussion

Compression caused by bleeding

ARM FRACTURES

SHOULDER BLADE OR COLLARBONE
- Use a classic sling to immobilize the arm.
- Or a T-shirt hem can be rolled up over the injured arm, and the back of the shirt can be cut and tied to hold the arm in place.

UPPER ARM
- Put a pad in the armpit.
- Place a splint from shoulder to elbow on the outside of the arm.
- Put a sling around the wrist and neck to support the arm.

ELBOW
- Support the elbow in a sling if bent.
- Bind the arm to the body by passing a bandage around the back.
- If the arm is not bent, support the arm with splints and padding, and bind it to the body.

FOREARM, HAND, OR FINGERS
- Immobilize the forearm and hand with a splint extending from the elbow to the fingertips.
- Use padding in the splint.
- Elevate the arm in a sling to prevent swelling.

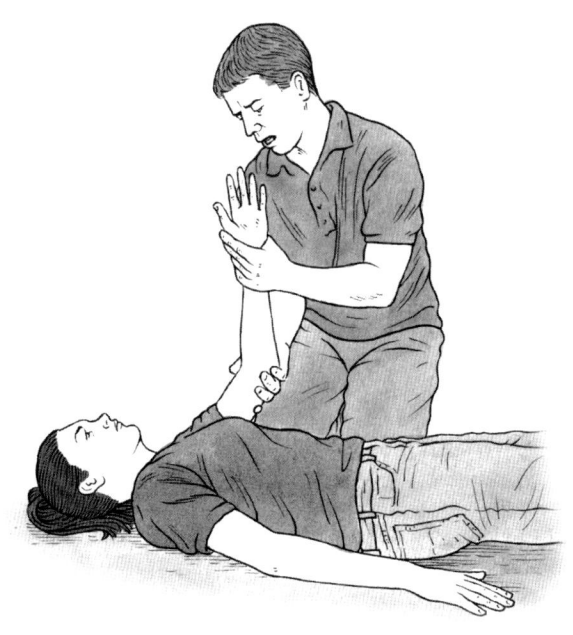

Different types of arm fracture

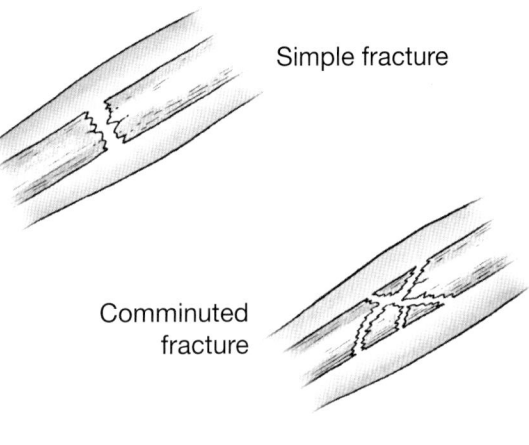

Simple fracture

Comminuted fracture

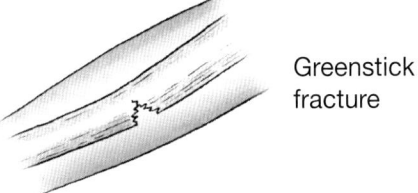

Greenstick fracture

Slings

A sling is a practical and easy way of supporting an injured arm.

Standard sling

One way to make a sling is to fold a square of material. For most people, a square that is 40 inches (1 m) is adequate, but if unsure of the size, it is better to use a square that is too large than one that is too small.

Position the arm at 90 degrees across the body. Have the patient support the bad arm with the good arm. Slip the triangle between the body and the injured arm so the two longest points can be gently pulled up and behind the neck. Tie the ends at the back of the neck with a square knot. Then gently twist any excess material over the elbow, and secure it with a safety pin. Ensure that the wrist is higher than the elbow.

Collar and cuff sling

When a large square is not available, wrap a strip of material, such as a necktie, pantyhose, or a strip of sheet, around the wrist, and tie the ends at the back of the neck.

Elevation sling

If the hand needs to stay elevated, rather than straight across the stomach, to keep bleeding to a minimum, allow the elbow to hang at the side, and extend the hand toward the shoulder on the uninjured side.
- Place the triangle over the chest, with one long end pointing toward the shoulder on the uninjured side.
- Tuck the material under the hand, arm, and elbow.
- Pull the other long end across the back toward the shoulder on the uninjured side.
- Extend the points of the bandage at the collarbone, and tie firmly with a square knot.
- Twist the end by the elbow gently, and secure with a safety pin.

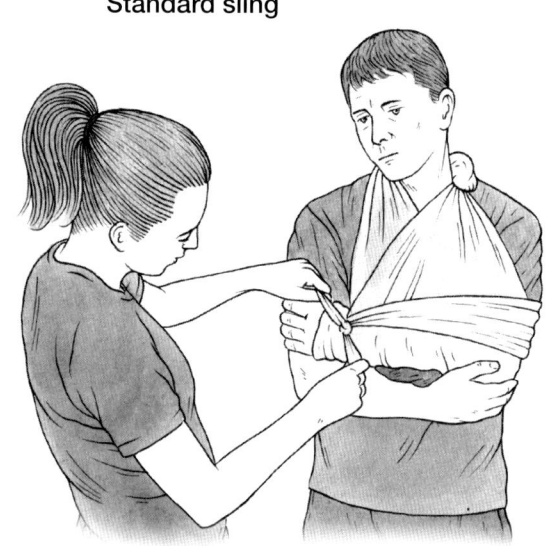

Standard sling

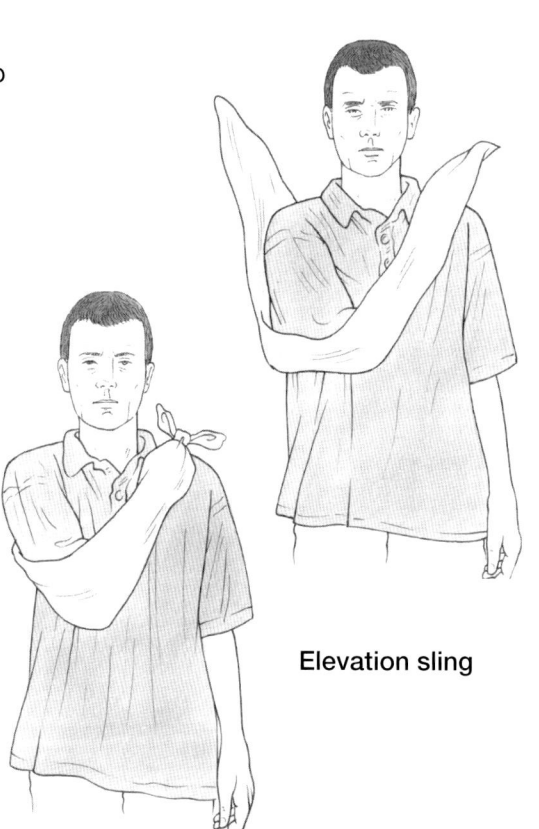

Elevation sling

PRICE

PRICE stands for Protection, Rest, Ice, Compression, and Elevation.

PROTECTION:
You should protect the affected area from further injury. For example, use a support.

REST:
Avoid further exercise, and reduce physical activity of any kind. A sling may help if a shoulder is injured, or use crutches if necessary for leg injuries.

ICE:
Apply an ice pack or a bag of frozen peas or similar to the affected area for 15 to 20 minutes every two to three hours. To avoid ice burn, wrap the ice pack in a towel, so that it does not directly touch the skin.

COMPRESSION:
To limit swelling, use elastic compression bandages during the day.

ELEVATION:
Ideally, the injured area should be raised above the level of the heart whenever possible. This also helps to reduce swelling.

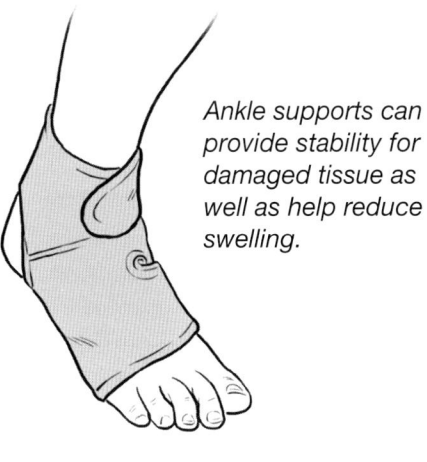

Ankle supports can provide stability for damaged tissue as well as help reduce swelling.

BITES, STINGS AND POISONS

Injuries from bites, stings, and poisons can vary from the relatively mild through debilitating to life-threatening. By acting promptly, you can help to prevent a poison or infection from spreading.

Animal bites

Clean the wound thoroughly by flushing it with clean water. Then cover the wound with a sterile dressing. If an arm or a leg has been bitten, you should immobilize it. Get medical help urgently, and provide detailed information of the type of animal that carried out the attack.

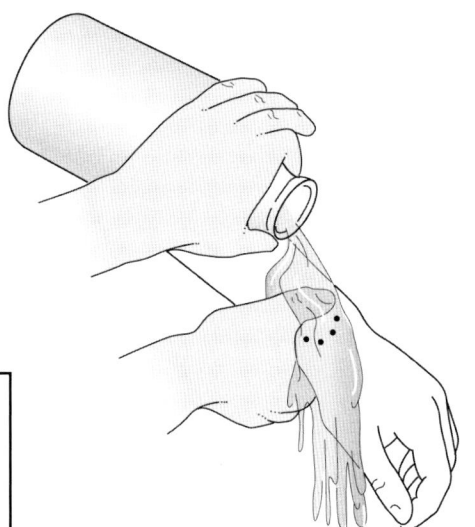

TICKS AND LYME DISEASE

Some ticks can infect you with Lyme disease. This can cause a rash and flu-like symptoms. Take the following steps:

- **Cover your body with insect repellent when walking outside.**
- **Regularly check your body and clothing, especially if walking in grassy or wooded areas.**
- **Carry a tick-remover tool and/or tweezers.**
- **If a tick is on your skin, grasp its mandibles close to your skin with the tool/tweezers and gently pull away. Do not squeeze the body of the tick.**
- **Rub isopropyl alcohol on the tick and wound to ease removal.**
- **Clean your skin with antiseptic or soap and water.**

Stings

If stung by an insect and the stinger remains in your flesh, rather than try to pull it out by the fingers, scrape along the skin with a reasonably sharp-edged item such as a credit card. Then wash the area with soap and water. An ice pack will help to reduce the spread of the poison.

When attacked by spiny fish, urchins, and the like, try to deactivate the toxin. Soak the wound in hot water for between 30 and 60 minutes. Seek medical attention.

Objects in the eye

Any object in the eye is an excruciating and disorientating injury. If you are in a survival context, as soon as a person is temporarily blinded, then you must immediately act.

- If a foreign body has entered an eye, immediately prevent the person from rubbing it.

- Inspect the eye yourself by carefully drawing back the eyelids with your finger and thumb. If the person can, get them to look in all directions. In this way they will be presenting all of their eye for your inspection.

- Once you can see the object, and if it is not embedded in the eye, then simply try to wash it out. You should irrigate the eye repeatedly with large quantities of water.

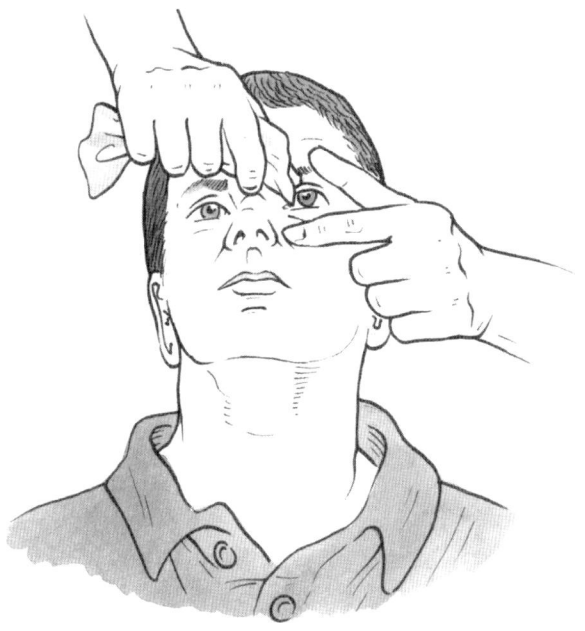

CHECK, CALL, CARE

In a remote emergency, check the scene, the available resources, and the patients. Then call for help, and provide care.

1. CHECK:
Check the scene, the resources, and the patient. Ensure that the area is safe. Check for available resources and for people who can help you in responding to the emergency. Is anyone hurt? Find out what the cause of injury is. Move the patient only if needed, such as if he or she is near danger. Assess if there is a life-threatening condition.

2. CALL:
If you are in a remote area or if there has been a disaster that prevents emergency services from reaching you fast, you should first call for help by either cell phone or radio, and then make a decision whether to evacuate the patient. This decision should be based on the level of severity of the injury or illness. You may opt for a slow evacuation if the injury or illness is not life-threatening or a fast evacuation if the patient needs immediate help.

3. CARE:
Provide whatever care you can for the conditions that you have managed to identify, giving priority to the most life-threatening injuries or illnesses.

PANDEMICS

A pandemic is the spread of a dangerous virus such as influenza over more than one country. Pandemics can be facilitated by fast modern travel, particularly air travel.

One of the most recent global pandemics was the spread of the H1N1 flu virus, also known as swine flu.

The virus originated among pigs and was passed from pigs to humans. A strain then developed which had no connection with pigs. In 2009, swine flu began to spread around the world. It was then classified by the World Health Organization (WHO) as an official pandemic.

During a pandemic, it is advisable to protect yourself by practicing strict hygiene. Hand sanitizer, a face mask, protective goggles, and vinyl gloves are useful items to carry with you.

FEMA ADVICE FOR ACTION DURING A PANDEMIC

During a pandemic, limit the spread of germs and prevent infection.

- **Avoid close contact with people who are sick.**
- **When you are sick, keep your distance from others to protect them from getting sick, too.**
- **Cover your mouth and nose with a tissue or your sleeve when coughing or sneezing. It may prevent those around you from getting sick.**
- **Washing your hands often will help protect you from germs.**
- **Avoid touching your eyes, nose, or mouth.**
- **Practice other good health habits. Get plenty of sleep, be physically active, manage your stress, drink plenty of fluids, and eat nutritious food.**

PHASES OF INFLUENZA PANDEMIC
BASED ON THE WHO PREPAREDNESS PLAN FOR PANDEMICS

PHASE 1
No viruses circulating among animals have been reported to cause infections in humans.

PHASE 2
An animal influenza virus circulating among domesticated or wild animals is known to have caused infection in humans, and is therefore considered a potential pandemic threat.

PHASE 3
An animal or human-animal influenza has undergone reassortment, and the virus has caused sporadic cases or small clusters of disease in people but has not resulted in human-to-human transmission sufficient to sustain community-level outbreaks. Limited human-to-human transmission may occur under some circumstances.

PHASE 4
This phase is characterized by verified human-to-human transmission of an animal or human-animal influenza virus able to cause community-level outbreaks. The ability to cause sustained disease outbreaks in a community marks a significant upward shift in the risk for a pandemic. Phase 4 indicates a significant increase in risk but does not necessarily mean that a pandemic is a foregone conclusion.

PHASE 5
This phase is characterized by human-to-human spread of the virus into at least two countries in one WHO region. While most countries will not be affected at this stage, the declaration of Phase 5 is a strong signal that a pandemic is imminent and that the time to finalize the organization, communication, and implementation of the planned mitigation measures is short.

PHASE 6
This is the pandemic phase; it is characterized by community-level outbreaks in at least one other country in a different WHO region in addition to the criteria defined in Phase 5. Designation of this phase will indicate that a global pandemic is underway.

ALTITUDE SICKNESS

Altitude sickness occurs when people at high altitudes have reduced blood oxygen levels due to low ambient pressure. Altitude illnesses can vary and the first treatment step is almost invariably to descend to a lower altitude.

Acute Mountain Sickness (AMS)

This condition is normally experienced only at altitudes higher than 8,000 feet (2,500 m). Symptoms include headache, nausea, weariness, insomnia, and loss of appetite.

Care should start with ensuring that the patient does not continue to ascend. If necessary, the patient should descend. Provide oxygen if you have the ability and training to do so. If the patient is able to swallow, he or she should take painkillers such as aspirin to relieve the headache.

Specific medications for AMS include acetazolamide and dexamethasone. Administration of any medications, however, is dependent on professional prescription and the patient's individual condition, contraindications, and needs. Anyone who is planning on ascending to high altitudes should have the necessary prescriptions already in place.

Cross-country skiers trek high in the Alpine mountains.

High Altitude Cerebral Edema (HACE)

This is a serious condition that results from swelling of brain tissue at high altitude. The swelling can lead to brain damage and to death. Symptoms of HACE may include loss of coordination, a severe headache that does not respond to conventional medications, personality disorders, seizures, and coma.

Treatment must start with descent to a more manageable altitude for the patient. Provide oxygen if you have the ability and training. Help the patient take altitude sickness medications, depending on his or her particular conditions, prescriptions, and label instructions.

High Altitude Pulmonary Edema (HAPE)

This condition is caused by the collection of fluid in the lung air spaces. This constricts breathing and may ultimately lead to death. Symptoms include a dry cough, lack of breath, chest pain, and frothy or reddish sputum from coughing.

Care should start with immediate descent to a lower altitude. Maintain a regular and balanced body temperature. Provide oxygen if you have the ability to do so.

CYBERATTACK

Cybersecurity is a wide-ranging term that covers the prevention of attacks via the Internet and computer systems. These can occur at a national level when a hostile state seeks to degrade the cybersecurity and technological activities of another state. They can also be directed at organizations, infrastructure, and individuals.

- At a personal level, a cyberattack can include identity theft or the blocking of access to personal information. If widespread, a cyberattack can cause disruption and confusion. Hacking and the introduction of malware are just two aspects. Individuals need to be constantly aware of the threat of cyberattacks as well as of malware and viruses.
- Some people favor particular computer operating systems. However, it is mainly important to check that the operating system you use is fully supported by the provider. Check when the support dates with the provider end. Check whether you are running the latest software packages and operating systems.
- Ensure that virus software updates automatically, and carry out regular scans, including regular deep scans. Use strong passwords, including letters, numbers, and special characters, and change them regularly.
- Do not reply to spam emails or to people and organizations you do not know. Do not open unknown links. Beware of browser site pop-ups that ask for unexpected updates. Keep backup files. That way, you can access files if your computer shuts down.

FEMA advice about cyberattacks

You can increase your cyber security by setting up the proper controls. The following are things that can protect individuals, groups, and property from a cyberattack:

- Use strong passwords that are 12 characters or longer. Use upper and lowercase letters, numbers, and special characters. Change passwords monthly. Use a password manager.
- Use strong authentication, such as a PIN or password that only you would know. Consider using a separate device that can receive a code, such as a cell phone, or use a biometric scan, such as a fingerprint scanner.
- Watch for suspicious online activity. If asked to do something right away, take an offer that sounds too good to be true, or give personal information, stop. Think before you click.
- Check account statements and credit reports regularly.
- Use secure Internet communications.
- Use HTTPS sites to access or provide any personal information. Do not use sites with invalid certificates. Use a virtual private network (VPN) that creates a secure connection.
- Use antivirus solutions, malware, and firewalls to block threats.
- Regularly back up files in encrypted files or encrypted storage devices.
- Limit the personal information you share online. Change privacy settings often, and do not use location features.
- Protect your home network by changing the administrative and Wi-Fi passwords regularly. When configuring a router, choose the Wi-Fi Protected Access 2 (WPA2) Advanced Encryption Standard (AES) setting, which is the strongest encryption option.

APPENDICES

Ten deadliest natural disasters by death toll

Rank	Event	Location	Date	Death toll (estimate)
1.	Flood	China	July–November, 1931	1,000,000–4,000,000
2.	Flood	Yellow River, China	September–October, 1887	900,000–2,000,000
3.	Earthquake	Shaanxi, Province, China	January 23, 1556	830,000
4.	Cyclone	Bhola , Bangladesh	November 13, 1970	500,000
5.	Cyclone	India	November 25, 1839	300,000
6.	Earthquake	Antioch, Byzantine Empire	May 20, 526 CE	250,000
7.	Earthquake	Tangshan, Hebei, China	July 28, 1976	242,000
8.	Earthquake	Haiyuan, China	December 26, 1920	240,000
9.	Earthquake/tsunami	Indian Ocean	December 26, 2004	230,000
10.	Flood	Banqiao Dam, Zhumadian, Henan Province, China	August 7, 1975	90,000–230,000

Deadliest natural disasters by type of event

Type	Event	Location	Date	Death toll (estimate)
Avalanche	Wellington avalanche	United States	March 1, 1910	96
Blizzard	Iran blizzard	Iran	February 1972	4000
Drought	Great Famine	India	1876–1878	25,250,000
Earthquake	Shaanxi earthquake	China	January 23, 1556	830,000
Flood	China floods	China	1931	2,000,000–4,000,000
Hailstorm	Roopkund, Uttaranchal	India	Ninth century	200–600
Heat wave	European heat wave	Europe	June–August 2003	37,451
Landslide	Vargas mudslides	Venezuela	December 1999	20,006
Limnic eruption	Lake Nyos	Cameroon	August 21, 1986	1746
Pandemic	Spanish influenza	Worldwide	1918–1920	750,000,000-100,000,000
Tornado	Saturia-Manikganj Sadar tornado	Bangladesh	April 29, 1989	1300
Tropical cyclone	Bhola cyclone	Bangladesh	November 13, 1970	200,000–500,000
Tsunami	Indian Ocean tsunami	Indian Ocean	December 26, 2004	230,000
Volcano	Mount Tambora	Indonesia	1815	92,000
Wildfire	Peshtigo Fire	United States	October 8, 1871	2000

GLOSSARY

ABS—Advanced Braking System

Acetazolamide—medicine used to treat glaucoma, altitude sickness, etc.

Anthrax—fatal bacterial infection; terrorists have targeted victims by mailing them letters containing anthrax spores

Carbon dioxide—colorless gas that forms part of the Earth's atmosphere

Carbon monoxide—colorless and odorless gas caused by combustion of carbon

CBRN—chemical, biological, radiological, and nuclear

CPR—cardiopulmonary resuscitation

Crust—hard outer layer of the Earth's surface

Dexamethasone—corticosteroid medication used for rheumatism, brain swelling, and other conditions

Dorsal muscle—upper side or back muscle

Epicenter—the point on the surface of the Earth directly above the focus on an earthquake

FEMA—Federal Emergency Management Agency, the government agency responsible for coordinating disaster relief across the U.S.

Fartlek—training for distance runners that involves constant changes in pace

Fault line—area of weakness in the Earth's surface where earthquakes can occur

Geomagnetic storm—a storm that interferes with the Earth's magnetosphere by, for example, a solar wind

High Altitude Cerebral Edema (HACE)—swelling of the brain with fluid due to high altitude

High Altitude Pulmonary Edema (HAPE)—dangerous accumulation of liquid in the lungs occurring in mountaineers above 8,200 ft (2,500 m)

Hydrogen sulphide—colorless, odorless, flammable, poisonous, and lethal gas formed by sulphur

Hyperthermia—abnormally high body temperature

Hypothermia—abnormally low body temperature

Keffiyeh—Arab headdress made from a square piece of cloth fastened around the crown of the head and often wrapped around the neck and face

Lyme disease—infectious disease caused by *Borrelia* bacteria transmitted to humans by ticks

Mantle—area of the Earth between the core and the crust

Maximum heart rate (MHR)—the highest number of beats per minute that your heart is safely capable of during high-stress exercise

Morse Code—an arrangement of dots, dashes, and spaces to represent letters of the alphabet communicated by electrical impulses or by flashes or sounds

Multi-stage Fitness Test (MSFT) or "Beep" test—a test used to measure aerobic capacity. It involves running a marked distance between ever decreasing beep sounds.

Novichok—a lethal nerve agent developed in the Soviet Union

Prefrontal cortex—cerebral cortex of the frontal lobe of the brain responsible for cognitive thinking and decision making

Pyroclastic flow—fragments of rock, hot ash, and lava flowing from a volcano

Resting heart rate (RHR)—the average number of beats per minute of your heart when not exercising

Sarin—nerve gas developed in World War II

Seismic—vibrations in the Earth's crust relating to earthquakes

Seismograph—an instrument that measures earthquake activity and duration

Solar wind—a stream of charged particles released from the upper surface of the sun

Tectonic plate—a piece of the Earth's crust

Torniquet—device for stopping flow of blood through a limb or artery

Training heart rate (THR)—an average, safe heart rate range established by calculating percentages of your maximum heart rate, resting heart rate, and heart rate reserve, depending on your goals, type of training, and intensity level

VX—a toxic synthetic chemical nerve agent

INDEX

A
abdomen crunches 24
abdominal plank 12
accidents
  cycling 196
  on trains 197
  while driving 192–93
active shooters, terrorism 169–71
Acute Mountain Sickness (AMS), first aid 246
air travel
  evacuation routes 203
  hijackings 199
  plane crashes 200–205
  seat belts 201
  turbulence 199
altitude sickness 246–47
animals
  bites from 242
  in cars 120
anthrax attacks 182
apartments, during fires 86
arm fractures 239
avalanches 139–44
awareness, situational 38–39

B
bandages, first aid 233–35
basement flooding 60
baseplate compass 51
beep test 29
bench press 19
bent lateral raise 21
biological attacks 180–82
bites 242
bleeding 231–35
blizzards 105–9
body mass index (BMI) 31
body signals 211
bombings, terrorism 167
bracing, on planes 201
breathing exercise 35
bunkers, hurricanes 104
burns and scalds 230

C
cadence, running 16
campfire safety 88
cars *see* vehicles
caving 154–59
chemical attacks 183–85
chilblains 228
choking 226
civil defense, biological attacks 180
cleaning up, after floods 60
climbing cams 152
clothing 46–47
  caving, for 154
  desert survival 129
  driving, for 189
  heatwaves and droughts, during 119, 120
  polar survival 146
  winter storms, during 106, 107
clouds, recognizing 112–13
coastal dangers
  floods 56–61
  storm surges 98
  tsunamis 62–65
  volcanoes 75
compasses 50, 214
concentration curls 23
concentration, importance of 34
condensation, water from 126
condos, during fires 86
confidence, importance of 39
countdowns, hurricanes 101
CPR, first aid 222–24
crunches 24
curls, arms 22
cyberattacks 248
cyclists 195–96

D
daytime running lights (DRLs), motorcycles 195
decontamination, nuclear explosions 176
defensive driving 194
dehydration, dangers of
  in the desert 128
  when driving 190
descent, mountain survival 151–52
desert survival clothing 129
diet 30–31
disassociation 38
disaster supplies kit 53
dome shelters 148
dorsal raises 25
double-layer tarp shelters 131
dressings, first aid 233–35
drinking water *see* water, for drinking
driving *see also* vehicles
  in blizzards 108–9
  safety 188–94
DRLs (daytime running lights), motorcycles 195
droughts *see* heatwaves and droughts
drowning 227
dumbbell press 20
dust and sandstorms 133
  finding water 123–28
  shelters 130–33
dynamic stretching 10

E
earthquakes 67–71
electrical storms 110–11
emergency conditioning (EC) 36
emergency kits 48, 49, 53, 101, 109, 189
endurance 40
equipment *see also* emergency kits
  avalanches 142–43
  backpacks 48–49
  carrying water 49
  caving 156–57
  compasses 50–51
  disaster supplies kit 53

INDEX

fires, for 83
first aid kits 48
flashlights 50
home essentials 52–53
mountain survival 150
navigation, for 50–51, 216
personal locator beacon (PLB) 50, 211
sleeping bags 49
waterproof bags 49
escape routes
 fires 85, 90
 tsunamis 62
 volcanoes 73
evacuations
 aircraft 203
 fires and 83
 hurricanes, during 103
examination technique, first aid 225
exercises
 abdominal plank 12
 arm curls 22
 bench press 19
 bent lateral raise 21
 breathing exercise 35
 concentration curls 23
 crunches 24
 dorsal raises 25
 dumbbell press 20
 lateral raise 19
 leg press 27
 leg raises 25
 pull-ups 13
 push-ups 12
 rowing 14
 seated leg push 25
 shoulder press 20
 side lateral raise 21
 sit-ups 14
 squats 26
 step-ups 27
 tricep dip 23
 twist sit-ups 24
eyes, objects in, first aid 243

F
facemasks
 biological attacks 181
 volcano, after a 73
fartlek 17
fast continuous running (FCR) 16
fight-or-flight response 33
finding bearings 214
fires
 detection 80–81
 home escape plans 84–87
 outdoor refuge 88–91
 response 82–83
 safety zones 81
 signaling 210
 vehicle fires 193
first aid
 altitude sickness 246–47
 bites, stings, and poisons 242–43
 bleeding 231–35
 choking 226
 cold and heat 228–30
 drowning 227
 examination technique 225
 first steps and CPR 222–23
 fractures 236–41
 jaw thrust technique 225
 pandemics 244–45
 the recovery position 224
 treating shock 225
first aid kits 48
five Ps, the 83
flashlights 50
flexibility, running 16
flood damage 56
 sandbags 58–59
floods *see also* tsunamis
 basement flooding 60
 cars in 60
 cleaning up after 60
 drinking water 59
 flash floods 57
flying debris, tornadoes 95
fog, driving in 188

food
 diet 30–31
 storing 52
 during winter storms 106
footwear, polar survival 146
fractures 236–41
frostbite 229

G
geomagnetic storms 111
glaciers 150
glide avalanches 140
ground shelters 132
ground signals 210

H
heart rate monitors 8
heat cramps 230
heat exhaustion 120, 122
heat related safety 119
heatwaves and droughts
 dehydration dangers 128
 finding water 123–28
heat exhaustion 120, 122
heatstroke 121–22, 229
 preparing for 117
 safety advice 119–20
 shelters 130–33
 water conservation 118
helicopter rescues 212–13
High Altitude Cerebral Edema (HACE) 247
High Altitude Pulmonary Edema (HAPE) 247
hijackings, planes 199
homes
 during and after earthquakes 68–70
 essentials 52–53
 fires and 81–87
 heatwaves and droughts 117–18
 hurricane safety 99–101
 security devices 84
 tornadoes and 96
 winter storms and 106–7

hot lava, volcanoes 75
hotels, terrorism awareness 163
HOT mnemonic, terrorism awareness 165
hurricanes 97–104
hypothermia
  caving and 157
  first aid for 228

I
ice, melting 147
igloos 148
interval training 17

J
jaw thrust technique, first aid 225

K
kitchen fires 87

L
landing zones, helicopters 213
landslides 136–38
lateral raise 19
layering principle, clothing 47
leg fractures 237
leg press 27
leg raises 25
lightning 110–11
limitations, accepting 43
long slow distance (LSD) runs 15

M
maximum heart rate (MHR) 9
measuring scales, volcanoes 76–77
measuring your fitness 8–9
media, checking on 70
meditation 35
mental preparation
  accepting your limitations 43
  breathing exercise 35
  concentration and planning 34, 39
  confidence 39
  disassociation 38
  distractions 42–43

emergency conditioning (EC) 36
endurance 40
meditation 35
motivation 37
negativity 39, 41
positive thinking 37
rule of three thinking strategy 43
sleep 34
stress, handling 32–33
team building 36
visualization techniques 37, 39
vulnerability 41
Mercali scale 76
mile run 15
military fitness 28–29
mirrors, for sending signals 209
moment magnitude scale 77
moon navigation 219
motivation 37
motorcyclists 195–96
mountain survival
  altitude sickness 246–47
  descent 151–52
  equipment 150
  glaciers 150
  shelters 153
multi-stage fitness test (MSFT) 29

N
Naismith's Rule, navigation 215
nature, navigation from 219
navigation 214–19
negativity, getting rid of 39, 41
nuclear explosion, terrorism 176–79
number six, distress signal 209
nutritional guidelines 30

O
outdoor refuge
  fires 88–91
  tornadoes 96

P
pacing, navigation 215
pandemics 244–45
pedometers 50

personal locater beacons (PLBs) 50, 211
pets see animals
phone calls
  during earthquakes 70
  first aid 243
  terrorism and 166
physical preparation
  core fitness 24–27
  interval training 17
  measuring your fitness 8–9
  military fitness 28–29
  running 15–17
  stretching 10–11
  testing your fitness 12–14
  weight training 18–23
plane crashes 200–205
planning, importance of 34, 39
plants, water from 124
PLOW, caving 155
polar survival
  clothing 146
  environment 145
  finding water 147
  shelters 148–49
  snowshoes 147
  temperature factors 146
police, and terrorism 166–68
positive thinking 37
posture, running 16
preparation
  diet 30–31
  distractions 42–43
  goal setting 40–41
  mental preparation 32–37
  physical preparation 8–29
  situational awareness 38–39
PRICE technique 241
pull-ups 13
push-ups 12

R
rainwater and dew, for drinking 125
recovery position 224
relaxation technique 41
rescue
  checking your situation 208
  helicopter, by 212–13
  navigation 214–19
  signals for help 209–11

INDEX

resting heart rate (RHR) 8–9
Richter scale 76
road accidents 192–93
rocky areas, water and 124
rowing 14
rule of three thinking strategy 43
running 15–17

S

safety equipment
  avalanches 142–43
  caving 156–57
  mountain survival 150
safety zones, fires 81
sandbags 58–59
sandstorms 133
seat belts, on planes 201
seated leg push 25
security devices, homes 84
self-defense, terrorism and 168–69
shelters
  desert survival 130–33
  hurricanes 99
  mountain survival 153
  polar survival 148–49
shock, treating 225
short-term shelters 130
shoulder press 20
side effects, of stress 33
side lateral raise 21
signaling 209–11
situational awareness 38–39
sit-ups 14
skids, driving out of 192
skull fractures 238
slab avalanches 140
sleep, importance of 34
sleeping bags 49
slings, first aid 240
smoke, dangers from 89
snowshoes 147
snow tree shelters 153
solar stills 127
speed play 17
splints, first aid 236–37
squats 26
stand, drop, and roll technique 87
stars, for navigation 217–18
steam plumes, volcanoes 75
steering position, vehicles 190
step-ups 27
stings, first aid 242
stopping distances 191
storage, water 117
storms
  electrical storms 110–11
  hurricanes 97–104
  recognizing clouds 112–13
  tornadoes 94–96
  tropical cyclones, typhoons, winter storms 105–9
stress, handling 32–33
  relaxation technique 41
stretching 10–11
stride, running 16
sun, navigation with 217
survival kits/equipment 49
  avalanches 142–43
  heatwaves and droughts 117
  hurricanes and 101
  vehicles, in 189
  winter storms 109
suspicious behavior, terrorism and 163–64
sutures, first aid 232
sweating, dangers of 126
swimming, through avalanches 144

T

team building 36
team checks, caving 155
temperature factors, polar survival 146
tempo running 16
terrorism
  biological attacks 180–82
  chemical attacks 183–85
  nuclear explosion 176–79
  prevention and awareness 162–65
  vehicle ramming 174–75
  weapons attacks 166–73
testing your fitness 12–14
tick bites 242
tire chains 108
tiredness, driving and 190
tornadoes 94–96
torniquets, applying 231
training heart rate (THR) 9
train journeys 197
transport safety
  air travel 198–205
  driving safety 188–94
  motorcyclists and cyclists 195–96
  train journeys 197
trench foot 228
tricep dip 23
tropical cyclones 97–104
tsunamis
  response 64
  warning signs 62
turbulence, air travel 199
twist sit-ups 24
typhoons 97–104

U

underground shelters 132
  see also bunkers

V

vehicle ramming, terrorism 174–75
vehicles
  air travel 198–205
  basic vehicle checks 189
  defensive driving 194
  dehydration dangers 190
  driving and tiredness 190
  driving in blizzards 108–9
  driving in fog 188
  driving out of skids 192
  earthquakes, in 69
  emergency kit 189
  fires, in 193
  floods, in 60
  heatwaves and droughts, during 120
  motorcyclists and cyclists 195–96
  road accidents 192–93
  steering position 190
  stopping distances 191
  terrorism awareness 162
  train journeys 197
visualization techniques 37, 39
volcanoes 72–77
vulnerability, embracing 41

INDEX/ACKNOWLEDGMENTS

W
warning signs
  landslides 136
  tornadoes 95
  tsunamis 62
  volcanoes 73
water conservation 118
water, for drinking
  carrying 49
  during fires 82
  during floods 59
  heatwaves and droughts 117, 118, 123–28
  polar survival 147
waterproof bags 49
weapons attacks, terrorism 166–73
weight training 18–23
winch rescues, helicopters 213
wind chill factor 105
winter storms 105–9
worry, getting rid of 39

ACKNOWLEDGMENTS

Picture credits:

Alamy: 61 (Robert Gilhooly), 65 (Dinodia Photos), 72 (Stuart Hunter), 74 (Xinhua), 75 (Travelpix), 80 (NASA Archive), 110 (Ron Niebrugge), 158 (Newscom/B J Warnick), 167 (Anette Selmer-Anderson), 206 (Xinhua), 212 (Ashley Cooper)

Dreamstime: 105 (Sergey Kichigin), 134 (Roman Lysogor), 138 (Gaspert), 145 (Claudia Tillmanns), 188 (Steve Allen), 190 (Antikainen), 191 (Joe Sohn), 219 top (Frank Luerweg), 246 (Michelangelo Oprandi)

FEMA: 92

Getty Images: 54 (AFP/Jiji Press), 71 (John T. Barr), 89 (Bloomberg), 142 (Aurora/Corey Hendrickson), 160 (Photonica World/Frank Schwere), 172 (Science Faction/U.S. Navy), 173 (Marc Piasecki), 174 (AFP/Jack Guez), 183 (AFP/Stan Honda), 185 (Kyodo News), 186 (AFP/Cole Burston), 193 (NurPhoto), 204 (Chris McGrath), 219 bottom (Bloomberg), 227 (Anadolu Agency), 229 (Robert Nickelsberg)

I-Stock: 200 (Skrum)

NASA: 111

Shutterstock: 34 (Gorodenkoff), 39 (Paul Aiken), 44 (Candy Box Images), 63 (AJE44), 66 (Sara Escobar), 77 (Frans Delian), 86 (SashkO), 98 (Benjamin Todd Shoemake), 114 (Idiz), 154 (Pedko Anton), 162 (TonyV3112), 195 (S_E), 196 (Nick Beer), 208 (Photka), 220 (Presslab)

U.S. Department of Defense: 6, 15, 16, 37, 38, 41, 42, 56, 78, 91, 102, 120

Text credits:

Text on pages 83, 100, 103, 107, 119, 124, 136, 138, 141, 164, 170–171, 181, 184, 244 courtesy "Official advice from the US Federal Emergency Management Agency (FEMA) on preparing for a [disaster]." The author and publisher are grateful to the US Federal Emergency Management Agency (FEMA) for permission to reproduce official advice in this book.

Text box on page 53 courtesy https://www.ready.gov/build-a-kit